Dislocating the frontier
Essaying the mystique of the outback

Dislocating the frontier
Essaying the mystique of the outback

Edited by Deborah Bird Rose and Richard Davis

ANU
THE AUSTRALIAN NATIONAL UNIVERSITY

E PRESS

ANU

E PRESS

Published by ANU E Press
The Australian National University
Canberra ACT 0200, Australia
Email: anuepress@anu.edu.au
Web: http://epress.anu.edu.au

National Library of Australia
Cataloguing-in-Publication entry

Dislocating the frontier : essaying the mystique of the outback.

Includes index

ISBN 1 920942 36 X
ISBN 1 920942 37 8 (online)

1. Frontier and pioneer life - Australia. 2. Australia -
Historiography. 3. Australia - History - Philosophy. I.
Rose, Deborah Bird. II. Davis, Richard, 1965- .

994.0072

Indexed by Barry Howarth.
Cover design by Brendon McKinley with a photograph by Jeff Carter, 'Dismounted,
Saxby Roundup', http://nla.gov.au/nla.pic-vn3108448, National Library of Australia.
Reproduced by kind permission of the photographer.

Table of Contents

List of Figures

Part I. Preface, Introduction and Historical Overview

Preface

Deborah Bird Rose
Richard Davis

This book jumps into the arena to 'bulldog' a deceptively simple idea. *Dislocating the frontier* goes beyond images of a progressive or disastrous frontier to rethink the frontier imagination itself. In re-imagining the frontier in Australia, we do not discount Aboriginal dispossession. Nor are we enjoined in a critique of colonialism, or a critique of a critique of colonialism. Confronted by the complexity of Aboriginal-Settler encounters and their long, entwined histories, we offer interpretative analysis that acknowledges resistance and indigenous autonomy as well as contingencies, contentions and complexities. As a mythic arena, the frontier is a site of violence, replacement and nation-building. And yet, this book shows that it is also a site of productive assertions of dilemmas, and of unexpected engagements toward change. It is, thus, a continuing site of cultural action. And as a number of authors to this volume advert, in some parts of Australia a post-colonial frontier is emerging that jostles and upsets the classical frontier imagination without, as yet, seeking to bury it.

This book began in September 1999 in Darwin. The geographic and mythic significance of North Australia as frontier territory has long been acknowledged; we believed that a located conference would draw on both the setting and the weight of history to enhance the vitality of the contributions. The conference and this collection acknowledge the frontier to be conceptually pervasive and elusive, as well as being provocatively catalytic. These essays show that a critical and comparative approach to analysing the frontier is an essential part of decolonising thought. Collectively, the essays reveal diverse aspects of the frontier; in representation, performance, society and politics. Individually and collectively, the contributing writers set out to chart meanings and experiences of the frontier in their contemporary multivalent complexity.

In 1999 we understood these issues to be part of an expanding discourse on the frontier, in the mode that Furniss discusses so eloquently in Chapter 2. Since then, however, Autralian public life has been captured by a debate over the meaning of history and historical method, the meaning of the frontier, and the meaning of conflict. Labelled 'history wars' this debate has clarified a conservative position that seeks to reconfigure analysis of the frontier by framing it in terms of how history is told and confining it to the past and to zones of conflict (for example, see Windschuttle 2002, Manne 2003, Macintyre 2003, Attwood and Foster 2003, Attwood 2005). The history wars are on-going. Attwood's recent (2005) work contextualises the debates and addresses the main issues in a profoundly scholarly and yet accessible way.

Dislocating the frontier stakes out a position that both speaks to, and refuses to be bound by, the terms of the current debates about the frontier. The history wars have shown a narrowing of focus: the frontier has been reduced from a zone of encounter and interaction to a zone of conflict; conflict has been reduced to killing; killing has been reduced to deliberate gunshots; body counts have become a measure of violence. In the process, historians have been stereotyped as people who seek to promote accounts of the past that focus on particular types of conflict and particular levels of body counts. Attwood (2005:191) reminds us that in debates about the past it is not only the past that is at stake:

> In the final analysis, it is not a conflict about the past .... but a conflict over the past in the present. More particularly, it is a conflict regarding the moral relationship of settler peoples to this history – to this relationship between past and present, present and past.

To the extent that the debate reduces the terms of engagement, to that extent it reduces the possibilities for understanding the complexities of the past and of the past in the present. These reductions impair our capacity to imagine the future as well as to engage fully with the present and the past.

Dislocating the frontier is provocatively multi-vocal when read in light of the history wars. In our emphasis on contemporary complexity, the authors implicitly argue for a multitude of types of interactions that are on-going. These essays allow the intricacies of real life to take precedence over the singularities that have come to dominate the history wars. They seek to examine and celebrate subtlety and complexity in an arena that is in danger of being turned into a shadow zone of caricature and stereotype.

We acknowledge the Co-operative Research Centre for the Sustainable Development of Tropical Savannas at the Northern Territory University which provided the main funding for the conference. The Northern Territory Museum hosted the event; the Aboriginal Areas Protection Authority supported the travel of some speakers, and staff of the North Australia Research Unit of the Australian National University helped in the organisation. ANU E-Press staff have been a delight to work with, and we gratefully acknowledge their dedication to the embattled project of scholarly publication.

References

Attwood, B. 2005, *Telling the Truth about Aboriginal History*, Allen & Unwin, Sydney.

Attwood, B. and S. G. Foster 2003, *Frontier Conflict: The Australian Experience*, National Museum of Australia, Canberra.

Macintyre, I. 2003, *The History Wars*, Melbourne University Press, Melbourne.

Manne, Robert 2003, *Whitewash: On Keith Windschuttle's Fabricaiton of Aboriginal History*, Black Inc, Melbourne.

Windschuttle, K. 2002, *The Fabrication of Aboriginal History*, Macleay Press, Sydney.

1. Introduction: transforming the frontier in contemporary Australia

Richard Davis

The frontier is one of the most pervasive, evocative tropes underlying the production of national identity in Australia. Although frequently used in various contexts, it is rarely defined, suggesting that as an idea it gains its strength and dynamism by virtue of ease of use and great flexibility of application. As an interpretation of indigenous-settler historical relations it is used across the spectrum of encounter, from race wars, conquest and imperialism, to less violent but no less consequential inter-cultural crossings between indigenous Australians and settler-colonists. In terms of scientific or intellectual endeavours the frontier evokes the edges of possibility, beyond which glimpses of new and exciting prospects can be seen. Indeed, it is the real and imaginative spaces where edges and borders between ideas are traversed, where identities can lose their certainty and be reassembled, and where power fluctuates between people and the world, that the frontier trope attempts to secure. Further, while the frontier trope carries not only the freight of historical encounters, it also reveals the postures of nationhood that inform inter-cultural relationships and that shape institutions and ideas. To take only one instance, the debate in Australia over the last 25 years over the nature of the violence that characterised early relationships between Aboriginal people and settler-colonists is most often conducted around the veracity of estimates of Aborigines killed in frontier conflict with settler-colonists, the benign or malevolent intentions of the killers and other factual evidence that supports or denies the various claims.[1] These are not simply matters of fact, however; the arguments are waged as part of a larger public concern about race relations and the use of history in shaping a national identity that strives for a confident wholeness or is expressive of more contingent, contested, mobile processes. Nevertheless, the unquestioned status of the frontier invites interrogation: why has such an omnipresent idea slipped unreflexively into discussions of nationhood, history and identity? This volume brings together leading scholars and activists to examine the discursive strategies with which the frontier concept is made to be intellectually productive in Australia.

[1] B. Attwood, *Telling the Truth about Aboriginal History*; B. Attwood and S. G. Foster, *Frontier Conflict: The Australian Experience*; I. Macintyre, *The History Wars*; R. Manne, *Whitewash: On Keith Windschuttle's Fabricaiton of Aboriginal History*; K. Windschuttle, *The Fabrication of Aboriginal History*; B. W. Smith, *The Spectre of Truganinni*; H. Reynolds, *The Other Side of the Frontier*; K. Windschuttle, 'The Myths of Frontier Massacres in Australian History'; G. Blainey, *The Tyranny of Distance: How Distance Shaped Australia's History*; R. Milliss, *Waterloo Creek*.

The genuine frontier

On February 23, 2000 the Mangarrayi people were handed the title deeds to Elsey Station, a Northern Territory cattle station immortalised in Jeannie Gunn's autobiographical novel *We of the Never-Never* (1907). Widely read by many generations of Australians, Gunn's novel has played an influential part in establishing the outback and its special privations as a critical cultural interlocutor in the development of national consciousness. Gunn wrote of struggles against economic hardship, Aboriginal cattle spearing, environmental capriciousness and social isolation as part of the process of colonists domesticating themselves to the Australian continent. For many Australian readers in the first half of the 20th century, her written experiences personalised the ideological process of settlement by bringing elements of a distant frontier into the realm of daily life to an encompassing, ordinary language of settlement.

We of the Never-Never was not intended to establish a definitive account of Australian settlement but it came to encapsulate that process as a relatively undifferentiated and uncomplicated myth of the psychological and moral accommodations needed to establish European ownership of the country and displacement of Aborigines. Much has been said about Gunn's original description of the murder of local Aborigines and subsequent sanitisation of this violence in later publications of the book where the description of the killings was removed. A film interpretation of the book, released in 1982, continued this elision, further cementing the virtuous elements of struggle with the land in the popular imagination.[2] Through these works Elsey Station became mobilised as a key sign of settlement in the theatre of Australian cultural history, while the Mangarrayi continued to be displaced and unrecognised as the original and enduring owners to that country. In a very modern evocation of the enduring iconicity of Elsey Station the local radio station – Radio Never Never – claimed the region to be the genuine frontier, the place in which specific events embodied broader process of invasion, settlement and displacement across the nation. At that 'genuine frontier' on February 23, a reversal occurred and a series of new questions was posed about the apparatuses of colonialism and the frontier. If the monolithic discourse of Australian history is motivated by the displacement of Aboriginal people and the establishment of settlers as the natural occupants of the land, to what extent has this process rested on an inscrutability that submerged dialogue, exchange and encounter by presuming their cataclysmic proportions?

This collection starts with the assumption that while the classical Australian frontier tends to be located in the imaginative fertility of the outback and is to be characterised by racial conflict, a more problematic and challenging frontier

---

[2] Auzins, *We of the Never Never*, 1982.

embraces a greater set of relationships than appropriation, and deals with more diverse circumstances than violence. Our aim is to move beyond the consensus that the frontier is a recognisable tale of woeful cross-cultural encounters. In our rejection of the tendency to homogenise the frontier as a single process we recognise the corresponding homogeneities implied by the discursive entities of settler, Aborigine and indigenous. We therefore address frontier encounters as having the simultaneous features of exchange, perpetuation, transformation, reclamation and a greater sense of the limit of colonising influences than resistance, capture, seizure and violence entails. We also recognise that the radically asymmetrical relations of power that have historically operated between settlers and Aborigines have tended to suppress differences within settler and Aboriginal peoples. Debate about Australian frontiers has not always recognised that the pervasive effects of encounter have sometimes been curtailed by autonomous indigenous spaces beyond frontier history. This point is eloquently expressed by Stephen Muecke in Chapter 10 in his discussion of Boxer's ability to enact an indigenous power based on an autonomous cultural geography that made contact with settlers discontinuous, fleeting and sometimes irrelevant in a period when the apparatuses of colonialism in the Kimberley exerted an abiding influence on indigenous lives.

Dislocating the frontier does not take as its place of departure a specific event or work that could be said to inaugurate the frontier as a distinctive process or idea. The essays that are collected here suggest continually occurring scenes of encounter wherein frontier is a conception of history and sociality that incorporates and moves beyond the assumption that history is a progressive embracement of modernity. The plurality of frontiers underlines the sense that it is a conception that rests on predicaments occasioned by difference and return, notions that are suggestively allied to evocations of nationhood. In Frederick Jackson Turner's celebratory historiographical interpretation of the establishment of the American nation, he concluded that by 1890 the process of frontier settlement across the north American continent had ended.[3] Frontier was, for Turner, variously assembled: it was 'the history of the colonization of the Great West ... an area of free land, its continuous recession, and the advance of American settlement'; the encounter of hierarchically ordered social groups in which European immigrants were characterised as more socially complex and more able than indigenous inhabitants; a line of development distinguishing the energetic New World from the declining Old World of Europe; the accomplishment of civil society. History breaks in Turner's historiography, little is left to the intervention of the past into the future, rather, the explanation of 'national origins and national character by reference to the ever-present frontier

---

[3] F. Turner, 1893.

of colonization' is imagined as a unique process occasioned by the influence of specific environments and the peculiarities of settlement.[4]

Much has been said about the ethnocentric, masculinist, nationalist biases in Turner's frontier hypothesis and in this volume, Elizabeth Furniss charts the criticisms and debates that have occasioned the rejection and rehabilitation of frontier concepts in recent North American scholarship. Feminist writers have argued for a more explicit focus on gender in frontier analyses noting that the dominant place of white men in frontiers around the country has tended to marginalise women, Aborigines and ethnic minorities, exposing the frontier concept as a vital component in the determination of ideals of gender relations and family structures in settler society. It is important to note how Turner's hypothesis about settler expansion and environmental influences on individual, social and civil development found its way into Australian literature and scholarship. Turner's clear, untangled narrative of the material and cultural aspects of American settlement had the compelling features of all good (nationalist) myths: the delivery of powerful stories that draw on familiar symbols with economy and resonance that can be interpreted and elaborated in diverse contexts without the loss of simple, dramatic, narrative elements. While Turner was primarily concerned to account for American ideals, he was convinced his ideas were more ecumenical than national. His short list of frontier countries included Australia, and his work inspired others to search for evidence of similar virtues and civil developments in their own national settings.[5]

Certainly the most influential interpretation of Turner in an Australian context is found in Russel Ward's, *The Australian Legend*. In this work Turner's emphasis on environment as a shaper of personal and national temperament is interpreted by Ward to account for the emergence of a 'different kind of man', a 'typical Australian' forged by 'the outback ethos', transformed from morally diminished convicts into a 'morally improved "bushmen"' by 'the brute facts of Australian geography'. Ward embraced Turner's combination of anti-imperial sentiments, characterisation of settlement as a process of opportunistically entering areas of 'free' land and the moral sovereignty granted by confrontation with Aborigines and environment as a process of the domestication of settlers. Ian McLean recognises that the employment of the Turnerian model by Ward was premised on the eradication of Aborigines, ideologically catered for by establishing the heritage of distinctive Australian characteristics borne of bush living and encounter.[6] McLean considers this process of settler domestication to have

---

[4] Bassin, 'Turner, Solov'ev, and the "Frontier Hypothesis"', p. 474.

[5] Webb, *The Great Frontier*; Winks, 'Australia, the Frontier, and the Tyranny of Distance'; W. T. Jackson, 'Australians and the Comparative Frontier'; Jull, *The Politics of Northern Frontiers in Australia, Canada, and other 'First World' Countries*; Allen, *Bush and Backwoods*, p. 59. Sharp, 'Three Frontiers'.

[6] Ward, *The Australian Legend*, p. 286.

produced a melancholic aesthetic informing much early colonial art.[7] In Peter Brunt's assessment of McLean's argument he registers his unease that racial violence should inevitably assume a central place in the foundational myths of settler nations such as Australia.[8] There is more, though, to be said about the complex and deeply embedded place of violence in the ideological field generated by the frontier.

Where it provides a confident and authoritative account of settlements, frontier discourse creates the conditions for the forgetting of original violences. This process of forgetting is more apparent than real though as the 'hidden histories' of violent encounter constantly haunt settlement.[9] At those moments that buried accounts of violence break through established history, the history of settlement is beset by a twin ambivalence. On the one hand, accounting for frontier violences asserts local histories of encounter over generalising national narratives of settlement. Operating in the opposite direction, violence becomes a precondition for nationhood, associating the shedding of blood with sacrifice and elevating violent encounter into a kind of civil action. To the extent that sacrifice and violence are more commonly recognised through the Gallipoli story as inaugurating Australian nationhood, they operate within longstanding discourses of masculine nationfounding in Western liberal democracies.[10] However, the capacity for indigenous Australians to 'speak back' and 'talk up' to dominant histories through their own long-standing generational memories besets celebratory encounter by destabilising the foundational heroism associated with sacrificial elements of violent encounter.[11]

Ward's willing evocation of the bushman as an Australian frontiersman counteracted any sense that the vigour and entrepreneurial attitudes implied by the Turnerian thesis could be replaced by less sanguine features. Fred Alexander had argued that the process of settlement had resulted in a deterioration in the Australian male character, such that by the 1940s laziness and subservience were prevalent.[12] Alexander regarded this depletion as resulting from the deep incorporation of English values and institutions in Australian settler-colonial society. When Paul Sharp later elaborated on this idea, he added that frontier expansion was also destructive to Aborigines, an expression of the view that Aboriginal people would inevitably decline in the face of prosperous, energetic northern European immigrants.[13] Alexander's bleak regard for male character and Sharp's account of ruinous race relations in

---

[7] McLean, *White Aborigines*, pp. 18, 89.
[8] Brunt, 'Clumsy Utopians', p. 271.
[9] Rose, *Hidden Histories*.
[10] Lake, 'Mission Impossible'; Taussig, *The Magic of the State*, pp. 3, 195.
[11] Moreton-Robinson, *Talkin' Up to the White Woman*.
[12] Alexander, *Moving Frontiers*, p. 35.
[13] Sharp, 'Three Frontiers'.

Australia faulted the seductive persuasion of the frontier as a series of heroic struggles by settlers against Aborigines. Their pessimistic musings on the imperial utopia of a distinctive Australian civil society are early examples, later exemplified in the diverse works of C. D. Rowley, Henry Reynolds, Noel Loos, Deborah Bird Rose, and Patrick Wolfe, of the desire to engage in redemptive history by confronting violent settler-Aboriginal encounters and wrestling with the enigmatic moral episteme that places that particular violence at the core of Australian nationhood.[14]

Contemporary Australian frontier studies have bifurcated into remnant interpretations of Turner's ideas on the one hand[15] to a diversity of approaches wherein frontier is taken to be a discursive trope that settler society generates to give authority to the formations of civil society and cultural and gendered hegemonies.[16] Certainly the most well-known contemporary works on Australian frontiers are by Reynolds whose chronicling of settler-Aboriginal conflict has found great purchase in Australian studies.[17] Less well known but no less considerable has been the attention Rowley gave in a trilogy of books published through the 1970s detailing the radical changes affected on Aboriginal people by Australian governments since British colonisation.[18] Despite their considerable differences both employ the frontier to interrogate the extent to which the nation-state 'Australia' is founded on the violence and depredation of colonial encounter. In doing so they confront the 'cult of forgetfulness' that characterised white Australia's ignorance of the effects of colonialism on Aboriginal people. Their work also encapsulates the paradox embedded in frontier logic: in confronting Aboriginal dispossession and slaughter as unacknowledged presences within settler naturalisation narratives, a consensus is created about the relationship between history, settler identity and social order and land.[19]

---

[14] Reynolds, *The Other Side of the Frontier*; Rose, *Hidden Histories*; Reynolds, *Frontier*; Loos, *Invasion and Resistance*; Wolfe, 'Nation and Miscegenation'.

[15] Winks concluded in his 1981 analysis whether the Turnerian frontier could be observed in Australia, that it is more appropriate to talk of Austalian frontiers rather than a single defining period of set of events. Ten years later Peter Loveday (1991) discusses Turner's frontier hypothesis in terms of political economy concluding that north Australia has been too far away from the rest of Australia to have any lasting impact on its national identity and that the frontier is a developmental stage that has passed in this region.

[16] In *Rednecks, Eggheads and Blackfellas* Cowlishaw (p. 17) uses the term 'racial frontier' to think through racism and racial differentiation in contemporary northern Australia, while in *Creating a Nation* Grimshaw et al. (p. 132) use the idea of the frontier to provoke questions about how class, ethnicity and gender worked their way through opposing groups in the 19th century. In 'Frontier Transgressions: Writing a History of Race, Identity and Convictism in Early Colonial Queensland' Thorpe and Evans expand the notion of identity frontiers.

[17] Reynolds, *The Other Side of the Frontier*; Reynolds, *Frontier*; May, *Aboriginal Labour and the Cattle Industry*; McGrath, *Born in the Cattle*, p. 9.

[18] Rowley, *The Destruction of Aboriginal Society*, *Outcasts in White Australia* and *The Remote Aborigines*.

[19] Stanner, *After the Dreaming*, p. 25.

Rowley's adherence to Turner's successive frontiers model and Reynolds's recognition of the plurality of Aboriginal reactions to European settlement does not shift 'frontier' as an ideological process that defines the privileged status of 'settler' by reference to encounter with Aborigines. In frontier logic Aborigines define settler – the alterity of Aborigines is respected because they are necessary to the constant reaffirmation of settlerhood. The most immediate problem with enjoining the complexity of encounter to the goal of creating a distinctive settler nation is the difficulty of acknowledging or accounting for the spaces of encounter beyond the encompassing rubric of frontier. It is precisely at this point that the authors here announce their intention to dislocate frontier historiography, and at the same time to probe the symbolic energy of the frontier in its refusal to relinquish its territorial hold over the terms within which settler Australia conceives an Australian social order.

Frontier, self and other

The focus on Aborigines as the defining 'other' to settlers in the Australian nation is no more than a recognition that the basic parameters of frontier ideology produces a set of relationships wherein the symbolic function of Aborigines is to create the privileged and naturalised status of the settler. But there is a further distinction to be drawn which extends from Juliet Mitchell's recognition that 'we live as ideas', that the circulation of symbolic order through social being and individual experience not only creates alliances of identity and power but allows for more negotiable, liminal, contested and transformative exchanges to occur between different groups of people. This is not to suggest that the grounds of exchange exist beyond forces of repression and intolerance or imply compatibility and free-flowing authentic reciprocity. More, that the discourses and practices of Australian frontier cross-cultural encounter that wend their way through to politico-economic structures already evince the influence of the subaltern symbolic systems and lifeways of Australia's indigenous peoples.

This infiltrative movement within an already established logic that establishes colonial rule over the lands and seas of Australia's indigenous peoples is most recently evident in the historic 1992 Mabo v. Queensland judgement of the Australian High Court. This case involved a claim by Meriam people to ownership of land on the island of Mer (Murray Island) in eastern Torres Strait, north Queensland. The Mabo decision recognised for the first time that indigenous, or native, title to land, which had hitherto been excluded from Australian common law, could be protected by the common law. Prior to this decision the principle of terra nullius, that Australia was uninhabited or at best inhabited by peoples who had no systems of social organisation and property ownership that compelled colonial recognition, gave exclusive radical title of Australian lands to the Crown. The Mabo decision overturned the legal basis of colonial sovereignty, recognising rights to indigenous use and ownership of land where they were not extinguished by the Crown, necessitating a series of legislative actions by the Commonwealth that validated pastoral and mining leases and constrained the procedures by which Australia's indigenous population could proceed on native title claims (Native Title Act 1993 and 1998).[20]

Despite the Commonwealth's legislative attempts to rein in the property law implications of native title, the moral hierarchies of colonised and coloniser established under the shelter of terra nullius became subject to searching investigation among the Australian population. If there was ever a consensus operating amongst the majority of the non-indigenous population about the moral rights to settlement that colonial occupation ensured, it was surely shattered in the Mabo decision. Ensuing cultural and political debates revealed agonistic and antagonistic public attitudes around the treatment of Australia's indigenous population, both past and present, and subjected the 'doctrine of the settled colony' to intense public scrutiny.[21] Legal entitlement became inextricably linked to questions of national identity. The seemingly inviolable ridge between legal precedent and settlement that was ruptured by Mabo also destabilises the demands of oppositional categories of self and other, settler and indigenous, colonised and coloniser that informs the presumptions of established frontiers. However, if this destabilisation amounts to no more than a vulgar deconstruction of types or narratives or lumps together all differences into a single 'other', then we have missed the responses to alterity that are the true terrain of the frontier trope. In this elusive, fragmented, fissured space the 'attractions and aversions' (to borrow a phrase from Adorno) of encounter are compellingly demonstrated. It is perhaps an overly didactic observation, but it should be stated that the acculturative, hybrid overtones are not the necessary endgame of cross-cultural interaction. In keeping with the project of 'dislocating the frontier,' theme, some chapters attest to the incommensurable differences of cultural attitudes and philosophies that inform encounter. They compel us to be alert to unacknowledged indigenous and non-indigenous expressions of describing encounter, force a re-evaluation of what constitutes frontier; how it is experienced, imagined, and absorbed; how it discriminates, and how it is opposed. If frontier mythology has traditionally been understood as indiscriminate apology for conquest then these recognitions show that this configuration has yet to determine a coeval indigenous register.

The notion that the frontier naturalises processes of inhabitation by colonisers to colonised lands is carefully explored by Liz Furniss's examination of the usages of frontier symbolism in recent Canadian and Australian political discourse (Chapter 2). She begins with a survey of the major theoretical trends in North American scholarship on the relationship between concepts of frontier and

---

[20] Bartlett, *The Mabo Decision*, p. 42.
[21] Reynolds, *Aboriginal Sovereignty*, p. 13.

14

nationhood. Of particular value is her overview of critical approaches to Turner's frontier thesis that have occurred since the 1960s and have come to be referred to as the New Western History. In concluding her overview she raises questions that point to the disjuncture between the analytical (in)adequacy of the term and the populist power of associated symbolisms. Through an insightful discussion of the anti-indigenous rhetorics that have recently been employed in Canadian and Australian political discourse, she demonstrates that the popular usages of frontier thinking in both countries are at once too fluid for concise analytical capture, and yet tend strongly to situate the autonomy and livelihood of Aboriginal peoples as a national threat. Furniss's analysis of these two issues leads her to conclude that scholarly uses of the term collude with populist understandings as shared moments in nationalist mythology.

Collusion between contrasting ideas or conflicting groups holds forth the possibility that on the way past the dispossessing aspects of encounter a qualitative exchange between cultures resulting in redemptive advancement might occur. Taken at face value, the story of Australian artist Ainslie Roberts's relatively benign experiences of relating to the Aboriginal people and country of Palka-karrinya (Central Mount Wedge station), Central Australia, suggests such an inter-cultural dialogue. But, as Deborah Bird Rose shows in Chapter 3, the devil is in the detail, and in Roberts's case his personal and artistic fascination with Aboriginal land sacrality mirrors that stream in the Australian imagination that seeks, through mystical yearnings, a cure for past injustices. Through an analysis of Roberts's Palka-karrinya influenced work and his relationship to the ethnologist Charles Mountford, Rose is able to show how Roberts's personal quest for meaning was not only an expression of national existential concern, but transformed local religious affinities into Jungian-like religious universals. Rose recognises that this transformation effects an effacement of Aboriginal cultural expressions and uses colonial land-based resource use language to evoke the subtle violences informing these processes. Thus, Aboriginal knowledge is an 'ore body that could be mined by anyone with the talent for tapping into the unconscious.' That said, Rose cautions that what looks like the erasure of Palka-karrinya specificity in Roberts's work should be understood in terms of the transportation of highly specific Aboriginal invocations of environmental connections and iconography to Australian metropoles. The original Palka-karrinya conceptions continue despite Roberts's personal encounters and artistic transformations.

The expansion of inward-looking boundaries by encounter with Aboriginal people and place are closely allied to an experience of frontier as an outward moving boundary between the ordered and familiar and the unfamiliar and disordered. Nicholas Gill's examination of immigrant pastoralists' narratives of settlement in Central Australia stands in a critical relationship to the sense that the frontier is an expanding, overcoming boundary (Chapter 4). Their tendency to define relationships to land largely in terms of personal and family bodily engagement with land leads Gill to question 'whether the relationship between settler pastoralists is comparable to that of Aboriginal people.' The answers are both mundane and surprising. At one level the employment by both Aborigines and settlers of the idea that creatively interacting with the land brings about social order and shapes the environment would seem commensurable. The linkages, though undeniably present, belie radically different affinities: the acts of ancestral beings unfold to weave Aboriginal people, land and law together in spiritual as well as experiential ways. By contrast settlers understand their arrival in Central Australia as a homecoming, awakening a vacant, unfamiliar land to its fertile potential. In contrast to the strong sense of masculine wrestling with land that Gunn describes, Central Australian settlers project a more feminine imagining of nurturance on to the landscape.

In Chapter 5 Jay Arthur takes an innovative approach to frontier landscapes by treating water as an active agent with whom settlers have had to contend and which forever disappoints them by failing to conform to expectations. She works with the transitional edges between watercourses and land and notes that their 'drying out', as they gradually disappear into man-made containers, mirrors an increasingly regulated hydrography in Australia. In the following chapter (Chapter 6) Pat Lowe shows how seemingly innocuous events, such as losing objects and coping with car breakdowns, are as rich with meaning about the frontier as are public conflicts over ownership of natural resources. Through her relationship with Jimmy Pike, a Walmajarri man, she moves from her initial experience of the Upper Sandy Desert as monotonous sameness to an understanding of the complexity of shapes and textures that inform Walmajarri relationships to these spaces. We are also reminded by Lowe that while she is able to develop understanding of and relationships with desert country, for many Aboriginal people who were originally resident in this region and who now reside in the Kimberley towns, separation from these lands, whether by force or force of events, induces a kind of disorienting exile.

The capacity to comprehend difference is presented by Libby Robin as a heroic process of subjecting what is alien to familiar principles of order (Chapter 7). The story Robin recounts is the quest for the scientific classification of platypuses found in northern Queensland in the latter decades of the 19th century by Australian and European scientists. The echoes of an antipodean fabulity play about this creature, as does the struggle to overcome the marginality of Australian science to the English scientific establishment. However, it is Robin's singular achievement to note that this famous moment of imperial traffic between the Australian colony and metropolis was entirely dependent on another imperial exchange between explorers and Aborigines. Platypuses and other anomalies such as lungfish and echidna, presented classificatory problems for scientists of the time as well as the enticing possibility that they might bridge between seemingly discrete classes of animals. Libby notes that 19th century scientists regularly hired Aboriginal assistance in scientific expeditions, but scientists on the hunt for platypuses, lungfish and echidna relied on huge numbers of Aboriginal people, up to 150 by William Caldwell, who were hired for both their labour and knowledge of ecology and animal habitat. While European scientists were yet to understand the developmental stages of these animals' growth, Aboriginal identification and capture of animals at various stages of their life cycle allowed scientific understanding to develop, making them genuine but unacknowledged co-workers in discovery. The exchange of labour and knowledge between Aborigine and scientific explorer translated into the traffic between colony and metropole of the denouement of discovery – names. Once classified and garbed with Latin names these animals were birthed into an imperial scientific order operating independently and indifferently to local symbolic or evaluative systems.

The scientific use of frontier concepts in gaining an imaginative purchase on remote Australia offers the possibility that national aspirations for economic self-sufficiency might be fulfilled. Tim Sherratt examines atomic utopias, and the fear/hope duality founded in frontier connections between science and progress (Chapter 8). He focuses particularly on the energy industry of North Australia, and interrogates the imagining of the nation's future embedded in the scientific frontier imagination. The progressive aspects of frontier thinking become glaringly obvious in the imagined post Second World War atomic age. Sherratt notes that the nationalistic language of expansion and opportunity attached to the atomic utopia, *Australia Unlimited*, has its own curious life and reappears in contemporary popular debates over Australia's economic future. He suggests that the futuristic implications of recurring alignments of science, frontier and economy are always shadowed by the accumulation of past dreams and hopes.

These chapters have explored aspects of settler's attempt to lodge themselves in land that is already invigorated by its own geographic distinctiveness and indigenous bearings. Each chapter remarked on a frontier tabula rasa imagining that ideally absents indigenous people, while uncovering the extent to which indigenous Australians are present or implicated in such imaginings. The following three chapters look to Aboriginal engagements with frontier practice, and examine some of the ways in which Aboriginal people's cultural practice destabilises and critiques frontier imagination. The authors work from spaces adjacent to the frontier, where transformations and distortions are possible.

In my own chapter, Chapter 9, I discuss the place of rodeo in frontier imagination, particularly Aboriginal organised rodeos that occur throughout the Kimberley. Rodeo events are sometimes regarded as carrying the symbolic structures of classical frontiers in that they replay, through competitive bovine and horse riding, relationships of racial and environmental dominance. In terms of their capacity to bring together people involved in cattle grazing, rodeos have replaced race meets as the most common rural festival in northwestern Australia. Also, Aboriginal rodeos draw attention to changes in land ownership in the Kimberley pastoral industry where Aboriginal people own almost a third of the pastoral leases there. This situation is immensely different to the ration life of station camps that Aboriginal people lived in prior to the late 1960s where they were unable to exercise proprietary control over station lands and cattle.[22] The performance of Aboriginal cowboys in rodeos prises open a provocative, inter-cultural space where the conditions for identity frisson and exchange across cultures does not suggest an inability to traverse turbulent pasts, cultural boundaries and distinctive geographic grounding of peoples in the world.

In Chapter 10 Stephen Muecke dramatically shifts our perception by describing a Kalkatungu man named Boxer, a maban, a 'magic' who created the *Djanba* cult and who lived with the Duracks in the East Kimberley. Boxer's life on the white-owned stations and his *Djanba* response implies different senses of 'order' and unsettling understandings of inside and outside. Just as importantly Muecke presents Boxer as both a cultural critic and a cultural innovator. As innovator Boxer heralded new social arrangements and world concepts amongst Aboriginal people; as critic Boxer shakes things up by inaugurating, through *Djanba*, a powerful intellectual response to whitefella ways and technology. And if, as Muecke says, Boxer is best approached through deconstructive method, then the rewards seem great for Boxer appears as a philosopher of renown, a man whose performative response to the Kimberley pastoral frontier opens up paths of understanding and investigation beyond the familiar landmarks of Aboriginal resistance to, or complicity with, the frontier situation. Through Boxer's *Djanba* we are granted an enhanced understanding of an Aboriginal intellectual and creative endeavour that acknowledges the critical and open-ended negotiations, which mark Aboriginal efforts towards survival in frontier situations.

The following chapter provides an account of Aboriginal reclamation of country that was abandoned by previous generations of Aboriginal people. In Chapter 11 Andrew McWilliam describes the movement of people and names through the Fitzmaurice River region in western Northern Territory. We are introduced to an unfamiliar Aboriginal frontier that is becoming increasingly familiar for many Aboriginal people around Australia. As a consequence of favourable accounts of the pastoral potential of the region generated by A. C. Gregory, a number of stations, including Victoria River Downs, were established during the 1880s, leading to a gradual out-migration of the Aboriginal population from the basin. McWilliam describes a number of other boundaries that the river demarcates: the extent of sub-section naming systems and ritual subincision

---

[22] See Rowse, *White Flour, White Power.*

practices; and newer land uses expressed by Aboriginal freehold land on the northern side and army-owned land on the southern side. Surprisingly, the different 'exdigenous' (settler) land uses have not resulted in a wide array of place names, Through his work for the Aboriginal Areas Protection Authority, McWilliam finds that the region is more of a terra ignomia than a known geography for settlers. Likewise for Aboriginal people with traditional attachments to the area, there is much enigmatic space around the river despite ongoing reaffirmation and reclamation of the area. The Aboriginal depopulation of the region has resulted in an emptiness.

References

Alexander, Fred 1969, *Moving Frontiers: An American Theme and its Application to Australian History*, Oxford University Press, Melbourne 1947, 2nd edition, Kennikat Press, Port Washington, New York.

Allen, Harry 1959, *Bush and Backwoods: A Comparison of the Frontier in Australia and the United States*, Angus & Robertson, Sydney.

Attwood, B. 2005, *Telling the Truth about Aboriginal History*, Allen & Unwin, Sydney.

Attwood, B. and S. G. Foster 2003, *Frontier Conflict: The Australian Experience*, National Museum of Australia, Canberra.

Bartlett, Richard H. 1993, *The Mabo Decision: and the Full Text of the Decision in Mabo and Others v. State of Queensland*, Butterworths, Sydney.

Bassin, Mark 1993, 'Turner, Solov'ev, and the "Frontier Hypothesis": The Nationalist Signification of Open Spaces', *Journal of Modern History*, vol. 65, pp. 437–511.

Blainey, Geoffrey 1966, *The Tyranny of Distance: How Distance Shaped Australia's History*, Sun Books, Melbourne.

Brunt, Peter 1999, 'Clumsy Utopians: An Afterword', in Nicholas Thomas and Diane Losche (eds) *Double Visions: Art Histories and Colonial Histories and the Pacific*, pp. 257-274 Cambridge University Press, Cambridge.

Cowlishaw, Gillian 1999, *Rednecks, Eggheads and Blackfellas: A Study of Racial Power and Intimacy in Australia*, Allen and Unwin, Sydney.

Grimshaw, Patricia et al. 1994, *Creating a Nation*, McPhee Gribble, Ringwood, Victoria.

Gunn, Jeannie 1907, *We of the Never Never*. Hutchinsons Colonial Library, London.

Jackson, W. Turrentine 1976, 'Australians and the Comparative Frontier', in Kenneth R. Philp and Elliott West (eds), *Essays on Walter Prescott Webb*, pp. 17–52, University of Texas Press, Austin.

Jull, Peter 1991, *The Politics of Northern Frontiers in Australia, Canada, and Other 'First World' Countries*, North Australia Research Unit, The Australian National University, Darwin. 1991.

Lake, Marilyn 1992, 'Mission Impossible: How Men Gave Birth to the Australian Nation: Gender, Nationalism and other Seminal Acts', *Gender and History*, vol.4, no. 3, pp. 305–22.

Loos, Noel 1982, *Invasion and Resistance: Aboriginal-European Relations on the North Queensland Frontier, 1861-1897*, Australian National University Press, Canberra.

Loveday, Peter 1991, 'Political History of the North', in Ian Moffatt and Ann Webb (eds), *North Australian Research; Some Past Themes and New Directions*, pp. 146–72, ANU North Australia Research Unit, Darwin.

Macintyre, I. 2003, *The History Wars*, Melbourne University Press, Melbourne.

Manne, Robert 2003, *Whitewash: On Keith Windschuttle's Fabricaiton of Aboriginal History*, Black Inc, Melbourne.

May, Dawn 1994, *Aboriginal Labour and the Cattle Industry: Queensland from White Settlement to the Present*, Cambridge Unoversity Press, Melbourne.

McGrath, Ann 1987, *Born in the Cattle: Aborigines in Cattle Country*, Allen & Unwin, Sydney.

McLean, Ian 1998, *White Aborigines: Identity Politics in Australian Art*, Cambridge University Press, Cambridge.

Milliss, Roger 1994, *Waterloo Creek: the Australia Day Massacre of 1838, George Gipps and the British Conquest of New South Wales*, UNSW Press, Sydney.

Moreton-Robinson, Aileen 2000, *Talkin' up to the White Woman: Aboriginal Women and Feminism* , University of Queensland Press, Queensland.

Reynolds, Henry 1982, *The Other Side of the Frontier: Aboriginal Resistance to the European Invasion of Australia*, Penguin, Harmondsworth.

— 1987, *Frontier: Aborigines, Settlers and Land*, Allen and Unwin, Sydney.

— 1996, *Aboriginal Sovereignty: Reflections on Race, State and Nation*, Allen & Unwin, Sydney.

Rose, Deborah Bird 1991, *Hidden Histories: Black Stories from Victoria River Downs, Humbert River and Wave Hill Stations*, Aboriginal Studies Press, Canberra.

Rowley, C. D. 1970, *The Destruction of Aboriginal Society: Aboriginal Policy and Practice – Volume 1*, Australian National University Press, Canberra.

— 1971, *Outcasts in White Australia – Aboriginal Policy and Practice – Volume 2*, Australian National University Press, Canberra.

— 1971, *The Remote Aborigines: Aboriginal Policy and Practice – Volume 3*, Australian National University Press, Canberra.

Rowse, Tim 1998, *White Flour, White Power: from Rations to Citizenship in Central Australia*, Cambridge University Press, Melbourne.

Sharp, Paul F. 1955, 'Three Frontiers: Some Comparative Studies of Canadian, American, and Australian Settlement', *Pacific Historical Review*, November.

Smith, B. W. 1980, *The Spectre of Truganini*, 1980 Boyer Lectures, The Australian Broadcasting Commission.

Stanner, W. E. H. 1968, *After the Dreaming*, Australian Broadcasting Commission, Sydney.

Thorpe, Bill and Raymond Evans 1999, 'Frontier Transgressions: Writing a History of Race, Identity and Convictism in Early Colonial Queensland', *Continuum: Journal Of Media And Cultural Studies*, vol. 13, no. 3, November, pp. 325–32.

Turner, Frederick 1893, 'The Significance of the Frontier in American History', in The Annual Report of the American Historical Association for 1893, pp. 199–227. By Professor Frederick J. Turner, then of the University of Wisconsin.

Ward, Russel 1958, *The Australian Legend*, Oxford University Press, Melbourne.

Webb, Walter P. 1952, *The Great Frontier*, Houghton Mifflin, Boston.

Windschuttle, Keith 2000, 'The Myths of Frontier Massacres in Australian History', *Quadrant,* vol. 11, no. 1.

—— 2002, *The Fabrication of Aboriginal History*, Macleay Press, Sydney.

Winks, Robert W. 1981, 'Australia, the Frontier, and the Tyranny of Distance', in George Wolfskill and Stanley Palmer (eds), *Essays on Frontiers in World History*, pp. 121–46, University of Texas Press, Austin.

Wolfe, P. 1994, 'Nation and Miscegenation: Discursive Continuity in the Post-Mabo Era', *Social Analysis*, vol. 36.

Filmography

Auzins, Igor, 1982, *We of the Never Never*. Adams Packer Film Productions, Film Corporation of Western Australia.

2. Imagining the frontier: comparative perspectives from Canada and Australia

Elizabeth Furniss

The idea of the frontier reflects a uniquely colonial view of a place and process of encounter between colonising people, indigenous inhabitants, and natural landscapes.[1] Within this colonial context, the idea of the frontier has been variously developed through history by natural and social scientists, popular historians, artists, writers, and government officials. This volume draws together a similarly diverse group of people who bring somewhat different conceptual approaches and theoretical interests to their studies of the frontier, which raises the immediate question: what do we mean when we talk about 'the frontier'? In the following pages, and before turning to the substantive matter of this paper, I wish to first explore this problem of conceptualisation and definition by surveying how scholars have used the concept of the frontier in studies of colonial societies. The idea of the frontier is not unique to Australia, but is one of the founding metaphors of all settler societies, finding its expression in a range of venues from official histories and literary and artistic productions to political discourse. In the remaining pages I take an ethnographic perspective on the idea of the frontier in settler cultures, and compare how the frontier is imagined within Canadian and Australian notions of national identity and history as expressed in the anti-native title discourse of two leading right-wing political parties: the One Nation Party in Australia and the Reform Party in Canada. I conclude by suggesting some ways in which a comparative analysis of frontier imagery can contribute to an understanding of the unique ways in which north Australian identity, history, and landscape are represented.

Frontier studies in academic scholarship

Frederick Jackson Turner

Any survey of academic studies of the frontier would have to start with a consideration of the work of Frederick Jackson Turner. In 1893 Turner delivered his paper 'The Significance of the Frontier in American History' to a meeting of the American Historical Association in Chicago. Over the next decade Turner's 'frontier thesis' received widespread acclaim among both academics and the

[1] This paper, written in 2000, draws upon research I conducted while on a postdoctoral fellowship from the Social Sciences and Humanities Research Council of Canada and based at the Centre for Cross-Cultural Research at The Australian National University, Canberra. I am grateful to both institutions for their support.

general public. Turner became a leading figure in the historical profession over the next decades, and his frontier thesis continued to have a profound influence through much of the 20th century.

What was the frontier thesis? Turner argued that American history, culture, and political institutions were shaped not by America's British heritage, but instead by the unique environment of North America. Specifically, it was from the frontier experience that uniquely American culture and political institutions were forged. As Turner so boldly and succinctly stated in the opening paragraph of his treatise: 'The existence of an area of free land, its continuous recession, and the advance of American settlement westward, explain American development'.[2] This is what Turner imagined: settlers moving westward to the frontier gradually shed the trappings of civilisation. Surrounded by wilderness, the settlers were in essence overwhelmed by nature. In order to survive and in the absence of a social framework and traditions, settlers were forced to revert to the 'primitive' ways of the 'savages' they encountered: the settler travelled by birch-bark canoe, survived by hunting, lived in a rough log cabin, and 'takes the scalp in orthodox Indian fashion'.[3] In short, he underwent a process of social devolution. But soon the settler began to master the wilderness: fields were cleared, towns were created, and a new society developed. The frontier environment, Turner believed, was selective of certain values: individualism, resourcefulness, self-sufficiency, and democracy. What emerged from the frontier crucible was not the old civilisation left behind, but the 'new American' who fully embraced these values, which in turn came to underlie American national character and democratic institutions. This, then, is how the frontier explains American development.

What did Turner mean by the term 'frontier'? Turner used various definitions, claiming that the term was 'an elastic one' that did not need to be clearly defined.[4] On the one hand, he defined the term by demographic criteria, following the convention of the US Census Bureau, as those zones on the peripheries of regions having a population density (of settlers) of two or more people per square mile.[5] Seen in these terms, the frontier was a largely uninhabited region (of course, erasing an indigenous presence), and therefore a region of 'free, unoccupied land' (free in the sense that the American government deemed the land open to pre-emption by settlers, regardless of Indian ownership or claims). Turner considered the frontier not as a fixed place, but rather a moving zone of occupation, a moving place that swept from east to west as settlers pushed further and further towards the Pacific. In the early days of settlement, he noted, the

---

[2] Turner, *The Frontier in American History*, p. 1.
[3] ibid., p. 4.
[4] ibid., p. 3.
[5] ibid.

frontier was on the Atlantic coast; in the 1820s the frontier was along the Great Lakes and beyond the Mississippi; by 1880 settlers had pushed the frontier westward well into the Great Plains. On the other hand, Turner defined the frontier in a second sense, envisioning it not only as a place but as a process of encounter. The frontier was 'the meeting point between savagery and civilisation',[6] between man and nature, between settler and Indian. The frontier was a zone of intensive social devolution and reformation, where settlers became stripped of the trappings of civilisation, only to be recreated and reborn into values, traditions, and social forms that Turner considered uniquely American. In short, Turner argued that 'The frontier is the line of most rapid and effective Americanisation'.[7]

Turner's frontier thesis emerged at a particular time in history. We can see the influence of the 19th century notions of environmental determinism, Social Darwinism, cultural evolutionism and Manifest Destiny. Nor was Turner the first to assert the importance of the frontier to American history and culture. Others before him, from Benjamin Franklin to Thomas Jefferson and Theodore Roosevelt, had linked the frontier experience to the creation of uniquely American democratic institutions and the values of independence, individualism, self-sufficiency, resistance to imposed authority, and so on.[8] For over a century American literature had described the frontier experience: in this corpus of work American history *became* the history of the frontier, which in turn came to define American national identity.[9] The immense popularity of Turner's frontier thesis had less to do with the novelty of his ideas – Turner merely adapted ideas and sentiments that had long existed about the frontier to the setting of academic history as an explanatory theory. But he did so at a time in which public attention was focused on the frontier region of the nation.

In the 1890s the frontier was officially announced to have closed: non-indigenous settlement had spread to all reaches of the nation, and there were no more tracts of 'free land' available for settlers to pre-empt. To many it signalled a critical juncture in American history. For three hundred years colonists and settlers had based their existence around the relatively unrestricted pursuit and exploitation of natural resources, from which a distinct set of political and cultural values had developed. What would happen to these values and traditions once the frontier had disappeared? By the late 1800s the closure of the agrarian frontier was coupled with an increasing industrialisation of the agrarian economy and a concentration of wealth and power in the hands of a few individuals and companies, while independent farmers were losing land to debt and becoming

---

[6] ibid.
[7] ibid., p. 304.
[8] Billington, *The American Frontier Thesis*, p. 108; Slotkin, *The Fatal Environment*, pp. 29-31.
[9] Slotkin, *Regeneration through Violence*; *The Fatal Environment*.

tenants on industrial properties.[10] Turner's frontier thesis, in this respect, had two functions. First, it served as a legitimisation and celebration of the processes of American colonisation and the dispossession of the lands of indigenous peoples. In Turner's account, indigenous peoples and their ownership to traditional territories were erased through the image of the 'free land with abundant resources' and the image of indigenous savagery, an image that only justified the purportedly retributive acts of settler violence, settlers having inevitably 'become like Indians' under the force of the frontier. Second and more significantly, Turner's frontier thesis, having established the legitimacy of settlement and dispossession, then idealised the agrarian past while crystallizing growing public concerns about the future of the nation. It served as a populist critique of the developing social and political inequalities in American society, inequalities that many believed threatened the very values and ideals that the frontier represented.[11]

Turner's frontier thesis enjoyed remarkable popularity through the early 20th century. Despite its origins in a Western populist critique, the frontier thesis was taken up by Eastern political conservatives who promoted, in the words of one critic, a 'complacent nationalist romanticism' in which 'the notion of an aggressive pioneering national spirit nurtured by repeated exposure to primitive conditions became a means to national self-glorification'.[12] Beginning in the 1920s the thesis was subjected to a number of significant challenges from within the discipline. Scholars critiqued the frontier thesis for overemphasizing the single determining influence of the frontier environment and for ignoring how other forces, such as class struggle, urbanisation, industrialisation, Protestantism, ethnic heterogeneity, the slave system, and the growth of international capitalism, had influenced the course of American history.[13] Nevertheless, and in part due to the frontier thesis's association with a strident American nationalism, Turner's influence lingered for many decades while interest in studies of the American west waned.

It was not until the 1960s and 1970s that interest again arose in the history of the American west, and a new approach began to emerge to challenge the frontier thesis. By the 1980s, under the influence of such historians as Patricia Limerick, Richard White, and Donald Worster, this new approach began to take form as the New Western History.

---

[10] Billington, *Frederick Jackson Turner*, pp. 108-110; Slotkin, *The Fatal Environment*, pp. 31-2.
[11] Slotkin, *The Fatal Environment*, pp. 108-110.
[12] Hoftstadter, 'The Frontier Thesis Under Attack', p. 23.
[13] ibid.; Billington, *The American Frontier Thesis*, pp. 5-9; Nash, *Creating the West*.

The New Western History

The New Western History movement has been shaped by a number of social forces in the 1960s and 1970s, namely the rise of public concern with race relations, women's rights, Indian rights, multiculturalism and ethnic pluralism. The New Western History reflects the intellectual influence of both feminist scholarship and the new social history in general, which emphasises the diversity of historical experiences and the need to recover voices of the 'ordinary' people often ignored by nationalist, grand-level historical studies. Much of the early writing took the form of polemic denunciation of the Turnerian legacy in Western history, with promoters attempting to mark off ways in which the new approach was unique. Following Patricia Limerick's characterisation,[14] and supplemented by other contributors to the volume *Trails: Toward a New Western History*,[15] we come up with the following features.

Scholars such as Limerick have entirely rejected use of the term 'frontier' as an object of study, the term being too 'nationalistic', 'racist', and ethnocentric to be useful.[16] Rather than focusing on the frontier as a process, a moving line of encounter (in Turner's second sense of the term), many New Western Historians focus on the West as a distinct place, the West being that region from the Mississippi to the Pacific, although these boundaries are also debated. Unlike Turner, who saw the purported disappearance of the frontier in the 1890s as a pivotal event signifying a radical disjuncture in Western history, the new historians argue that there has been no such discontinuity, and that the West has remained a distinctive region into the present.[17] These historians are interested in recovering the voices of the multiple populations that inhabited and settled the West: different indigenous peoples, Hispanics, Chinese, blacks, women, and others. This contrasts sharply with Turner's simplistic formulation of the frontier encounter involving only two groups: white male settlers and generic 'Indians'. The new historians are interested in looking at the environment not as a barrier to Western expansion, but a component that changes with human interaction. They highlight how ecological factors, and human/environment interactions, influenced the path of Western history. Challenging Turner's celebratory approach that emphasised frontier social harmony and egalitarianism, the new historians are examining also the tragedies of western expansion: the destruction of the environment, the massacres of indigenous populations, the ambiguities, difficulties and disappointments of settlers' lives. As a result, they are stripping the frontier, the expansion of settlement Westward, of much of its sacredness as a source of national values. Finally, the new historians are

---

[14] Limerick, 'What on Earth is the New Western History?'.
[15] Limerick, Milner and Rankin, *Trails: Toward a New Western History*.
[16] Limerick, 'What on Earth is the New Western History?', p. 85.
[17] For example, Limerick, 'The Trail to Santa Fe', pp. 70-71.

redefining the historian's social role, and (in at least some instances) are abandoning their image of neutral objectivity and displaying an empathetic and critical concern with their subjects of study.

Despite the above summary, the New Western History is by no means a coherent field. Indeed, a significant literature debates just precisely what this approach constitutes and just how unique it really is from the Turnerian legacy. For example, Faragher,[18] Steiner,[19] Klein,[20] Wrobel,[21] and Bogue[22] all highlight continuities between the 'old' and 'new' Western histories. There has also been a move to reclaim the 'f-word'.[23] Simply abandoning the term 'frontier' does not protect historical analyses from ethnocentrism, Klein believes, and in his view the term is not too laden with implicit ethnocentrisms that it cannot be successfully resuscitated. Several scholars have recently re-introduced the term into their analyses, defining the frontier as a zone of cultural interaction.[24] In all, what the new Western histories provide is not so much a new paradigm, but an opening up of multiple perspectives and possibilities for new critical intellectual inquiries into the study of the American West.

Richard Slotkin and the frontier myth

A third figure that has contributed immensely to contemporary frontier studies is Richard Slotkin, Professor of English and Director of American Studies at Wesleyan University. In a sense, Slotkin's mission is similar to that of the New Western Historians: to escape the ideological baggage of the frontier thesis, and to look anew at American history. Slotkin, instead, turns the idea of the frontier in the United States itself into a subject of critical inquiry.

Slotkin has written three volumes tracing the development of the 'frontier myth' over three centuries of American history.[25] The frontier myth, he argues, is one of the most important cultural myths shaping public understandings of European colonisation and settlement in the United States. It consists of a constellation of narratives, symbols and metaphors that flow through American literature (including the earliest of settler autobiographies of the 18th century, 19th century dime novels, and contemporary pioneer literature); performative arts (including early Wild West shows and today's Hollywood movies), and 19th and 20th century political discourse legitimizing American domestic and foreign policy. Despite

---

[18] Faragher, 'The Frontier Trail'.
[19] Steiner, 'From Frontier to Region'.
[20] Klein, 'Reclaiming the 'F' Word'.
[21] Wrobel, 'Beyond the Frontier-Region Dichotomy'.
[22] Bogue, *Frederick Jackson Turner*.
[23] Klein, 'Reclaiming the 'F' Word.
[24] Limerick, 'The Adventures of the Frontier in the Twentieth Century' and Klein, 'Reclaiming the 'F' Word, provide overviews of this debate.
[25] Slotkin, *Regeneration Through Violence; The Fatal Environment; Gunfighter Nation*.

the different formulations of the frontier myth in these very different social, economic and historical contexts (and Slotkin includes Turner's frontier thesis as one expression of the frontier myth), in its most common 'progressivist' formulation the frontier myth has several standard features.[26]

The frontier myth portrays North America as an empty, unoccupied wilderness (not withstanding occasional acknowledgment of the indigenous presence) where resources are rich and land is free for the taking; or, if not exactly free, the land becomes the rightful spoil of war for those representing the interests of civilisation and progress. The symbolic landscape of the frontier narrative is marked by boundaries and by the encounter of opposites: civilisation and savagery, man and nature, Whites and Indians, good and evil. These encounters are characterised in terms of conflict and violence as the protagonist struggles against the harsh environment, the unknown and potentially hostile Indians, the savagery of the empty land. Eventually these encounters are resolved through domination and conquest, through the subordination of Indians, nature, and evil to the forces of progress, civilisation, and the ultimate will of God. The triumph of the protagonist highlights the triumph of the values of self-reliance, democracy, competition, and freedom, values that continue to define American ideals in the present.

The frontier myth thus provides a theory of history in which conflict, violence, and the subjugation of nature and indigenous peoples are legitimated as natural and inevitable for ensuring the 'progress' of civilisation. The frontier myth provides a master narrative of 'regeneration through violence', through which American identity was initially defined, and continues to be continually reasserted, through acts of aggressive violence.[27] Slotkin sees this key metaphor of regeneration through violence, and this foundational narrative of history, to be continually expressed in diverse arenas of cultural and political activity, ranging from the military aggression of American foreign policy to the crop of urban vigilante movies produced by Hollywood in the 1980s. It is through such acts of heroic, aggressive intervention that American national identity is continually expressed and celebrated.

The resilience of the frontier myth as a dominant cultural myth is due to two features. The first is its flexibility: it provides a set of narratives, symbols, images and metaphors that can be used either to affirm or to contest existing social and political arrangements. Populist forms of the frontier myth, Slotkin argues, have been among the most important vehicles for public criticism in the 20th century.[28] These narratives construct ideal images of the past (ranging from romantic notions of pre-contact Aboriginal life to the idyllic images of 19th century agrarian

[26] Slotkin, *Gunfighter Nation*, pp. 22-24.
[27] Slotkin, *Regeneration through Violence*.
[28] Slotkin, *Gunfighter Nation*, pp. 22-26.

communities of the American West) and launch critiques of the policies and developments that have brought about an abandonment of older traditional values and the destruction of social ties. Turner's frontier thesis is one such example. What remains consistent in populist versions is the standard narrative structure of the frontier myth: the binary encounter of opposites on the frontier, the centrality of conflict and violence to their encounter, and the outcome of absolute conquest; now however, the moral weighting of these agents and outcomes is reversed.

Second, the frontier myth conveys historical truths not so much through explicit, argumentative forms of discourse, but indirectly through narratives rich in symbolism and metaphor. 'The language is metaphorical and suggestive rather than logical or analytical', Slotkin asserts. 'The movement of a mythic narrative, like that of any story, implies a theory of cause and effect and therefore a theory of history (or even of cosmology); but these ideas are offered in a form that disarms critical analysis by its appeal to the structures and traditions of storytelling and the clichés of historical memory.[29] Of particular importance are 'mythic icons', which stand as condensed symbols of the frontier myth's narrative, and which 'effect a poetic construction of tremendous economy and compression and a mnemonic device capable of evoking a complex system of historical associations by a single image or phrase'.[30] The symbol of the 'pioneer', the 'empty wilderness', and even 'the frontier' are classic examples of mythic icons. Their power, thus, lies in their ability to convey certain myths of history intuitively and indirectly in such a subtle manner that often lies beyond our critical awareness.

What can we conclude about the concept of the frontier in academic studies of colonial histories? First, the term has been used in two quite distinct senses: as a descriptive/analytical term describing a presumably empirical reality, and as a social construction having no reality outside of the cultural imaginings of colonial societies. Is there such a thing as the frontier? In one of Turner's definitions, the frontier was a demographic phenomenon, a region where white settlers were scarce. In another definition, it was a more ambiguous zone of interaction between early settlers/fur traders and Indians/wilderness. In later definitions, the frontier becomes a specifically cultural frontier, a zone of cultural interaction.[31] The term retains its ethnocentric vantage: in its implicit association with expansion into an unknown region, it remains the view of the coloniser, the view from one 'side' of the encounter. There are alternatives; for example,

[29] ibid., p. 6.
[30] ibid.
[31] Limerick, 'The Adventures of the Frontier in the Twentieth Century'; Klein, 'Reclaiming the 'F' Word'.

the more neutral term 'borderlands' has been used instead to describe early processes of cultural encounter between colonizing and indigenous peoples.[32]

But what about the term's analytical adequacy? If we use 'frontier' more in an analytical than a descriptive sense, is it useful in assessing patterns of contact between indigenous and colonizing peoples and cultures? Scholars such as Patricia Limerick remain opposed on various grounds, including the term's ethnocentricity, the impreciseness of its definition, and the fact that it leads scholars to only reproduce the error of previous historians who overemphasised the role of the frontier in shaping American history.[33] Further, it is difficult to define the boundaries of the frontier. In many regions of North America, for example, both the material and ideological products of colonizing peoples (the horse, metal goods, ideas and symbols of Christianity) long preceded any direct contact between indigenous peoples and colonisers. This zone of cultural contact is complex and cannot be easily narrowed to a particular place or a span of time. And if, as Slotkin argues, the frontier is a classical mythic icon that carries the burden of the frontier myth through implicit associations and meanings, can the term be stripped of its ethnocentric meanings to be successfully resuscitated and applied to contemporary analyses? Despite careful attempts to define and contextualise our use of the term, can we in fact control how the term is understood by our readership? What meanings may we be inadvertently communicating when we use the term?

There is no easy solution to these questions; that the term seems to be making reappearance in Western American history is indicative of its compelling force, although I would caution scholars (including myself) that we continue to use the term as an analytical device at our own peril. On the other hand, that frontier is an ethnographic reality (as opposed to a descriptive reality or an analytical construct) is beyond question: it is one of the key, founding metaphors of virtually all settler-colonial societies, and serves as a continual source of symbols in the construction of national histories and identities. These are the issues that I now turn to examine.

The 'frontier' in Canadian and Australian anti-native title discourse

All settler-colonial societies face similar dilemmas. As new societies with populations that include both indigenous peoples and immigrants from diverse cultures and world regions, how can a collective sense of national identity, with a shared set of values, goals, and experiences, be constructed, or even imagined? How can settler societies explain and legitimate the process of nation-formation, and the original colonisation and dispossession of indigenous lands? How do

---

[32] Anzaldúa, *Borderlands/La Frontera*.
[33] Limerick, 'The Adventures of the Frontier in the Twentieth Century'.

they rationalise their historically exploitative and oppressive relations with indigenous peoples? How do they conceive of ongoing relations, and the place of indigenous peoples in contemporary society? These problems are particularly acute in the present, as indigenous peoples are asserting rights to land and self-government, in so doing challenging the very authority of the state and its official histories. How are conservative elements of settler societies responding to the questioning of official history, and to indigenous assertions of native title?

There is a remarkable similarity in the rhetoric of resistance to indigenous claims in settler societies today. In Canada, Australia, and New Zealand, individuals and groups opposed to indigenous claims all argue that these claims violate the basic values and principles of liberal democratic societies: the equality of all citizens, the emphasis on individual rather than collective rights, and democratic (majority rule) government. While public opposition to Aboriginal rights is somewhat similar, the way in which claims to Aboriginal rights are perceived to conflict with national values and to be threats to the very integrity of the nation varies significantly according to the ways in which ideas of colonial nationhood have historically been constructed. In the remaining pages I wish to compare how ideas of settler history, nationhood, and 'the frontier' encounter between colonisers and indigenous peoples/wilderness are imagined in Australia and Canada. I do so by tracing the anti-native title discourse of two prominent right-wing political parties, Pauline Hanson's One Nation party in Australia, and the Reform Party in Canada.[34]

Australia

Pauline Hanson first entered the political scene in the 1996 Commonwealth elections, when, after being disenfranchised from the Liberal party for her controversial views on Aboriginal issues, she was elected as an independent in the Queensland seat of Oxley. In her maiden speech to parliament, Hanson denounced Aboriginal land rights, multiculturalism and Asian immigration as policies encouraging racial separatism and national divisiveness. She called instead for an Australia of 'one people, one nation, one flag'. Hanson officially launched her new One Nation political party in 1997. Despite predictions that the 'Hanson phenomenon' was transient and lacking serious public appeal, One Nation through the late 1990s became a formidable threat to the Coalition (Liberal/National) and Labor parties. It enjoyed widespread public support in rural regions in northern and western Australia, and achieved an unprecedented success in the Queensland state elections of 1998, electing eleven candidates. By 1999, however, the One Nation Party had become wracked by bitter internal

---

[34] In 2000 the Reform Party changed its name to the Canadian Reform Conservative Alliance, which merged with the Progressive Conservative party in 2004. This paper traces the political rhetoric of the Reform Party during the 1990s.

disputes and defections – largely over the undemocratic structure of the party – placing its future in serious doubt.

Pauline Hanson's One Nation is a typical example of rural, conservative populism.[35] It is critical of the totalitarian powers wielded by the ruling classes, the intellectual elites, and other 'special' groups that are perceived to have an inordinate influence on government. It demands that democracy be restored to make government more fully representative of the interests of 'ordinary' members of 'mainstream' Australia. Hanson is vigorously opposed to multiculturalism and Asian immigration. She has stated: 'I believe we are in danger of being swamped by Asians … they have their own culture and religion, form ghettos and do not assimilate … A truly multicultural country can never be strong or united …'[36] Hanson is against economic globalisation, stating: 'Government … must stop kowtowing to financial markets, international organisations, world bankers, investment companies and big business people'.[37] She is opposed to foreign investment in Australia and has called for the immediate cessation of aid to foreign countries, stating that governments must 'apply the savings to generate employment here at home'.[38]

The threat to the nation's integrity comes not only from international capitalism and immigration, but also from within. Hanson believes that Australian indigenous people are a 'privileged' class who receive far more benefits than white Australians. She has called for an abolition of ATSIC, the federal government agency responsible for administering Aboriginal affairs, and which she has called 'a corrupt organisation run by an Aboriginal Mafia'.[39] She has called for the rejection of indigenous land rights and the abandonment of all special programs geared to improving the health, employment and living conditions of indigenous peoples. These programs, she insists, are dividing the country into 'black' and 'white', and she demands that all Australians be treated equally. Hanson's deep opposition to indigenous people (and the deeply undemocratic nature of the One Nation party) were made all too clear when Hanson stated that, as an elected politician, she intended to fight for 'the white community, the immigrants, Italians, Greeks, whoever, it really doesn't matter – anyone apart from the Aboriginals and Torres Strait Islanders'.[40]

What conditions allow Hanson to get away with such undemocratic and hostile political rhetoric? How is it that such an inherently intolerant, racist political

---

[35] Melleuish, 'Pauline Hanson and Australian Conservative Populism'.
[36] From Pauline Hanson's first speech to the federal Parliament, reprinted in 'The Speech that Unified a Nation', *Pauline Hanson's One Nation*, July 1998, p. 2.
[37] ibid.
[38] ibid.
[39] From a press conference in Adelaide, 13 February 1998, printed in 'Abolishing ATSIC', *Pauline Hanson's One Nation*, July 1998, p. 5.
[40] Wells, 'One Nation and the Politics of Populism', p. 21.

party has suddenly emerged and gained such a groundswell of public support? Here I am less concerned with the political and economic conditions that give rise to such a conservative political movement – rising unemployment levels, increasing internationalisation of the economy, and backlash attitudes towards earlier Labour Government policies that sympathetically addressed Aboriginal issues. Rather, I'm interested in culturally situating Hanson's political rhetoric – at looking at how this rhetoric draws upon and resonates with key understandings of nationhood, of history, and of settler identity in Australia.

First, Hanson defines the Australian nation as an ethnic nation. It is this Britishness that she imagines to be under attack from multiculturalism and Asian immigration. There is indeed a long tradition in Australian politics, popular culture and historiography of defining the Australian nation in terms of its British roots. Politicians at the turn of the last century were concerned with maintaining not only the cultural heritage, but also more precisely the 'racial purity' of Australia's British stock as Australia transformed from a British colony to an independent Commonwealth nation. Political parties and leading newspapers warned of the dangers of racial mixing and advocated 'Australia for the White Man'.[41] In 1901 the Commonwealth government passed the Immigration Restriction Act, inaugurating what became known as the White Australia policy, which effectively restricted non-European immigration to Australia until the late 1940s. The increase of non-British immigration since has fundamentally challenged conservative, established notions of national identity that now sit uneasily alongside newer models of Australia as a multicultural nation.

Australian identity has been traditionally constructed not just in terms of Britishness but also in opposition to Asia. Hanson opposes not just immigration, but Asian immigration in particular. Her rhetoric is an expression of what scholar Ien Ang has called the 'psycho-geographic logic' of the Australian national imagination.[42] Since Federation, Ang argues, Australia has had a split identity emerging from its unique geographical position in the southern hemisphere. On the one hand imagined as a British colony, Australia was yet far from Britain, isolated in the southern hemisphere and surrounded by Asian countries often imagined as foreign and potentially threatening. Indeed, at the turn of the last century the threat of an Asian invasion was one of the most pressing issues faced by the new federal government, a fear reflected in an outpouring of 'invasion novels' that embedded this perceived vulnerability in the popular imagination.[43]

[41] Macintyre, *A Concise History of Australia*, pp. 143, 148.
[42] Ien Ang, 'The Psycho-Geographical Effect', The New Racism: The Politics of Race and Nationalism in Australia. This paper was presented to 'The New Australian Racism?' colloquium organised by the Australian Studies Graduate Program Colloquium, The Australian National University, 13 October 1997. No published version yet.
[43] Macintyre, *A Concise History of Australia*, p. 141.

More recently, the fear of an Asian invasion was again raised in public debate in 1984 when controversial historian Geoffrey Blainey publicly condemned what he saw was a 'massive increase in immigration from Asia'.[44] Significantly, he criticised Asian immigration using the rhetoric of military invasion. In the subsequent furor, Blainey defended his views in letters to leading national newspapers, stating: 'I do not accept the view ... that some kind of slow Asian takeover of Australia is inevitable. I do not believe that we are powerless'[45] and 'So we jump as a nation from extreme to extreme. The old White Australia policy said rudely to half the world: Keep out. The new Surrender Australia policy says to that half of the world: Come in'.[46] Other anti-immigration proponents likewise made use of militaristic metaphors to describe the perceived Asian threat. Ian Sinclair, the leader of the National Party, supported the anti-immigration movement, arguing 'If there is any risk of an undue build-up of Asians as against others in the community, then you need to control it. We need ... to reduce the number of Asians'.[47] Extremist organisations spread posters and graffiti urging governments to 'stop the Asian invasion'.[48] Pauline Hanson's concern with being swamped by Asian immigrants is a direct reflection of these established modes of conceiving and defining Australian nationhood in terms of its geographic, military and demographic vulnerability to an Asian takeover. These military themes illustrate how Australian nationhood is imagined to be chronically vulnerable to external Asian threat, and how Australians should be compelled to react swiftly, aggressively, and defensively to protect the nation's integrity.

Pauline Hanson's call to aggressively defend the Australian nation from perceived threats also taps into wider concepts of settler identity and history. Historian Ann Curthoys has argued that master narratives of Australian history typically are stories of victimisation.[49] In contrast to frontier narratives in the United States, in which settlers confidently, aggressively encounter and ultimately triumph in their battle against the wilderness and Indians,[50] and in contrast to those frontier narratives in Canada in which settlers are surrounded by and passively endure a fearful landscape and are frozen into passive inactivity in the process,[51] in Australia the master narratives are of a kind of victimisation that necessitates not a passive endurance but an ongoing, aggressive battle for survival. This master narrative 'is a story of battlers, victims of huge forces,

[44] Ricklefs, 'The Asian Immigration Controversies', p. 41.
[45] *Age*, 20 March 1984, cited in Ricklefs, 'The Asian Immigration Controversies', p. 41.
[46] *Sydney Morning Herald*, 3 April 1984, cited in Ricklefs, 'The Asian Immigration Controversies', p. 42.
[47] ibid., p. 48.
[48] ibid., p. 43.
[49] Curthoys, 'Entangled Histories'; 'Expulsion, Exodus and Exile'.
[50] Slotkin, *The Fatal Environment; Gunfighter Nation*.
[51] Atwood, *Survival*; Frye, *The Bush Garden*.

their heroism one of survival, in war as in peace. The frame-story begins with a tale of convict suffering, of pioneers who had to endure the harshest continent on earth, endless drought and flood ... near starvation ...'[52] These narratives also extend to accounts of war, of being used as 'cannon fodder for the British military in World War One' and of chronic vulnerability as a continent to attacks from foreign nations.[53] One of the best known of the battler narratives is the Anzac legend, which emerged from the tragic deaths of thousands of Australian troops at Gallipoli in 1915. The Anzac legend has become one of Australia's most important founding myths, in which war is glorified as the proving ground for the Australian nation and national character, and death in war is upheld as the ultimate nationalistic sacrifice.[54] But this heroic victimisation also comes from within: Aborigines, too, are the aggressors, 'inflicting violence on the innocent settler and his family'.[55] And the landscape also victimises settlers and explorers. Australia's explorer-heroes — Burke and Wills, Edmund Kennedy, Leichhardt — are all individuals who died a heroic, mysterious death while exploring the continent, disappearing into the vast outback never to be found. In all, these master narratives of history reinforce the obligation, the ongoing imperative, to fight aggressively and defensively to protect one's rights, property and nation. Battling, in short, is an Australian imagined tradition.

These national themes and images pervade Hanson's rhetoric. She presents herself as an ordinary battler standing up to defend her nation. Her rhetoric is full of militaristic images of a nation under attack both from outside and within. In her 1997 speech at the launch of the One Nation party Hanson rallied her audience with a virtual call to arms: 'Australians can no longer afford the luxury of apathy. We must stand up. We must win this battle, or lose the war'. The One Nation Party, she claimed, represented 'a chance to stand against those who have betrayed our country, and would destroy our identity by forcing upon us the cultures of others ... if we fail ... we will lose our country forever, and be strangers in our own land ... Ladies and Gentlemen, who of you would not join this fight? Who of you would not stand up for your country?' She explicitly aligns her struggle with the heroic Anzac battlers of World War One: One Nation offers 'the chance to turn this country around, revitalise our industry, [and] restore our ANZAC spirit and our national pride'. She says: 'We must always remember the sacrifice of so many Australians who fought to save our country from outsiders who would have taken it. We must not now allow our country to be taken from within'.[56]

[52] Curthoys, 'Entangled Histories', p. 120.
[53] ibid.
[54] Dennis et al., 'Anzac Legend'.
[55] Curthoys, 'Entangled Histories', p. 121.
[56] Pauline Hanson's speech to the One Nation Party launch, 11 April 1997, reprinted in 'Party Launch Speech', *Pauline Hanson's One Nation*, June 1998, pp. 3-4.

Similar images of nationhood and national history permeate Hanson's anti-native title rhetoric. She argues for the extinguishment of native title, the abolition of ATSIC, and the end of all special programs for indigenous people. These arguments are framed by a series of concerns having to do with a demographic and pseudo-military takeover of Australia from within. She expresses alarm at being demographically overwhelmed by a rising Aboriginal population: 'The Aboriginal population increased 33% from 1991-1996 while the rest of the population of Australia increased by only around 6%', she warned a crowd gathered at Longreach, Queensland in September 1998. At the same meeting she raised fears that Aboriginal corporations could potentially buy up pastoral properties in Queensland, engaging in a kind of economic takeover of the land and pastoral industry in that state: 'Most Australians are not aware the Indigenous Land Corporation will have the financial ability to transfer the ownership of Australia's pastoral leases to Aborigines ... by 2004 the Indigenous Land Fund will have received over $1.2 Billion in taxpayers' funds ... Given the chance the Corporation could buy all the pastoral properties in Cape York in just one year. This taxpayer created fund could take only about thirty years or so to buy all the Pastoral Leases in Queensland'.[57] Significantly, Hanson envisions Aboriginal-run pastoral stations not as contributing in significant and important ways to the economy of the country, but somehow as threats to the nation's integrity. Along similar lines, Hanson claims that Queensland Labor and Coalition parties are in a conspiracy to create a separate, sovereign Aboriginal state. As evidence of an international conspiracy to this effect, she points her finger at the Canadian government and the new territory of Nunavut, which she incorrectly portrays as a separate, independent, 'race-based' state separate from Canada.[58] And she blames 'new class elites' for 'surrendering' Australia to indigenous Australians.[59]

While this kind of paranoid, militaristic rhetoric is also found in the extreme right-wing populist movements in North America, in Australia this rhetoric has a particular salience when placed alongside established foundational histories and images of nationhood. The success of One Nation during the mid- to late 1990s, in part, must be associated with its ability to appeal to these sentimental

[57] Pauline Hanson's speech at Longreach, 11 September 1998, from the One Nation website (http://www.gwb.com.au/onenation/speeches/long.html), October 1998.
[58] Pauline Hanson, speech to the Australian House of Representatives, 1 October 1997, as recorded in Hansard; also 'Hanson claims Aboriginal State conspiracy', *Sydney Morning Herald*, 3 June 1998. Nunavut, created in April 1999, and like every other province and territory in Canada, is headed by a government elected democratically by the majority vote of territorial residents, irrespective of ethnicity or 'race'. By virtue of the fact that the majority of Nunavut residents are indigenous, in can be said to be an 'indigenous' government, but this is subject to change should the demographic balance of indigenous/non-indigenous residents shift in the future.
[59] Pauline Hanson, cited in Bohill, 'For the Record', p. 74.

symbols of Australian identity and history and to tap into lingering fears about the tenuousness of the nation's security.

Canada

Anti-native title arguments in Canada show some significant differences. As in Australia, indigenous people in Canada are often constructed as undeserving of 'special rights': they 'sponge' off government, they don't use the land they have, they are incapable of self-management – these are the common stereotypes. There are concerns that the settlement of Aboriginal land claims and the implementation of forms of Aboriginal self-government will result in 'race-based' territories with governments operating outside the context of the Canadian federation. Opposition to indigenous land claims is justified in terms of a defense of the principle Canadian values of equality, democracy, and individual rights. But while similar to the anti-native title arguments in Australia, Canadian opposition to indigenous claims is couched in particular images of Canadian national identity and history that convey an unshakeable conviction of the imagined Canadian traditions of benevolence and generosity.

Popular histories in Canada, both at the national and local level, construct the frontier expansion as a series of benevolent extensions of Euro-Canadian colonial authority. This is quite unlike either American frontier narratives, where conquest is portrayed as a result of violence, or Australian versions, where – when settlement has been successful – indigenous peoples are either completely erased from the landscape or, as in the case of the Kalkadoon of north-western Queensland, have died a heroic, Anzac-like death in the face of Australian colonial expansion.[60] In Canadian popular narratives, when settlers are not portrayed in a kind of passive, frozen state surrounded by a hostile wilderness (as Atwood describes), the successful colonisation of the frontier is imagined as being achieved through a process of 'conquest through benevolence': through Aboriginal peoples' willing subordination and 'loyalty' to the paternalistic care of government agents, missionaries and settlers.[61] Canadian frontier heroes are not usually the Indian fighters of American versions; in fact, popular historians often deny the occurrence of overt Aboriginal resistance. Instead, the frontier heroes are the Mounties, the enforcers of law and order. Pierre Berton, Canada's foremost popular historian, has described the North West Mounted Police as 'civil servants and social workers' whose paternalistic qualities were appreciated by the Indians, who called the Mountie 'father'.[62] This narrative of 'conquest through benevolence' has permeated Canadian stories of national identity and history for over a century. It has translated into a heavily paternalistic Indian

[60] For example, Armstrong, *The Kalkadoons*; Grassby and Hill, *Six Australian Battlefields*.
[61] Furniss, *The Burden of History*, pp. 53-78.
[62] Berton, *Why We Act Like Canadians*, pp. 28-32.

Affairs policy of coercive power masked as benevolent guidance, and a set of paternalistic attitudes among non-Aboriginal Canadians in which racism is masked in a language of benevolence and good will.[63] This narrative of benevolence is echoed in the widespread belief, often heard, that in Canada 'we have treated our Aboriginal people well'.

This narrative of Canadian benevolence and generosity frames much of the anti-native title discourse today. For example, in contrast to Australian discourse, in which governments are accused of being traitorous and surrendering the country to Aborigines, in Canada governments are accused of being overly generous to Aboriginal people. Land claims are constructed as yet another massive government 'giveaway' to Aboriginal people – an excessive benevolence.

These themes of Canadian benevolence and government over-generosity infuse the anti land-claims rhetoric of the Reform Party (now known as the Canadian Reform Conservative Alliance), the conservative populist party that could be described as the Canadian version of Australia's One Nation. Like One Nation, the Reform Party is opposed to the recognition of special Aboriginal rights, arguing that 'all Canadians are equal', and that treaties would perpetuate 'racial' divisions among Canadians. The Reform Party opposes land claims settlements in the Western Arctic and Yukon because 'the generosity of the land claim agreements was excessive'.[64] The Reform Party's Aboriginal Affairs critic, Mike Scott, evoking a self-image of a benevolent parent to Canada's indigenous people, has stated that land claims settlements are not in the best interests of Aboriginal people. British Columbia's resource economy would be destroyed by land claims settlements, he argues. 'As the least well off British Columbians, Indians more than anyone will be harmed if the government makes deals that help destroy the economy'.[65] Another Reform party member has stated: 'The real villians [sic] [in the land claims movement] are the federal and provincial governments and their bureaucrats. Since 1982, these culprits have been leading the native people to expect that their wish lists would be fulfilled, that indeed Canada's native people have a right to expect preferential treatment.'[66] Thus, the land claims movement is a result of naïve Aboriginal 'children' being misled by overly generous, paternalistic governments.

This image of excessive government paternalism is even more explicit in the arguments of Mel Smith, a key Reform party supporter and recent author of a book on the land claims issue in British Columbia.[67] Smith argues that the British

---

[63] Furniss, *The Burden of History.*
[64] 'Native Land Claims: What's Going On', informational poster circulated by the Reform Party of Canada, 1995.
[65] Mike Scott, Town Hall Public Meeting in Williams Lake, B.C., March 1995, cited in Furniss, *The Burden of History,* p. 145.
[66] 'Only One Law for Canadian People', Williams Lake *Tribune,* 1 August 1995, A5.
[67] Smith, *Our Home or Native Land?*

Columbia government has addressed the native title question by establishing Indian reserves. '70% of the reserves in Canada are in British Columbia! It is a myth to say the government has not met its obligations to the Indians!'[68] Of course, colonial officials did not establish reserves to address Aboriginal title, but to protect settlers from growing threats of violence from indigenous peoples whose lands they were taking. Further, many of the reserves in British Columbia, in contrast with the large prairie treaty lands, are only a few acres in size – the number of reserves does not equate with the size of reserves. These facts, however, are obscured in Smith's rhetoric of generosity. The concept of Aboriginal self-government, now recognised and supported by the federal government, 'causes all sorts of problems, because it raises expectations, it causes the Native people, the leadership, to feel that they have their own rights', Smith suggests.[69]

These images of Canadian national identity and benevolence are also encountered in rural debates. For example, one writer to a rural B.C. community paper stated: 'Everyone agrees that land claims should be settled, but how? How many years have we been pouring funds into this abyss [reserve communities]? It apparently has done the natives on the reserves no good at all ... Where has this money gone? The native people of Canada should be the best dressed, the best housed, the best educated people in the world!'[70] Another writer similarly drew on the images of Canadian benevolence and Aboriginal ingratitude:

> There's a lot of concern over the land claims issues ... Who and what is really behind this, as we get along well with the native Indians? They now have warm houses to live in, warm clothing to wear, education privileges, and much more [than] before the white people came. Canadians are nice people and try to give everyone a fair chance. Some are taking advantage of this goodness.[71]

The images of history, of identity and of the nature of Aboriginal/non-Aboriginal relations contained within such anti-land claims rhetoric all resonate with dominant assumptions of Canadian identity and national history. The Canadian self-image of benevolent paternalism is juxtaposed to the image of a now-excessive government generosity and the passive, childlike Indian who is being misled into false expectations of their Aboriginal rights by sympathetic governments.

---

[68] Mel Smith, Reform Party Town Hall Meeting, Williams Lake B.C., March 1995, cited in Furniss, *The Burden of History*, pp. 143-44.
[69] ibid.
[70] Letter to the Editor, Williams Lake *Tribune*, 24 November 1994, A5.
[71] Letter to the Editor, Willliams Lake *Tribune*, 31 March 1994, A5.

Conclusion

How might this comparative perspective help us to understand how Australian history, indigenous/settler relations, and the northern 'frontier' have been imagined? To me, what is most striking about Australia is the deep sense that conquest has never, truly been achieved. In responding to the native title movement, opponents clearly convey a deep sense of pervasive victimisation. During the recent Wik debate over the existence of native rights on pastoral leases, pastoralists in Queensland were reported to be 'taking up arms' to defend themselves against an anticipated indigenous attack.[72] As previously mentioned, Pauline Hanson herself has expressed concern that indigenous corporations in Queensland were buying up pastoral properties and engaging in a kind of economic takeover of the country. There is, in short, a lingering culture of terror in Australia – a constructed fear of indigenous reprisal – that permeates much of the public opposition to the native title movement.

This contrasts significantly with public discourse in Canada. To be sure, in Canada there are the armed indigenous blockades, occupations, and so on. Such protests and blockades have become even more frequent through the 1990s as land claims remain unresolved and a younger indigenous population becomes increasingly impatient with government intransigence over the land question. There certainly are unresolved fears of indigenous reprisals against non-indigenous settlers and governments.[73] Yet public opposition to Aboriginal land claims is less often characterised by fear than it is by a paternalistic smugness in which governments are criticised for being excessively 'generous' to indigenous peoples, and politicians and the police both are criticised for 'putting up' with acts of indigenous 'disobedience', again evoking the image of indigenous children getting away with bad behaviour.

I don't mean to oversimplify the kinds of nationalist, historical narratives in either Canada or Australia, narratives which are much more complex, fluid and variable than I've portrayed here. I haven't traced at length, for example, how supporters of the native title movement draw upon particular images of national culture and history to support their cause. But these dominant narratives do

[72] 'Whites would quit the north', *Sunday Times*, 7 December 1997; 'Pastoralists taking up arms, says MP', *Sydney Morning Herald*, 5 December 1997.
[73] In my work in the British Columbia interior I have on occasion heard rural Euro-Canadians express fears that the local indigenous peoples were 'stockpiling arms' for a future uprising against local non-Aboriginal residents. Recently an RCMP report similarly claimed that militant Aboriginal people were 'stockpiling weapons' such as high-powered rifles, machine guns, and anti-tank weapons ('First Nations deny stockpiling weapons', *Vancouver Sun*, 28 February 1999.). This report must be viewed in the context of the 1990 Oka confrontation, in which armed members of the Mohawk nation barricaded a highway near Oka, Quebec to protect a sacred site from encroachment and to protest government inactivity on their land claims. The Canadian government responded to the Mohawk blockade by sending in the Canadian army, complete with armoured tanks and machine-gunned soldiers, to dismantle the blockade, an action that focused national attention and sparked critical public debate over the state of Aboriginal/government relations.

seem to constrain the possibilities of public discourse. For example, in Australia Henry Reynolds has played a critical role in bringing these historical questions to the attention of the general public, and has been one of the most popular and effective advocates for native title. Yet he has captured public attention not by challenging, but by modifying dominant historical narratives. Reynolds attempts to secure some positive public space for Aboriginality by constructing Aboriginal people as 'black pioneers' who contributed to the building of the Australian nation, thus retaining the image of pioneering progress that is central to the frontier myth.[74]

What influence might these narratives of victimisation, of a lack of faith in the completion of colonisation, have on portrayals of north Australia and the northern 'frontier'? Deborah Bird Rose has identified these themes in north Australian pastoralists' sense of relationship to the northern landscape. While pastoralists have a deep love for the country they have 'conquered' and now inhabit, they nevertheless feel a deep sense of their transience in that country. Pastoralists, Rose suggests, are living in a moment of perpetual liminality, a 'Ground Zero' in the colonial moment, unable to imagine the survival of the pastoral lifestyle and their future generations in those regions.[75]

While local narratives in north Australia resonate with the more general victimisation narratives elsewhere, these narratives are also strongly shaped by local conditions. In part, the uncertainties of northern pastoralists are linked to local economic conditions: the difficulties of the pastoral industry in the north, the insecurity over pastoral leases, and so on. Quite in contrast are the public histories found in the north-western Queensland city of Mount Isa, where the mining industry has been booming since the 1950s, has brought a level of almost unprecedented wealth to local workers, and has only in the last few years begun to decline. Here the histories encountered in the public spaces around town – tourism displays, the city's historical festivals, popular books, magazine and newspaper articles – all are proud, brash, confident, and arrogant. They speak of a linearity of history, of successful colonisation, of the 'disappearance' of local indigenous tribes (and thus the resolution of any outstanding historical questions concerning native title), and of a future of unlimited progress and prosperity for all.[76]

Thus both local factors and national traditions contribute to the process of imagining the north Australian 'frontier'. But this process also reflects similarities with other settler-colonial societies. In both Canada and Australia, the cultural problematic inherent to settler societies – being newcomers in a land once controlled by indigenous peoples – requires stories legitimizing arrival,

[74] Reynolds, *With the White People*.
[75] Rose, 'The Year Zero and the North Australian Frontier'.
[76] Furniss, 'Timeline History and the Anzac Myth'.

occupation, dispossession, and continued domination of indigenous peoples. And in both countries, the 'frontier' – the early process of encounter between colonists and the new land, its unknown territories, its indigenous peoples – retains its salience as a key source of symbols for the ongoing construction of official histories and national identities.

References

Anzaldúa, Gloria 1987, *Borderlands/La Frontera: The New Mestiza*, aunt lute books, San Francisco, CA.

Armstrong, R. E. M. 1980, *The Kalkadoons: A Study of an Aboriginal Tribe on the Queensland Frontier*, William Brooks, Brisbane.

Atwood, Margaret 1972, *Survival: A Thematic Guide to Canadian Literature*, Anansi, Toronto.

Berton, Pierre 1982, *Why We Act Like Canadians: A Personal Exploration of Our National Character*, McClelland and Stewart, Toronto.

Billington, Ray Allen 1971, *The American Frontier Thesis: Attack And Defense*. American Historical Association Pamphlets, no. 101, American Historical Association, Washington, DC.

— 1973, *Frederick Jackson Turner: Historian, Scholar, Teacher*, Oxford University Press, New York.

Bogue, Allan G. 1998, *Frederick Jackson Turner: Strange Roads Going Down*, University of Oklahoma Press, Norman.

Bohill, Ruth 1997, 'For the Record: Hanson, Equality and Native Title', in Bligh Grant (ed.), *Pauline Hanson: One Nation and Australian Politics*, pp.163–87, University of New England Press, Armidale NSW.

Curthoys, Anne 1997, 'Entangled Histories: Conflict and Ambivalence in Non-Aboriginal Australia', in G. Gray and C. Winter (eds.), *The Resurgence of Racism: Howard, Hanson and the Race Debate*, pp.117–27, Monash Publications in History, Clayton, Vic.

— 1999, 'Expulsion, Exodus and Exile in White Australian Historical Mythology', *Journal of Australian Studies*, vol. 61, pp. 1–18.

Dennis, Peter, Jeffrey Grey, Ewan Morris and Robin Prior, with John Connor 1995, 'Anzac Legend', in *The Oxford Companion to Australian Military History*, Oxford University Press, Melbourne.

Faragher, John Mack 1993, 'The Frontier Trail: Rethinking Turner and Reimagining the American West', *American Historical Review*, vol. 98, no. 1, pp. 106–17.

Frye, Northrop 1971, *The Bush Garden: Essays on the Canadian Imagination*, Anansi, Toronto.

Furniss, Elizabeth 2001, 'Timeline History and the Anzac Myth: Settler Narratives of Local History in a North Australian Town', *Oceania* 71(4):279–297.

— 1999, *The Burden of History: Colonialism and the Frontier Myth in a Rural Canadian Community*, UBC Press, Vancouver.

Grassby, A. and M. Hill 1998, *Six Australian Battlefields*, Allen and Unwin, St Leonards, NSW.

Hofstadter, Richard 1970, 'The Frontier Thesis under Attack', in Michael S. Cross (ed.), *The Frontier Thesis and the Canadas: The Debate on the Impact of the Canadian Environment*, Copp Clark Publishing, Toronto, 1970, pp. 23–8.

Ieng, Ang, 'The Psycho-Geographical Effect', The New Racism: The Politics of Race and Nationalism in Australia, Humanities Research Centre, The Australian National University, October 1997.

Klein, Kerwin Lee 1995, 'Reclaiming the "F" Word, or Being and Becoming Postwestern', *Pacific Historical Review*, vol. 65, no. 2, pp. 179–216.

Limerick, Patricia Nelson 1991, 'What on Earth is the New Western History?', in Patricia Nelson Limerick, Clyde A. Milner II, and Charles E. Rankin (eds.), *Trails: Towards a New Western History*, pp.81–8, University of Kansas Press, Lawrence, Kansas.

— 1991, 'The Trail to Santa Fe: The Unleashing of the Western Public Intellectual', in Patricia Nelson Limerick, Clyde A. Milner II, and Charles E. Rankin (eds.), *Trails: Toward a New Western History*, pp. 59–77, University of Kansas Press, Lawrence, Kansas.

— 2001, 'The Adventures of the Frontier in the Twentieth Century', in P. Limerick, *Something in the Soil: Legacies and Reckonings in the New West*, pp. 74–92, W. W. Norton & Company, New York,.

Limerick, Patricia Nelson, Clyde A. Milner II, and Charles E. Rankin (eds.) 1991, *Trails: Toward a New Western History*, University of Kansas Press, Lawrence, Kansas.

Macintyre, Stuart 1999, *A Concise History of Australia,* Cambridge University Press, Cambridge, Melbourne.

Melleuish, Gregory 1997, 'Pauline Hanson and Australian Conservative Populism', *Quadrant*, September, pp. 25–9.

Nash, Gerald D. 1991, *Creating the West: Historical Interpretations 1890-1990*, University of New Mexico Press, Albuquerque.

Reynolds, Henry 1990, *With the White People*, Penguin, Ringwood, Vic.

Ricklefs, M. C. 1997, 'The Asian Immigration Controversies of 1984-85, 1988-89 and 1996-97: A Historical Review', in Geoffrey Gray and Christine Winter (eds.), *The Resurgence of Racism: Howard, Hanson and the Race Debate*, pp. 39–61, Department of History, Monash University, Clayton, Vic.

Rose, Deborah Bird 1997, 'The Year Zero and the North Australian Frontier', in D. Rose and A. Clarke (eds.), *Tracking Knowledge in North Australian*

Landscapes, pp.19–36. North Australian Research Unit, ANU, Casuarina, NT.

Slotkin, Richard 1973, *Regeneration Through Violence: The Mythology of the American Frontier, 1600-1860*. Wesleyan University Press, Middletown, Connecticut.

— 1985, *The Fatal Environment: The Myth of the Frontier in the Age of Industrialization, 1800-1890*, Atheneum, New York.

— 1992, *Gunfighter Nation: The Myth of the Frontier in Twentieth Century America*. Atheneum, New York.

Smith, Melvin H. 1995, *Our Home or Native Land?* Melvin H. Smith, Victoria, BC.

Steiner, Michael 1995, 'From Frontier to Region: Frederick Jackson Turner and the New Western History', *Pacific Historical Review*, vol. 64, no. 4, pp. 479–502.

Turner, Frederick Jackson 1920, *The Frontier in American History*, Henry Holt and Company, New York.

Wells, David 1997, 'One Nation and the Politics of Populism', in Bligh Grant (ed.), *Pauline Hanson: One Nation and Australian Politics*, pp.18–28, University of New England Press, Armidale, NSW.

Wrobel, David M. 1996, 'Beyond the Frontier-Region Dichotomy', *Pacific Historical Review*, vol. 65, no. 3, pp. 401–430.

Part II. Landscape and Place

3. The redemptive frontier: a long road to nowhere

Deborah Bird Rose

This chapter is an invitation to journey along a tangle of tracks. The first track is a brief excursion across some of the analytic terrain. The analysis I present is founded in a theory and practice of dialogue. There are two main precepts for structuring ethical dialogue.[1] The first is that dialogue begins where one is, and thus is always situated; the second is that dialogue is open, and thus that the outcome is not known in advance. Openness produces reflexivity, so that one's own ground becomes destabilised. My concern here is with the first precept: to engage in dialogue as ethical practice one must understand one's own situatedness. One practical consequence of this precept is that our gestures toward others must not exclude analysis of our own histories, geographies, and cultures. I have been particularly attentive to our cultures of violence because their effect is to foreclose on dialogue before we even properly begin. The purpose in analysing violence is to understand where it is located and how it is embedded in our cultural work, and the end goal is to uncover paths that may lead toward reparative action in the world.

In a series of essays devoted to analysis of the frontier in Australian society, I have sought to interrogate violence in many of its contemporary forms.[2] I have argued that the frontier is a matrix of modernity, a time and place where modern culture simultaneously reveals its capacity for destruction and re-invents its own myth of creation. The conventional view of the frontier is that it is sequential: it is an historical moment of encounter that will be overcome by civilisation. This linear view obscures many things: the violence of civilisation, the coevalness of the frontier, the formative interactions of destruction and creation. To put it another way, the sequential theory of the frontier treats a tension-laden and interactive relationship as if it were a linear progression in which violence is always about to be overcome. In contrast, I contend that the frontier is a key site for reflexive critique of contemporary society.

The tension between presence and absence is integral to 'New World' frontier mythology. On the one hand the conquerors imagine themselves in the midst of savage people and wild places; on the other hand, the savage person and the wild place are defined by the absence of civilised man (the coloniser), and thus as living absences: tabula rasa (in respect of the people) and terra nullius (in

---

[1] Fackenheim, *To Mend the World*, p. 129.
[2] Rose, 'Reports from a Wild Country'; 'Hard Times'; 'Dark Times'; and 'Rupture and the Ethics of Care'.

respect of the land). Terra nullius is a particularly interesting concept for the way it combines presence – *terra,* with absence – *nullius.* The two are packed together in this one concept, and thus the one concept actually references relationship, interaction, and tension.

My purpose here is to examine frontier violence when the conquerors set out not to destroy but to redeem. As Richard Slotkin says, 'the fable of redemption through immersion in the wilderness ... lies at the heart of the Myth of the Frontier.'[3] The American myth offers redemption through violence very explicitly. In contrast, Liz Furniss draws an excellent comparison with the Canadian frontier, arguing that it is not violence but rather paternalistic benevolence that is the key to Canadian frontier mythology.[4]

In the Australian context we can locate a powerful stream of thinking that offers redemption through the landscape itself.[5] Redemption through landscape suggests that this place – this continent – has a power that can act on people, provided that civilisation does not interfere. The foundational concept of terra nullius thus has the potential to say so much more than we might have thought. Our attention has been on the *nullius* part of the term, on this absence of ownership whose unmasking threw the nation into crisis. But we need to think also about the *terra* part of the term – this continent, and how settler Australians have imagined an elemental power of place.

My argument is that the desire for exclusive presence is itself an act of violence. I will follow one man's flight to the frontier where I have encountered a site at which is visible much of what I am discussing: the conqueror's knowledge of his own loss, his own experience of absence as emptiness, his own recoil at the implications of his morally conflicted presence. That is one of the journeys of the paper, as it tracks the life and work of the artist Ainslie Roberts.

A track of decolonisation

I began by discussing dialogue. The conqueror's story is not the only story, and if I were to present the conqueror as if he stood alone I would perpetuate the violence I am seeking to work against. For that reason, I will begin with a track that aims toward decolonisation.

In 1997 I worked as the consulting anthropologist to the Aboriginal Land Commissioner, Justice Gray, when he went to Central Mt Wedge station, northwest of Alice Springs, to hear a claim to Aboriginal traditional ownership of the relinquished pastoral lease. Central Mt Wedge, in Central Australia, is located between the Aboriginal communities of Yuendemu and Papunya. This

[3] Slotkin, *Gunfighter Nation*, p. 246.
[4] Furniss, *Burden of History*, and this volume.
[5] See Haynes, *Seeking the Centre*.

is an extremely arid part of Australia, and the Mt Wedge area consists of hills and plains, with no rivers at all. There are few soakages, and only two rockholes of substantial size where the water has been regarded as permanent (although it has been known to fail). The station consists of 3245 square kilometers; it was taken up in 1947, much later than most of the stations in the Northern Territory.[6]

Some of the Aboriginal people for this country had fled into the area after the Coniston massacre in 1928, and had been adopted into the local groups. These groups moved in and out of neighbouring stations, alternating between life in the bush and station life. Some of them had been caught up in the brutal regime of Mt Doreen station where the station owner used them as slaves.

In 1947 Bill Waudby gained the grazing license over Central Mt Wedge. Waudby was not an experienced pastoralist at the time, and he relied on Aboriginal workers:

> I was a pretty new chum at all this. As I say, I had a good team of Aboriginals who knew what the game was about, and we managed to get along quite well, and we got the cattle home.[7]

Waudby had little difficulty recruiting Aboriginal labour: conditions on a number of the neighbouring stations were unbelievably bad, and Waudby was a decent bloke. When he took up the station, and proved to be a fair and reasonable man to work for, Aborigines who belonged there came to stay. Waudby kept the station running with Aboriginal labour until the mid-60s when drought and award wages altered the situation. Many of the Aboriginal workers then cleared out. Internationally acclaimed artists such as Daisy Jugudai Napaljarri, and Paddy Carroll Jungarrayi are Central Mt Wedge people who were introduced to commercial art in Aboriginal communities such as Papunya.

During this period of exile, people became committed to returning to their own country. In 1984 they started registering sacred sites on the station, and one of the senior men set up an outstation on the station. In 1987 they incorporated and were granted a community living area. The Aboriginal Benefits Trust Fund purchased the station in 1995. In 1997 the claim was heard; in 1998 the Aboriginal Land Commissioner made the finding that the claimants were traditional owners within the terms of the Act, and the title was handed over to the Aboriginal traditional owners in 1999.

In the course of the claim, the traditional owners took us to a particularly spectacular site called Palka-karrinya, translated as 'Behold karrinya'. It is a monolith in a narrow gorge. Several Dreamings are located here, and the site is

---

[6] This and following information is summarised from Vaarzon-Morel & Sackett, *Central Mount Wedge Land Claim*, and from Justice Grey, Aboriginal Land Commissioner, *Central Mount Wedge Land Claim No. 154*.
[7] Vaarzon-Morel & Sackett, p. 27.

connected with a number of the Dreaming tracks of major significance in Central Australia, as well as having its own local significance. Along with these Dreaming connections, the monolith at Palka-karrinya was identified with the grandfather of a number of members of the group. Creation and the present moment were connected through a known human ancestor. On our approach some of the people communicated to him.

The site is not only a place of past action, but of present action; not only a source of life but also a repository for life. It is a mutually interactive place where encounters contribute to the lives of all the parties. Stephen Muecke gets into the thick of interactive relationships in his discussion of the signs he saw in his northern travels: these signs announced a 'site of significance'. Muecke takes a more subtle and action-oriented view:

> Significance is the wrong word, these sites are not full of meanings, cluttered with signs like a library. Ask the locals: *something there* they will say.... You have to ask yourself, what has that site been doing over the years, getting people to do things, or producing meanings?[8]

Action toward a site is intended to be nurturant, and to elicit more life from the site. At Palka-karrinya women sang the bush plum Dreaming. The song is part of the work people do to keep the country productive or nurturant, and it is a communicative event as well. It tells the place that the people are here, and that they are doing the work that keeps the place engaged with everyday life and time.

In the context of the hearing women sang before the Judge as part of the evidence of their ownership. The song had the potential to influence legal proceedings as well as bush plums. Other demonstrations of ownership were presented in the form of art and ritual. Over the course of a day women of two groups made ground paintings, and danced and sang; a select portion of their actions were witnessed by the Judge and other men of the legal parties.

In sum, the traditional owners of Central Mt Wedge experienced the frontier under a number of historical positions: they experienced massacres, near slavery, starvation, chains, and floggings; they experienced the pastoral industry as valued workers; they removed into Aboriginal settlements such as Papunya, and gained national and international fame as artists. They launched a successful claim to land, and have regained a portion of their land under Aboriginal Freehold Title. Some of the oldest claimants experienced all of this in their own lifetimes. And in their extraordinary lives they learned and carried the knowledge that enabled them to engage reflexively in their own country – to act toward sites, and to be acted upon by sites.

---

[8] Muecke, *No Road*, p. 35.

Flight to the frontier

In 1950 an advertising artist and executive named Ainslie Roberts woke up, got out of bed, and collapsed. He was subsequently diagnosed as being in the midst of a nervous breakdown, and when he was well enough to get out of bed again, his wife and his business partner decided the best thing to do would be to buy him a one-way ticket to Alice Springs. There he recovered almost instantaneously, and there he made some major decisions: to spend more time on his art, to ease himself out of the advertising industry, and spend as much time as possible in Central Australia.[9] He was not the first Australian artist to go to the bush for inspiration; in fact, Sidney Nolan had made his famous trip to the Centre only two years earlier.[10]

According to Hulley, Roberts's biographer, Roberts was born in England in 1911. His parents were theosophists, which was a spiritual movement that aimed to blend the sacred wisdom of the East with the scientific materialism of the West. Roberts grew up in a home in which seances, photographs of the supernatural, and discussions of ectoplasm and other arcane matters were part of the domestic culture.

The family migrated to Australia in 1922 (when Roberts was eleven), and they spent the first months with relations on a farm in South Australia where he fell deeply in love with the bush. Once the family settled in Adelaide and Roberts was back in school he proved to be a top student and a gifted artist, but was unable to fulfil his early promise because he had to leave school at age fourteen. Over the years he put himself through art school, founded his own business, married and had a family, and achieved success in the world of commercial art.

In 1952, not long after his collapse and recovery, he met Charles Mountford, and the two of them became good friends. They started making short expeditions to the bush: Mountford to record rock art; Roberts to draw, paint and photograph. Mountford was an amateur ethnographer (he subsequently gained formal qualifications, but never found significant acceptance within the academic community). He had a great interest in Aboriginal art and culture, and the two men came to be collaborators in the retelling of Aboriginal myths, and the creation of works of art inspired by them. The first exhibit was in 1963; the first book came out in 1965. Both ventures were wildly successful. As Mountford said, 'No Australian artist has painted like this; he has followed no school – he has copied no previous artist'.[11]

Mountford and Roberts made their first major expedition together in 1956, and (as you will have anticipated) they went to Central Mt Wedge station. Their host

---

[9] This and subsequent information is summarised from Hulley, *Ainslie Roberts*.
[10] Schaffer, *In the Wake*, p. 153.
[11] Summarised from Hulley, *Ainslie Roberts*; quote p. 85.

was Bill Waudby, and their Aboriginal guide was One Pound Jimmy, an Aboriginal man whose face was the most well known of Aboriginal faces because it had been reproduced on a 1950 series of Australian postage stamps.[12] The artist came back in 1966, just after his first big successes, and was flooded in for a month during an uncharacteristic period of rain.

The first visit, in particular, with its interactions with Aborigines and opportunities to gain an understanding of myth and landscape, was formative for Roberts. He made two visits to Palka-karrinya, and according to Hulley, 'of all the places in the North that Ainslie [Roberts] came to know, this is the one that would hold the most deeply personal meaning for him'.[13]

Roberts brought his fascination with this site to fruition in 1983, shortly before he died. Hulley says that the story Roberts knew and painted was that Palka-karrinya was sacred to an Owl Dreaming.[14] In the course of the land claim a great deal of evidence concerning Palka-karrinya was presented to the Aboriginal Land Commissioner, and none of the public evidence made any mention of an Owl Dreaming. Let us simply hold to the fact that the site made a huge impression on Ainslie Roberts. According to Hulley, it 'would haunt his imagination until he could exorcise it in a major painting twenty-five years later'.[15]

This painting is not typical of Roberts's work, but it does go to the heart of his endeavour. He depicts a site, and alludes to a Dreaming or story for that site; the place and its power are refracted through the 'surrealism' of Roberts's imagination.[16] Most of Roberts's paintings depict a more generic landscape. Similarly, most of the stories are unsourced; while specific, they are unlocated. In most of the work, most of the particular knowledge of place and people is erased and the final product speaks to a far more generalised sense of place and to a homogeneous mass of 'brown people'. A number of the books are dedicated to 'the brown people who handed down these Dreamtime Myths'.[17] Not only are the storytellers generic, but they are positioned as putative ancestors who hand down stories – to us, when we read these books.

On the track of the lone artist

Whilst flooded in at Central Mt Wedge in 1966, Roberts painted directly on to the walls of the homestead. One painting is labeled 'Lasseter's Last Ride', and it

[12] ibid., p. 57.
[13] ibid., p. 56.
[14] ibid., p. 59. It is difficult to source this story properly, but it seems pertinent that a near identical story is told by Bill Harney, *Life Among the Aborigines*, p. 212. I have no explanation for why Roberts understood it differently. Probably there were miscommunications, perhaps it is more complicated.
[15] Hulley, *Ainslie Roberts*, p. 58.
[16] ibid., p. 96.
[17] Roberts & Mountford, *The Dreamtime*, and *The Dawn of Time*.

can also be imagined as a self-portrait. The wedge-shaped hill is very similar to Central Mt Wedge.

Lasseter, as is well known, was a dreamer and a con artist who claimed to know the location of a gold reef in Central Australia, and in 1930 he got backing to mount an expedition. Although spectacularly unsuccessful, Lasseter's expedition added another chapter to the legend of gold in the Centre, and Lasseter himself, having died in the bush, became a legend in his own right. The story gained more popularity in 1931 with the publication of Ian Idriss's book *Lasseter's Last Ride*.[18] In Ainslie's painting, the lonesome figure of Lasseter making his solitary way through the bush in search of a dream gives us a fair portrait of Roberts himself, as well as linking his project with the prominent 'motif of modern artist as nomad'.[19]

What did Ainslie Roberts think he was doing when he made his paintings of Aboriginal mythology? His description of his method tells us about his intent. He says that he studied the long versions of the myths, but that: 'The paintings always come first, and the big job is to get rid of me, the things I know, the conventional ideas I was taught and brought up with, so that the myth can come through. I become a channel, a communicator, scarcely a painter at all'.[20] He certainly acknowledges his debt to Aboriginal people: 'I just consider myself as the agent only, the communicator… I must always keep in mind my debt to the aborigines who created these myths … If my paintings continue to be accepted as readily as the first exhibition, I have the opportunity and responsibility of communicating to my fellow whites that here is a rich culture that deserves to be noticed, respected, and explored…' Roberts held the view that Aboriginal culture was 'very old' and 'very nearly extinct', and he wanted his paintings to be 'speaking for an ancient culture'.[21]

The underlying theory of Roberts's art is the Jungian view that there are universal archetypes which manifest in myth, and which are present in the unconscious of all humans. Like Nolan and other modern Australian artists, Roberts claims universal significance for his work through its expressivity in relation to a universal consciousness or universal soul.[22] To become a channel, for Roberts, was to open one's self to one's own unconscious, where one will connect with the universal archetypes which Aboriginal mythology also expresses. This theory of artistic channeling situates the artist as a medium through whom the archetypes, and by extension that which is universal in Aboriginal culture, can flow into the modern world.

[18] Carment et al., *Northern Territory Dictionary of Biography*, pp. 176-7.
[19] Schaffer, *In the Wake*, p. 155.
[20] Hulley, *Ainslie Roberts*, p. 81.
[21] ibid., p. 86.
[22] Schaffer, *In the Wake*, pp. 152, 155.

There is a more historically conscious intention in Roberts's work as well. The generic landscapes and homogenous indigenous people he presents in his work are totally Australian, and his work contributed to the making of Central Australian landscapes occupied by Aboriginal people as a primary symbolic Australian landscape.[23]

Mountford put his views on landscape and nationalism into words:

> The spirit of a locality evolves from its history. By virtue of thousands of years of usage, the history of Australia belongs to the Aboriginal ... The white man, because of his relatively brief tenancy of Australia, lacks such rich identification. Access to the original spirit of the land can only be gained through the mind of the Aboriginal. Through his myths, his art and his ceremonies, we can catch a glimpse of history as old as time itself'.[24]

I will set aside the gender issues here. In discussing Aboriginal action toward the place I have deliberately drawn on women's action in order to combat the generically gendered articulation of indigenous belonging.[25] Mountford apparently takes it as given that localities have a power or spirit, and he believes that the power or spirit of Australian localities can be accessed through Aboriginal people because of their long history here. The argument is that the shallowness of settler culture is due to its short chronology, and that it can be overcome by being grafted onto Aboriginal culture. It is thus a completely non-provocative theory of history. It rests on a sedimentary view of history and meaning, suggesting that both accumulate with time. It does not even dream of suggesting that shallowness might be linked to frontier violence or the concept of terra nullius.

Mountford's argument toward nationalism runs on a parallel track to Roberts's channeling of universalised archetypes. Whereas Roberts wanted to dip into what he believed to be a common pool and channel out messages that are both universal and located (at least at a continental scale), Mountford wanted to bore into historically grounded spirits of place, and thus to build up a modern history that connects with ancient powers. The artist and the anthropologist share this penetrative action in which Aboriginal people and their knowledge are mined to serve the interests of settlers. Even as Roberts attempted to channel respect for Aboriginal people, he was erasing their own particularity, their own representations, their own knowledges. And as he erased theirs he superimposed his own visions of what he imagined might once have been theirs.

---

[23] See Haynes, *Seeking the Centre*. My discussion here parallels that of Dorst who writes that the American West is 'a primary symbolic landscape through which the nation defines itself and the face by which it is most readily recognized throughout the rest of the world.' Dorst, *Looking West*, p. 102.
[24] Hulley, *Ainslie Roberts*, p. 85.
[25] Rose, *Reports from a Wild Country*.

In Mountford's nationalistic theory of the power of place the relationship of channeling seems to be reversed. The white man uses Aboriginal culture as a channel to sacred geography and to history. So, on the one hand, Roberts claims or hopes to channel myths into modernity. On the other hand, Mountford hoped Aboriginal culture would channel or bore the white man's presence into the landscape. In both forms of encounter we see the tension between desire and erasure, presence and absence, love and violence. This is nationalism in the settler society mode. Its own autogenesis is enacted through the dynamic tensions of love and death. Thomas suggests in his article 'Home décor and dance' that the business of simultaneously exhibiting and exterminating natives is part of the enduring invasive logic of a settler colonial nation.[26] Philip Deloria makes a similar point concerning the United States: that American (settler) identities are 'built not around synthesis and transformation, but around unresolved dualities themselves'. Those dualities include the simultaneous desire to exalt and 'extirpate' the Indian.[27]

This tension finds a complex articulation in the work of Mountford and Roberts. Commercially their collaborations were enormously successful. Roberts's first exhibit sold out in two days, a subsequent exhibit sold out in two hours; there was a waiting list of persons wishing to buy paintings. The books sold out and were reprinted; they remained in print for over 20 years, and thus became an Australian publishing phenomenon.[28] Along with the widespread enthusiasm, there was also criticism. At the time, many critics spoke of appropriation. Hulley took those criticisms seriously and sought to answer them by claiming that the intent was not to replicate Aboriginal art, but to find a new western art. He wrote, 'the paintings have nothing to do with the forms of Aboriginal art. They relocate this timeless material in a Western inner landscape. They do not falsify it, for in itself it is the product of something universal; but they give it a new range, and a wider context of immediacy'.[29] Hulley's reclamation of integrity is arrived at through recourse to this universal and timeless common pool. So the colonising logic of exhibition and erasure goes round and round.

The appropriative elements of both nationalist and universalising encounters are the subject of huge amounts of analysis, and, more recently and more interestingly, of law suits over the copyright of intellectual property. I would just note that in both nationalist and universalising contexts, the theory of a universal unconscious quite conveniently displaces indigenous people as the privileged artists and experts of their own culture. It treats Aboriginal knowledge as an ore body that could be mined by anyone with the talent for tapping into

[26] Thomas, 'Home décor and dance', p. 28.
[27] Deloria, *Playing Indian*, p. 185.
[28] Hulley, *Ainslie Roberts*, p. 112.
[29] ibid., p. 99.

the unconscious. This invasion via mysticism replicates the process of colonisation of land; it discovers, claims, and opens up indigenous culture as another unowned region, a cultural terra nullius.

Furthermore, while mysticism can be seen to be in contradiction to the pragmatics of both colonisation and modernity, the Mountford/Roberts project is in its structure completely modern. It claims access to universals, and it breaks, dissects and fragments in order to find the meanings of things.[30] It breaks into the mother lode of inspiration, pulling out and disconnecting pieces, and reducing parts to fragments. It relocates the fragments into new configurations and it markets this new work with a claim for non-native authenticity. The authenticity or integrity of the market product is based in part upon the fragments of an indigenous life world, which are worked into the piece or alluded to by the piece, which claims to transcend them.

There is a hollowness at the heart of this enterprise that is exactly the hollowness and emptiness created by more familiar frontier violence. One name for this hollowness is monologue: it constitutes its own closed circle and declares that circumscribed arena to be the true basis of all culture. As Said says, it mistakes 'one idea as the only idea'.[31]

Hulley tells a story which he believes symbolised the spiritual meaning of the 1956 trip for Roberts: 'As he walked through a ... [stone arrangement] on the east side of the hill, he picked up a sacred stone that lay there, broken into two pieces. Joining the pieces together in his hand, he stood for a long time looking down at them'.[32] There is an amazing amount of information about the modern artist and about redemption through landscape expressed and exposed in this little story. The white man fled civilisation and went to the frontier. He went with a white expert in Aboriginal matters, and with a love of Central Australia and respect for Aboriginal people. Whilst there, and ostensibly under the guidance of an Aboriginal man, he went walking around alone and he found what he took to be the broken remnants of Aboriginal culture. This is to say that he found confirmed in a stone his own expectations of what Aboriginal culture could be – ancient and nearly extinct.[33] The meanings he attributed to the stone – that it was sacred, that it was broken (in the sense that it should have been whole), that it needed to be mended – these meanings, as far as we know, were solely in his imagination. With his own two hands he tried to make these broken pieces whole again, and in that act he found a mission. He would heal himself by restoring or repairing Aboriginal culture.

---

[30] I am drawing a brief point out of a much more complex argument presented by Everdell, *The First Moderns*.
[31] Said, 'The text', p. 188.
[32] Hulley, *Ainslie Roberts*, p. 66.
[33] ibid., 86.

According to Hulley's account of this pivotal event, Ainslie Roberts did all of this as a solitary act. He did not ask One Pound Jimmy (or even Mountford) about the place, the stones, or the need for healing. Indeed, One Pound Jimmy does not seem to figure in this vignette at all. The guidance of this Aboriginal man meant a lot to both Mountford and Roberts, but it seems they wanted him to navigate and to answer questions as asked. On the basis of available information, One Pound Jimmy was asked to walk, point, carry, and provide pieces of information. His circumscribed presence enables us to realise how deeply Roberts was on a white man's quest. One Pound Jimmy facilitated the journey; he *travelled* with the white men, but he did not *journey* with them.[34]

As I read the accounts of the interactions with One Pound Jimmy, it looks to me like he was treated as a marvelous repository of fragments – an ore body in his own right. I am not accusing Roberts of using a poor methodology, of failing to consult, or of being insensitive to Aboriginal people's knowledge and feelings, although all of these things might, anachronistically but realistically, be said. What fascinates me is the solitariness of it all. This is monologue: the self talking to the self, and the self structuring encounters so that he will hear only reflections of the self. Violence lurks here: in monologue, where the possibilities for dialogue are erased. Roberts's experience with the stone is a solitary act of imaginary repair. It is emblematic of the larger project, and captures both the longing for a transcendent presence and the erasure of the real people and knowledge of the place. These two intertwined acts of imagination – longing for an imaginary presence / oblivion toward the real presence of others – together configure the violence of frontier redemption.

Let us recall that 'of all the places in the North that Ainslie [Roberts] came to know, … [Palka-karrinya was] … the one that would hold the most deeply personal meaning for him'.[35] This painting is on the wall in the kitchen at the old Waudby homestead on Central Mount Wedge. It was painted in 1966, just a few years after Roberts's first public successes. It is labeled 'Palka-karrinya', but for me it is a stunningly insightful portrait of the frontier.

[34] See Mathews for a discussion of the difference between travel and journey.
[35] Hulley, *Ainslie Roberts*, p. 56.

The painting leaches all the colour from the country, and shrinks the stone to a peanut. The foreground is an oversized skull, which I take to be an eagle skull, but it could be any predatory bird. It is not asking too much to see the predatory skull as *both* the colonising project and the artist himself. Death dominates here. The eye socket is a reversed telescope, making everything seem small, distant, and terribly faded. This frontier gaze kills the country; we see that very clearly. Through the reversed telescope of the death head the sacred site looks lost and lifeless. Not just its presence, but its meanings too are absorbed, erased, strained through the dominating eye socket of death. The artist came for redemption; he imagined a mission to make whole that which had been broken by frontier violence, but here he recognises himself as one of the predators.

Dancing for Palka-karrinya

Ainslie Roberts's death head exposes the open secret at the heart of terra nullius – that *nullius*, the erasure, ends up destroying the beloved *terra*.

Frontier redemption is here displayed as a violent commingling of desire and death. The violence is omnipresent because what settlers desire they cannot achieve without killing everything in the long run. Desire produces death. Death produces a hollowness that fills with desire. Desire produces more death. Ainslie Roberts showed us this when his desire to paint outback Australia took him to Palka-karrinya. His long-term action toward the site was to imagine it on paper and on canvas. On the kitchen wall in the Central Mount Wedge homestead it may be that he painted the devastating knowledge that he had nothing to give that could enhance the life of the place.

When we were at Central Mt Wedge for the land claim, we camped in the old Waudby homestead. We lived with these paintings and I, for one, couldn't eat in the kitchen. I worried about our own gaze – it seemed to flatten everything before us. We dredged the mother lode for evidence, and roamed voraciously across landscapes, lives, sites, and ritual actions. I told myself that we were there to listen, and that from this courtroom drama could come legal standing with respect to the land that would make a genuine difference in the life of the place and the people. This was true, and I am not aiming to denigrate a piece of legislation that was benevolent in its inception and that is radically altering power relations in the Northern Territory. Nor would I wish to denigrate the evident pride and pleasure with which the traditional owners displayed their knowledge. Legal practice, however, ensured our right to know a great deal, and I slipped back and forth between an appreciation of the positive aspects of this drama, and an awareness of the predatory quality of our high beam gaze as it worked across other people's lives in search of the bits and pieces that it labels evidence.

In the interests of natural justice, evidence in a land claim has to be accessible. People's words are recorded, translated if necessary, transcribed, and printed out for all to consult, except in the case of 'restricted' evidence that is not freely available to all but is fully available, as appropriate, within the context of the judicial process. Legal practice, formulated to protect the interests of all parties, fragments knowledge before it even encounters it because it asserts that some, and only some, forms of information count as evidence. The best lawyers cast a narratival net over the fragments and pull them into a drama of proof. Cross-examining lawyers seek to undo the drama – to hammer, probe, disconnect, and thus further to disintegrate the bits and pieces that were, in any case, fragments to begin with.

At Central Mt Wedge, as on many other land claims, Aboriginal people interrupted legal practice. At Palka-karrinya and other sites they sang. These were beautiful moments: people's faces lit up, their voices rose and worked in the gorges, resonating to the place, and filling the area with invocative communication. Back at camp, people made paintings on the ground and on their bodies. They sang the country as they painted it, and they sang it as they danced it. Their performatives were for the country, and at the same time they captured legal practice and brought it into their own law. People melded the power of place with their own performative power to convince everyone present that they were the owners of the place in their own terms as well as in the terms of the Land Rights Act. Their action folded legal practice, its flattening gaze and its fragmenting search for evidence, into reparative and regenerative ritual.

My analysis has landed me back in the binary stated so succinctly by Stephen Muecke: Aborigines are providing the eros to our thanatos.[36] He has a good point, and even as we reject binaries in favour of the more complicated and entangled journeys of life in the time of rapidly shifting powers, it is proper, I believe, to honour eros wherever it may be found. With that in mind, I wish to note that Roberts's work appeared at a time when relations between Aboriginal people and settler-descended people were on the cusp of major change. He hoped that his work would foster respect among white people for Aboriginal people, and his immensely popular work helped bring about the social changes that led to citizenship, land rights, and the Mabo decision. In spite of what now appears as an overwhelming presence of thanatos, Roberts gave eros a worm hole into settler consciousness.

Mountford spent a large portion of his life studying Aboriginal cultural fragments, and his views about the spirit of place were percipient in their insistence on the locality of it all. But while the work carried out by traditional owners may indeed have its roots in millennia of history (as Mountford contended), the power of place continues in the world not out of some passivity of endurance or timeless universalism. The power of place is interactive, reflexive, mutual. The Aboriginal owners of this place do the work that keeps the place vital, active in the world, and reflexively engaged with living time. The

---

[36] Muecke, *No Road*, p. 15.

astonishing thing about frontier violence is that death does not always have the final word.

References

Carment, D., R. Maynard, & A. Powell 1990, *Northern Territory Dictionary Of Biography, Volume 1*, Northern Territory University Press, Casuarina, NT.

Deloria, Philip 1998, *Playing Indian*, Yale University Press, New Haven, Conn.

Dorst, John 1999, *Looking West*, University of Pennsylvania Press, Philadelphia.

Everdell, William 1997, *The First Moderns: Profiles in the Origins of Twentieth-Century Thought*, University of Chicago Press, Chicago.

Fackenheim, Emil L. 1994 [1982], *To Mend the World, Foundations of Post-Holocaust Jewish Thought*, Indiana University Press, Bloomington.

Furniss, Elizabeth 1999, *The Burden of History; Colonialism and the Frontier Myth in a Rural Canadian Community*. UBC Press, Vancouver.

Gray, Justice 1998, Aboriginal Land Commissioner, Central Mount Wedge Land Claim No. 154, Report and Recommendations of the Former Aboriginal Land Commissioner, Australian Government Publishing Service, Canberra.

Harney, Bill 1980 [1963], *Life Among the Aborigines*, Rigby Ltd., Adelaide.

Haynes, Roslyn 1998, *Seeking the Centre: The Australian Desert in Literature, Art and Film*, Cambridge University Press, Melbourne.

Hulley, Charles 1988, *Ainslie Roberts and the Dreamtime*, J. M. Dent, Melbourne.

Mathews, Freya 2005, *Reinhabiting Reality*. SUNY Press, Albany.

Muecke, Stephen 1997, *No Road: Bitumen All the Way*, Fremantle Arts Centre Press.

Roberts, Ainslie & Charles Mountford 1965, *The Dreamtime*, Rigby Ltd., Adelaide.

— 1969, *The Dawn of Time*, Rigby, Ltd. Adelaide.

Rose, Deborah 2004, *Reports from a Wild Country: Ethics for Decolonisation*, University of New South Wales Press, Sydney

— 1999, 'Hard Times, An Australian Study' in K. Neumann, N. Thomas, & H. Ericksen (eds), *Quicksands: Foundational Histories in Australia and Aotearoa New Zealand*, pp. 2–19, University of New South Wales Press, Sydney.

— 1997, 'Dark times and excluded bodies in the colonisation of Australia,' in G. Gray and C. Winter (eds), *The Resurgence of Racism: Hanson, Howard and the Race Debate*, pp. 97–116, Monash Publications in History, Monash University, Melbourne.

Said, Edward 1979, 'The Text, the World, and the Critic' in J. Harari, (ed), *Textual Strategies: Perspectives in Post-Structuralist Criticism*, pp. 161–88, Methuen, London, 1979.

Schaffer, Kay 1995, *In the Wake of First Contact: The Eliza Fraser Stories*, Cambridge University Press, New York.

Slotkin, Richard 1992, *Gunfighter Nation: The Myth of the Frontier in Twentieth-Century America*, Atheneum, New York.

Thomas, Nicholas 1997, 'Home décor and dance: the abstraction of Aboriginality' in Rebecca Coates and Howard Morphy (eds) *In Place (Out of Time): Contemporary Art in Australia*, pp. 24-28, Museum of Modern Art, Oxford.

Vaarzon-Morel, P. & L. Sackett 1997, Central Mount Wedge Land Claim, Anthropologists' Report, Prepared on behalf of the claimants for the Central Land Council, Alice Springs, NT.

4. Transcending nostalgia: pastoralist memory and staking a claim in the land

Nicholas Gill

The strength of Australian outback mythology in providing a blueprint for what Australian society, landscapes and history ought to be, lies at least partly in its 'lack of specificity in time and space'[1] , coupled with retrospect. Deborah Bird Rose has argued that such free-floating retrospect diverts attention from 'here and now of our lives', and militates against dealing with the consequences of Australia's colonial past and present.[2] The inland and north of Australia, the so-called 'frontier', in a spatial sense, are, and have been, places where optimistic non-indigenous assessments of land have been subject to regular appraisal and debate.[3] They are also areas where the treatment and status of indigenous people have remained significant social and political issues, and where national and regional conflicts over indigenous land ownership and title have been most focused, particularly in relation to extensive pastoralism. Despite this, outback, or frontier, mythology remains important in providing symbols and normative ideals that shape perceptions and landscapes of the inland and north. The avenues by which this occurs are manifold and are diffused across Australian political and cultural life.

This chapter examines one avenue by which pastoral landscapes are represented and validated, the production of pastoral memory and historical writing from the Alice Springs pastoral district in the southern Northern Territory (NT). This analysis arises from fieldwork and examination of documentary sources undertaken in the period 1996–98.[4] The production and consumption of memory and history in the Alice Springs area are significant for the authority they carry at various scales, but particularly in the context of the NT[5] where differences in indigenous and non-indigenous values, aspirations and interpretations of the past are features of everyday life and politics.

Recent debates over the future of land use and management in the inland and conflicts over the existence of native title on pastoral leasehold land have

---

[1] Rose, 'Rupture and the Ethics of Care in Colonized Space'; Rose, 'Australia Felix Rules, Ok!'.
[2] ibid.
[3] Ratcliffe, *Flying Fox and Drifting Sand: the Adventures of a Biologist in Australia*; Heathcote, *Back of Bourke: A Study in Land Appraisal and Settlement in Semi-arid Australia*; Heathcote, 'Drought in Australia: A Problem of Perception'; Powell, 'Taylor, Stefansson and the Arid Centre: An Historic Encounter of "Environmentalism" and "Possibilism"'; Heathcote, 'Manifest Destiny, Mirage and Mabo: Contemporary Images of the Rangelands'.
[4] Gill, 'Outback Or At Home?: Environment, Social Change and Pastoralism in Central Australia'.
[5] Riddett, 'Think Again: Communities Which Lose Their Memory: The Construction of History in Settler Societies'.

illustrated many aspects of contemporary frontier ideologies in Australia.[6] These conflicts are struggles not only over land as a material resource, as a factor of production, but also over landscapes as loci of personal, group and national identity, meaning, belonging, experience and what Furniss calls the 'burden of history', the consequences of indigenous dispossession.[7] These struggles are not simply over legal property rights, but also over property rights grounded in moralities based in relationships to land. These are matters of legitimacy, not simply legality. Confronted by the consequences of past acts of Aboriginal dispossession, and the survival of Aboriginal cultures, rural settler Australians have largely looked to the land to build a sense of legitimacy, and to tell a story of benign settlement, rather than state-sanctioned and enforced land occupation and control of indigenous people.

In inland Australia, where the physical transformations of agriculture have not been possible and are not visually evident, the strategies required for this have been somewhat different than in other areas. As elsewhere,[8] however, the strategies of legitimation and the mutually constitutive process of building identities and landscapes, has relied, at least partially, upon particular traditions of remembering the past to interpret the present and to provide normative guidance for the future.

It might be imagined that Australian outback mythology with its images of vast stations, droving, skilled horse work, and dusty and laconic stockworkers would provide a solid basis for pastoralists to establish a legitimate place in the land. Certainly, it is an influential mythology and has a place in the cultural politics through which pastoral landscapes are maintained symbolically and materially. Outback mythology is, however, not a monolithic edifice. As to whether it alone can constitute a mythology adequate for the maintenance of pastoral landscapes among contemporary (post)colonial politics of land is more questionable. There are two ways in which this may be seen. First, is the adequacy of this conventional outback mythology in relation to how pastoralists see themselves. We should not assume that popular, dare I say urban, conceptions of outback lands and people, are consistent with identities and conceptions held by those who dwell within lands characterised as 'outback'[9] . We are familiar with this in relation to critiques of non-indigenous perceptions of indigenous people,[10] but less so in relation to non-rural perceptions of rural, non-indigenous people.

---

[6] Heathcote, 'Manifest Destiny, Mirage and Mabo: Contemporary Images of the Rangelands'; Hiley, *The Wik Case: Issues and Implications*.

[7] Furniss, *The Burden of History: Colonialism and the Frontier Myth in a Rural Canadian Community*.

[8] Dominy, 'Lives Were Always Here: The Inhabited Landscape of the NZ High Country'; Dominy, 'The Alpine Landscape in Australia: Mythologies of Ecology and Nation'; Furniss, *The Burden of History: Colonialism and the Frontier Myth in a Rural Canadian Community*.

[9] Fergie, 'Unsettled'.

[10] Sackett, 'Promoting Primitivism: Conservationist Depictions of Aboriginal Australians'.

Pastoralists do not see their identity as wholly portrayed in the heroism of the conventional outback tale, they do not find their conception of their place in the land wholly provided for in such narratives.

Second, even as outback mythology celebrates the pastoral industry, it is also characterised by emptiness, wilderness and arguably, by settler transience in the face of a land that has not been transformed according to the mythical progression from wilderness to garden. In the conventional outback tale, the wilderness remains ever present. Without the transformative self-evidence of agriculture and the emergence of a 'garden' landscape, pastoralism remains either imaginatively or imminently absent and its roots in the land remain tenuous. As seen in the Native Title debates in 1996-98, many critics of pastoralists described pastoral lands in terms of vastness and emptiness, and suggested that pastoral leasehold tenure provided merely a readily removed veneer of occupation rather than a more deeply rooted presence.[11] For pastoralists, then, imaginatively establishing permanence, persistence and presence has emerged as an important aspect of establishing legitimacy for their place on the land.

Memory and public history in central Australia

Historical tales play a key role in Central Australian assertions of legitimacy. Pastoral historical narratives of self and land locate people and activities in time and space. They link the present to a past that provides much to guide pastoralists' normative views of the present and future. History, for the pastoralists of Central Australia, has become an important means by which to present their sense of belonging in a landscape generally seen in Australia as one from which the frontier has not fully passed.[12] Outback mythology provides little room for settlers to hold the reciprocal relationships with land central to culturally legitimate occupation. Historical accounts of settlement are one forum in which the establishment of such relationships between pastoralist and land occurs and are placed into public history.

Times of social change can spark 'crises of individual and collective remembering'.[13] Central Australian pastoralists appear to be going through such a phase as their vision of Central Australia is eroded. For example, Judy Robinson, local historian and member of a pastoral family, worries that the labours of early pastoral families are being forgotten, and has expressed concern that pastoralists are being 'pushed out of [their] own history'.[14] One of the outcomes of this anxiety, and of the sense that the 'pioneering generation' is rapidly disappearing, is a small body of biographical and autobiographical texts that recall pastoral

[11] Horstmann, 'The Dead Heart of the Wik Backlash'.
[12] Rose, 'Australia Felix Rules, Ok!'
[13] Pred, 'Memory and the Cultural Reworking of Crisis: Racisms and the Current Moment of Danger in Sweden, or Wanting it Like Before'.
[14] Northern Territory Archives Service TP 858/1 and interview with author 26/10/96.

settlement. Recent texts include Robinson's story of her family in 'Bushman of the Red Heart' and Powell's 'By Packhorse and Buggy'.[15] These histories are important for they are a means by which pastoralist memory authoritatively enters the public realm and contemporary struggles over land, landscape and identity. They 'transcend nostalgia'[16] because of their role in naturalising Central Australia as a pastoral landscape and in constituting Central Australian history through pastoralism. In the dominant whitefella culture of the NT, these histories, and the memories that they embody, gain authority partly through a claimed direct and unmediated access to the past. In this culture, such exclusive access to the 'pastoral true story'[17] of the NT, grants a vantage point from which to interpret and shape the present.

Memory, however, is not simply a passive process by which objective records of the past are retrieved. Both individual and group memory is an active social process, located, like all human activities, within race, class and gender and other social relations. Memory is constituted as individuals and groups seek coherency and meaning in the past, and is as much a product of the present as the past. Memories are built up as groups and individuals tell their stories, receive additional information or criticism and modify their stories for retelling. In this process, while the stories may change, there are key elements that provide stability and consistency over time.[18] This process of building memories and group histories is so much a part of everyday life that we:

> Fail to recognise not only why we alter history but often that we do. Thus we tend to misconceive the past as a fixed verity from which others have strayed but to which we can and should remain unswervingly faithful.[19]

Shared memory is a key building block in the development of group identity and culture. Memory is the medium through which a group develops and traces a shared past, shared meanings and shared values. Through collective identification of the material and symbolic signposts that mark a group's past, a sense of continuity, stability and legitimacy develops.[20]

In the public histories of pastoral Central Australia, the authors write of the constitution of the Central Australian landscape though pastoral settlement and station development. In the process, signposts of shared significance are created

---

[15] Powell and McRae, *By Packhorse and Buggy*; Robinson, *Bushman of the Red Heart: Ben Nicker 1908-1941*.
[16] Lowenthal, *The Past is a Foreign Country*.
[17] Hill, *The Rock: Travelling to Uluru*.
[18] Barclay, 'Schematization of Autobiographical Memory'; Brewer, 'What is Autobiographical Memory'.
[19] Lowenthal, *The Past is a Foreign Country*.
[20] ibid.; Edensor, 'National Identity and the Politics of Memory: Remembering Bruce and Wallace in Symbolic Space'.

and a sense of landscape accretion through pastoral lives and labour built up. There are a number of key features to this process in the histories.

History begins – the arrival as homecoming

In the pastoral histories such as those listed above, the arrival by pastoral families in Central Australia constitutes a key moment in delineating a past that is gone and a present that is about to unfold. The story of a land without history, a tabula rasa upon which the settlers could create not only a new nation, but also fresh lives and new starts for themselves in a youthful landscape unwearied by humanity is an old one in Australian historiography.[21] The currency and continued publication of histories that reiterate this theme indicate that it is one that is not necessarily losing its vigour. The journeys to Central Australia by early pastoral families such as the Nickers, Price and Chalmers[22] feature significantly in pastoral historical narratives.

These three families were coming to Central Australia after problems and losses elsewhere. Central Australia represented a new start. For example, the Nicker family came to the Centre and saved for years to buy a station in order to 'leave behind their former lives and start again beyond the boundaries of what they had individually experienced'.[23] Initially the land tests these families, throwing up unfamiliar landscapes, aridity and seemingly impenetrable mountain ranges. Ultimately, however, the land softens in the accounts, and becomes welcoming and full of potential. The station envisaged by these families seems to only require labour to assume their full but quiescent form.

In the published accounts, the arrival of these families at the sites of their future homesteads is portrayed as much homecoming as arrival. After saving for eleven years, the Nicker family is able to purchase Ryans Well station. Their arrival there is a transition from harshness to verdant bucolism:

> Yesterday they had trailed across a spinifex plain, relieved by sparse grey shrubbery and this morning everything had changed. They'd wound across a creek-bed in a gap in the Hann Ranges where pine trees sprinkled the hillsides and gums nodded in the early morning breeze. Bloodwoods harboured flights of brilliantly-green budgerigars and cockatoos prattled raucously as they wheeled and dipped.

> Past the gap, they came into a wide, shallow valley where shadows dappled their road and softer grasses and herbage grew more abundantly.

[21] Hamilton, 'The Knife Edge: Debates About Memory and History'.
[22] Ford, *Beyond the Furthest Fences*; Powell and McRae, *By Packhorse and Buggy*; Robinson, *Bushman of the Red Heart: Ben Nicker 1908-1941*.
[23] ibid.

The fierce spinifex lay behind them was restrained from entering or infringing by the stolid demarcation of the Hann Hills[24]

From the Nicker's first camp at the future site of their homestead, Robinson paints a picture of a family at home and at peace in this landscape: 'there weren't any walls to surround them but they were home'.[25] This arrival is also represented as a new beginning, of activity and life not known by this landscape:

> An owl 'whoo-d enquiringly at all the unaccustomed activity and who could doubt his question because rarely had there been such movement, so many people, animal and sounds within his knowledge. He settled himself on a branch of a mulga tree and absorbed these new sights, swivelling his head now and then towards a new sound. The fire's glow mesmerised him. It was beyond his ken.[26]

The fundamental story being told in these accounts of arrival is of the *discovery* of a pastoral landscape. The pastoral landscape does not have to be created; it already exists. It exists in an unformed state, and requires only labour to bring out its full potential and to make it a place for family life. In effect, the 'arrival tales' in these pastoralist accounts begin the pastoral story of a process that went on for many years, and which through labour, revealed the envisaged stations much as a sculptor reveals the sculpture within the stone. It is also a landscape that is largely empty of Aboriginal people. Those who are present are generally those who become 'trusted companions' and childminders. They are, except in Ford's[27] account that emphasises benign paternalism on the part of pastoralists, presented as isolated and alienated figures, rather than as coherent groups of landowning people. Consistent with the portrayal of a virginal land, the pastoral histories do not generally canvas the possibility of settler-caused Aboriginal dispersal and fragmentation prior to the arrival of the settler protagonists.

The new day dawning in such accounts involved transforming this welcoming but 'untouched' landscape into a home. The welcoming nature of the places which were to become homestead sites and centres of family life stands in stark contrast to stories of struggle, sacrifice and loss that also pervade pastoral narratives. The apparent poles of welcome and struggle are not, however, incompatible in the pastoral story. Both are important constituents of it and together tell a story of a land that, in pastoral culture, is harsh and often fickle, but which is fundamentally productive and which rewards faith in its capacity to support those who stay and learn its ways.

---

[24] ibid.
[25] ibid.
[26] ibid.
[27] Ford, *Beyond the Furthest Fences*.

Indeed at this early stage some key elements of the pastoral story of Central Australia are emerging. In the accounts, the families are forced to engage with the land early on, mentally and physically, to reach their destinations and the possibilities, harshness notwithstanding, they still envision. The qualities of endurance and patience in the face of the land's enormity and implacability are highlighted. This quality, to become a key element in pastoral relationships to land, is seen not only in the families' continued faith in what lay ahead but also in their dogged acceptance of the trials imposed by the cycles of flood and drought. As pastoralists would see it, this is the beginning of an acceptance of the hardships of Cental Australia. For pastoralists, this acceptance brings a morality to their presence in the country. In the pastoral histories, the land enfolds and engulfs the pastoralists. Pastoralists use and extract from the land, but are ultimately unable to significantly transform it as the spatial and temporal enormity of the land overshadows them, yet simultaneously shapes and sustains them, rewarding their persistence. In Central Australian cattle culture, the persistence is significant in setting pastoralists apart from others and in claiming a legitimate and righteous presence. That the land rewards faith and persistence is illustrated in these accounts most clearly by events in the years following arrival.

The land is transformed

In the years that followed arrival the pastoral narrative trace the development of a pastoral community and the landscape it inhabits. Tents and bough sheds gave way to homesteads and families grew. The landscape is domesticated and native and stock animals are both equally naturalised in the land.

Powell's[28] description of a 1920s childhood visit to the Bloomfields Loves' Creek station, east of Alice Springs illustrates the nature of this domesticated landscape. Powell weaves European stock seamlessly into the landscape. They were visiting Atnarpa on Love's Creek in order to purchase horses. There was 'lush and plentiful grass. We saw kangaroos everywhere … there were quite a few joeys … we also saw a flock of seven emus and several wedge tail eagles'.[29] The horses at Atnarpa 'were all such beautiful animals'[30] that it was hard to make a selection. As the unwanted horses were released and galloped off 'they made a fine sight'.[31]

In this account there is a richness and productivity to Central Australia and a unifying acclamation of native flora and fauna, and of the European world of yards, stock skills, and fine horses. Such childhood memories describe a blooming Central Australia. This is not a barren and difficult landscape, but one in which

[28] Powell and McRae, *By Packhorse and Buggy*.
[29] ibid.
[30] ibid.
[31] ibid.

settlers' animals and enterprises are thriving, at home in a landscape that is rewarding their efforts.

European stock also materially transforms the land in pastoral memory. From her vantage point on the homestead verandah at Ryan's Well, Liz Nicker watches the country:

> The country around them grew better with every wet. From the homestead vantage point Liz noticed an improvement in grasses and a slow but steady greening and developing density of shrubbery. Because she was a gardener at heart, she believed the cattle were responsible. Their hooves broke up the topsoil and their bodily waste nourished the soil. Where they foraged on low bush branches, the canopy grew taller and shaded more grasses and infant trees. Moving away from their watering places, they distributed grass and herbage which better anchored what already grew. Every hoof indent left a cradle for new seeds to develop, protected from wind on the open plains and held little pockets of water when it rained.[32]

This belief in the 'gardening' effect of stock remains widespread among pastoralists today.[33] This observation and belief has material aspects but its true import lies in the manner these observations have entered and informed pastoral culture. It is not only that cattle have changed the landscape; they are seen as at least partially responsible for creating what is seen today, and as having improved it. The pastoral presence is thus written everywhere on the very structure of the land itself, not only through the visibility of homesteads, bores, fences and other pastoral infrastructure. Stories about these environmental changes circulate within the pastoral community and pastoral families.

On one level, these narratives might be dismissed as mere romanticism for a golden rural past. Rural nostalgia, however, is rarely as innocent as its surface form might suggest.[34] In a pastoral culture where deeply embedded presence and insider/outsider identity counts in the cultural politics of land,[35] these histories do more than establish an early presence. They establish a role in the very creation of a Central Australia that pastoralists take as the norm and which takes its form from the pastoral industry. This presence and its geographies are given moral weight in the narratives. For example, the stability and strength of the pastoral settlers is emphasised and contrasted with the mobility and fecklessness of miners. Moreover, pastoral settlement is not associated with the

---

[32] Clewett and Smith, et al. *Australian Rainman Version 3: An Integrated Software Package of Rainfall Information for Better Management*; Robinson, *Bushman of the Red Heart: Ben Nicker 1908-1941*.

[33] Gill, 'Outback or at Home? Environment, Social Change and Pastoralism in Central Australia'.

[34] Williams, *The Country and the City*.

[35] Gill, 'The Contested Domain of Pastoralism: Landscape, Work and Outsiders in Central Australia'.

wider colonising processes that made the land available for settlement by non-indigenous people. Settler actions seem to take place within a self-contained world. The infamous children's home, the 'Bungalow', recently described as the 'government's most determined act of social engineering by segregation'[36] and which was part of a suite of measures by which settlers intensively regulated the Aboriginal population, is represented in one account as the outcome of the impulses of generous and giving folk. It is described as a creation of the townspeople of Stuart (Alice Springs) as a means of providing for the Aboriginal children left behind by miners. Pastoralists are described as doing their bit by getting into the 'habit of dropping off beef'.[37]

Knowing the land

The land itself features significantly in pastoral history. The focus however, is not the land itself, but the evolution of pastoral society and landscapes. In this development, the bodily aspects of memory take on significance as the pastoral body and land permeate each other through physical presence, observation and labour.

In a complex and arid biophysical environment that is highly variable in time and space[38] and greatly variable in its ability to support stock, pastoralists require a good knowledge of their land. For example, to control their herds, particularly prior to widespread fencing and establishment of sub-artesian bores, pastoralists needed considerable knowledge of the limited natural waters and of where cattle were likely to congregate. In many cases, pastoralists were often dependent on local Aboriginal people in these regards, at least initially, although this is not generally evident in these pastoral histories.

Pastoralists gain this knowledge through work and experience. They come to gain not only knowledge of the physical features and layout of the land, but also to develop a way of knowing it that provides them a place within it. This knowing is specific to their mode of land use and occupation, and arises in part from the variability of the land.

The Chalmers, Price and Nicker families all had sheep. Whereas cattle can be largely left to their own devices much of the time, sheep required shepherding. For this reason, they had largely disappeared from the area by the 1960s. Shepherding sheep forced the Chalmers to engage in some desperate searches for water that almost cost the lives of family members. New to Central Australia and to arid zone pastoralism, the Chalmers were reassured by rainfall records that indicated regular summer rainfall and by assurances from 'old timers in the

[36] Rowse, *White Flour, White Power: From Rations to Citizenship in Central Australia*.
[37] Robinson, *Bushman of the Red Heart: Ben Nicker 1908-1941*.
[38] Friedel and Foran, et al. 'Where the Creeks Run Dry or Ten Feet High: Pastoral Management in Arid Australia'.

district, that in at least twenty years of history there had never failed to be a rain before Christmas'.[39] They did not realise that twenty years is inadequate in assessing the highly variable rainfall pattern of Central Australia. According to Ford,[40] in 1926 they and their stock were forced to their limits when summer rains failed to materialise. Ford paints a picture of despair as the previously welcoming land dries out and stock begin to die and as hopes for the future turn to dust.

From such disasters, however, is forged the mythic stoicism of the outback. In outback mythology, the outcomes generally remain at the level of rather vague admiration and worthy stoicism, the value of which is taken to be self-evident. More detail, however, is required to tease out the specific resonances of such elements of frontier mythology today. In the Chalmers case, rain finally came in March, when the country flooded and brought forth an 'unbelievable carpet of vitality and fertility' where stock had been dying their thousands.[41] The Chalmers sheep flourished and the region 'had become a land flowing with milk and honey, and the pastoral scene breathed serenity, prosperity and contentment' as 'once again the remarkable recuperative powers of the country had been proved'[42] . This experience provided the Chalmers with a steep learning curve about Central Australia, but it also had a more significant effect. As noted above, Ford is evidently told of another observation, that the country can recuperate and bloom, when it is apparently ruined, and the pastoralists labour and commitment destroyed with it. From this perspective, for those who are there to see it, the country shows its true nature, its true productivity. This is a productivity that is felt or known for those who have seen the cycles and seen their families and stations survive; there to see for those who wait, for those who persist and place their faith in the land.

In pastoral historical memory, experiences such as the Chalmers etch the families into the land. They carve out a place for themselves through suffering, and in turn the experience is carried by them and their heirs. In pastoral culture, those who pass through such events in Central Australia embody the events and carry them within their person. Indeed, among pastoralists the shared embodiment of these experiences is an important part of collective identity and memory, marking them off from others whom they assume to have no understanding of Central Australia due to lack of presence. It is a culture of faith that persists strongly to this day. This was exemplified by pastoralist Bernie Kilgariff's assertion to a 1996 Landcare meeting that 'we [pastoralists] know the good of Central Australia'. The 'good' appeals to shared understandings and meanings

[39] Ford, *Beyond the Furthest Fences*, aide.
[40] ibid.
[41] ibid.
[42] ibid.

about the nature of the land between pastoralists and to the value of their occupation of it. It is a singular 'good', one that has meaning only within the context of pastoralism, yet which underpins a presumption in favour of a universal pastoral landscape. It is a concept that is perhaps nostalgic in form, but it is central to the fabric and maintenance of the pastoral landscape for it expresses both a domestication of the land according to powerful notions of landscape progression[43] and reciprocity between land and pastoralist.

Knowing the land also develops through labour. In pastoral culture, the labour on a station creates a geography that is an amalgam of the land and of those who labour; a geography of work that is specific to those who created it. A great familiarity is generated in the course of developing and working a station, and this is portrayed in the pastoralist histories. In her autobiographical account of establishing a station in the Tanami Desert, Marie Mahood,[44] describes her husband's labours. In setting up the station, Joe Mahood travels continuously over its 1620 square kilometres, determining the best locations for the bores, yards and other facilities. Successfully determining the best location of such infrastructure required observation of pasture and water resources, and their relationship to landforms and routes around the station. In concert with these tasks is a sense of how the station is to function as a whole. The station is the outcome of the merging of the physical makeup of the land, and of the pastoral ideals and plans that are both imposed upon the land and shaped by the encounter with it. In the process the land is marked by the pastoralists' efforts, and, while in cattle culture land retains its enormity and separateness from the human realm, it is nonetheless transformed to a personalised and pastoral landscape. Due to the effort involved in starting the station, Mongrel Downs became a home for the Mahoods 'as no other place had ever been because the challenges and responsibilities were so much greater'.[45] Knowledge of the land is also knowledge of oneself.

The relationship of the pastoral families with the land is not only one of inscription of themselves and of meaning onto the land. In the pastoral histories, the land also shapes and works it way into the pastoralists, shaping their bodies, actions and ways of thinking. For example, Joe Mahood gave 'eight years of his life to establishing Mongrel Downs' and Rosemary Coppock, recalling her days on a station she and her husband began, writes of how they 'used up muscle, sweat and tears'.[46] Pastoralists are portrayed as giving themselves to the land and to an unspecified higher goal. In these histories, this is a selfless process of forging a landscape for the social good, not the realisation of personal ambitions.

---

[43] Anderson, 'A Walk on the Wild Side: a Critical Geography of Domestication'.
[44] Mahood, *Icing on the Damper*.
[45] ibid.
[46] Coppock, *Central Australian Cattle Station Woman*; Mahood, *Icing on the Damper*.

Why this might be a worthy activity is not asked; the teleology of landscape is assumed in pastoral culture.

The permeability of land and people that underlies much of these pastoral accounts is a central part of the pastoral relationship to land. This relationship is founded on establishing presence in the landscape through work or observation. This is a presence defined as much by the presence of the land within pastoralists as the presence of the pastoralist in the land. This presence is articulated through remembering such that memory is at once histories and geographies of self, family and pastoral community. Memory and landscape constitute each other and the remembered self is present at all times. Indeed without the remembered self, or the presence of those pastoralists who have succeeded and built upon previous labour, there is no meaning in the land. Such are the silent foundations of present day pastoralist objections to transfer of pastoral land to Aboriginal landowners or national parks.

Conclusion

One of the questions raised by these accounts is whether the relationship between settler pastoralists and land is comparable to that of Aboriginal people. On the face of it pastoral relationships based on a sense of ancestral origins and on permeability between land and people appear similar to Aboriginal relationships to land. This topic requires more elaboration than possible within the task tackled here. Suffice here to say that there appear to be some fundamental differences, in particular that the pastoral sense of connection appears to be a process of *becoming* connected, whereas for Aboriginal people it is always a question of being. Moreover, pastoral relationships, based as they are in labour and reproduction, may be recreated in different places. Aboriginal relationships, though far from static, are not so readily transported and recreated.

This chapter has focused on selected elements of pastoral memory and histories. I have sought to lay out those elements that illustrate pastoralists' conceptions of landscape evolution in Central Australia, and which validate their habitation and land use. Although the histories present these elements as self evident in their worth, their underlying strength derives from two broader structural features of the narratives.

One pertains to Raymond Williams's concept of the 'knowable community'[47] .This is a 'strategy in discourse'[48] through which value is bestowed on certain and powerful sections of society, such that those sections, their members, their activities and their values stand as definitive of society as a whole. The 'knowable community', as presented in any one narrative is a community 'wholly known, within the essential terms' of the narrative, yet as an 'actual community [it is]

[47] Williams, *The Country and the City.*
[48] O'Connor, *Raymond Williams: Writing, Culture, Politics.*

very precisely selective'.[49] The appearance of wholeness emplaced and built in emptiness, as we see in pastoral histories, conceals selectivity and fragmentation. In addition, the land itself is drawn into the pastoral 'knowable community' as its capacities and variations are woven into pastoral concepts of productivity, persistence and faith that naturalise the pastoral presence. The pastoral mode of knowing the land becomes *the* 'good of Central Australia'.

The second structuring feature is further buried within the stories told. This is a feature alluded to at points in the text, the mythic landscape progressions from wilderness to cultivated garden. In times of European expansionism these idealised and strongly hierarchical geographies were mapped onto the globe, positioning Europe as civilised and the colonies as wilderness. By the late 19th century such geographies came to be mapped in nationalist terms onto European colonies.[50] As European nations expanded their empires, these ancient ideals 'functioned as ideology and legitimation for settlement of the New World'.[51]

The wilderness landscape is essentially unformed, chaotic, innocent and uninhabited. Classically, the garden is a step towards culture. It is the crucible of domestic life and the active transformation of the earth for human ends, and is a place of labour within nature's cycles. In classical mythology, it is superseded by the city, the pinnacle of culture, itself to be returned to wilderness as it degenerates. By the colonising period, however, the garden had become an endpoint in itself as the classical cycle of landscape destruction and creation was replaced by a linear progression from wilderness to the recovery of the garden from the Fall.[52] In relation to colonising practices, recovering the garden landscape involved emptying the landscape of indigenes and establishing agriculture and reciprocal relations with land.

In their representations of the construction of Central Australia, the pastoral histories replicate the creation of the garden from an empty wilderness. Upon these potent ideals they build a version of yeoman agrarianism that includes reciprocal relationships between settler and land in territory unmodified by the plough. Pastoralists tell a story of closing the frontier, but one that freezes the landscape just after closure, does not countenance change and celebrates frontier activities. They tell of a process of settlement but rather than seeing this as something that can evolve and go on, pastoral settlement brings closure. Although pastoralists bring and carry out change, they see this as teleological process; the pastoral landscape is an endpoint. That their changes and their labour, are themselves part of broader social processes that vary regionally, nationally, globally and in time, is disavowed. History ends with them. In pastoral histories

---

[49] Williams, *The Country and the City*.
[50] Cosgrove, 'Habitable Earth: Wilderness, Empire and Race in America'.
[51] Merchant, 'Reinventing Eden: Western Culture as a Recovery Narrative'.
[52] ibid.

and memory, all value, as a 'general... condition',[53] is to be found in the past. Even as the frontier is ended in these histories, it is made available for retelling as a model of society and landscape for today.

In these retrospective responses to change, pastoralists derive their morality from the very colonising structures that are under challenge. They look to a simplified past for guidance, rather than fully responding to the complexities of the present. They draw on a highly selective recollection of the past that is not simply an outcome of colonialism but is constructed from the very mythical foundations that have informed, driven and justified non-indigenous settlement of Australia and the dispossession of indigenous people. These histories portray their protagonists one-dimensionally as deserving 'battlers'. Until more complex pasts are admitted within the dominant 'whitefella' culture of the NT, however, these histories simply give further voice to a group that still wields considerable political and cultural power.

[53] Williams, *The Country and the City*.

References

Anderson, K. 1997, 'A Walk on the Wild Side: A Critical Geography of Domestication', *Progress in Human Geography*, vol. 21, no. 4, pp. 463–85.

Barclay, C. R. 1986, 'Schematization of Autobiographical Memory', in *Autobiographical Memory*, D. C. Rubin, pp. 82–99, Cambridge University Press, Cambridge.

Brewer, W. F. 1986, 'What is Autobiographical Memory', in *Autobiographical Memory*, D. C. Rubin, pp. 25–49, Cambridge University Press, Cambridge.

Clewett, J. F., P. G. Smith, et al. 1999, 'Australian Rainman Version 3: An Integrated Software Package of Rainfall Information for Better Management', Brisbane, Department of Primary Industries.

Coppock, R. R. 1993, *Central Australian Cattle Station Woman*, Alice Springs, Rose Rawlins Coppock.

Cosgrove, D. 1995, Habitable Earth: Wilderness, Empire and Race in America, in *Wild Ideas,* D. Rathenberg. pp. 27–41, University of Minnesota Press, Minneapolis.

Dominy, M. D. 1993, '"Lives Were Always Here": The Inhabited Landscape of the New Zealand High Country', *Anthropological Forum*, vol. 6, no. 4, pp. 567–85.

Dominy, M. D. 1997, 'The Alpine Landscape in Australia: Mythologies of Ecology and Nation', in *Knowing your Place: Rural Identity and Cultural Hierarchy*, B. Ching and G. W. Creed. pp. 237–65, Routledge, New York.

Edensor, T. 1997, 'National Identity and the Politics of Memory: Remembering Bruce and Wallace In Symbolic Space.' *Environment and Planning D: Society and Space*, vol. 29, pp. 175–94.

Fergie, D. 1998, 'Unsettled' in *The Space Between: Australian Women Writing Fictocriticism*. H. Kerr and A. E. Nettelbeck, pp. 173–200, University of Western Australia Press, Nedlands.

Ford, M. 1978, *Beyond the Furthest Fences*, Rigby, Adelaide.

Friedel, M. H., B. D. Foran, et al. 1990, 'Where the Creeks Run Dry or Ten Feet High: Pastoral Management in Arid Australia', *Proceedings of the Ecological Society of Australia,* vol. 16, pp. 185–94.

Furniss, E. 1999, *The Burden of History: Colonialism and the Frontier Myth in a Rural Canadian Community*, University of British Columbia Press, Vancouver.

Gill, N. 1997, 'The Contested Domain of Pastoralism: Landscape, Work and Outsiders in Central Australia' in *Tracking Knowledge in North Australian Landscapes: Studies in Indigenous and Settler Knowledge Systems*. D. B.

Rose and A. Clarke. pp. 50–67, ANU North Australian Research Unit, Darwin.

—— 2000, Outback or At Home? Environment, Social Change and Pastoralism in Central Australia. *School of Geography and Oceanography*, University of NSW, Canberra.

Hamilton, P. 1994, 'The Knife Edge: Debates About Memory and History', in *Memory and History in Twentieth Century Australia*, K. Darian-Smith and P. Hamilton, pp. 9–32, Oxford University Press, Melbourne.

Heathcote, R. L. 1965, *Back of Bourke: A Study in Land Appraisal and Settlement in Semi-arid Australia*, Cambridge University Press, Melbourne.

—— 1969, 'Drought in Australia: A Problem of Perception', *The Geographical Review* vol. 59, no. 2, pp. 175–94.

—— 1994, 'Manifest Destiny, Mirage and Mabo: Contemporary Images of the Rangelands' *The Rangeland Journal,* vol. 16, no. 2, pp. 155–66.

Hiley, G. 1997, *The Wik Case : Issues and Implications*, Butterworths, Sydney.

Hill, B. 1994, *The Rock: Travelling to Uluru*, Allen and Unwin, Sydney.

Horstmann, M. 1997, 'The Dead Heart of the Wik Backlash', *Habitat Australia*, vol. 25, no. 3, pp. 34–5.

Lowenthal, D. 1985, *The Past is a Foreign Country*, Cambridge University Press, Cambridge.

Mahood, M. 1995, *Icing on the Damper*, Central Queensland University Press, Rockhampton.

Merchant, C. 1996, 'Reinventing Eden: Western Culture as a Recovery Narrative' in *Uncommon Ground: Toward Reinventing Nature*, W. Cronon, pp. 132–59, W. W. Norton and Co., New York.

O'Connor, A. 1989, *Raymond Williams: Writing, Culture, Politics*, Basil Blackwell, Oxford.

Powell, J. 1980, 'Taylor, Stefansson and the Arid Centre: An Historic Encounter of "Environmentalism" and "Possibilism."', *Journal of the Royal Australian Historical Society,* vol. 66, no. 3, pp. 163–83.

Powell, P. and E. McRae 1996, *By Packhorse and Buggy,* Self-published, Alice Springs.

Pred, A. 1998, 'Memory and the Cultural Reworking of Crisis: Racisms and the Current Moment of Danger in Sweden, or Wanting it Like Before.' *Environment and Planning D: Society and Space*, vol. 16, pp. 635–64.

Ratcliffe, F. 1947, *Flying Fox and Drifting Sand: the Adventures of a Biologist in Australia*, Angus and Robertson, Sydney.

Riddett, L. 1995, 'Think Again: Communities Which Lose Their Memory: The Construction of History in Settler Societies', *Journal of Australian Studies,* vol. 44, pp. 38–47.

Robinson, J. 1999, *Bushman of the Red Heart: Ben Nicker 1908-1941*, Central Queensland University Press, Rockhampton.

Rose, D. B. 1996, 'Rupture and the Ethics of Care in Colonized Space', in *Prehistory to Politics: John Mulvaney, the Humanities and the Public Intellectual*, T. Bonyhady and T. Griffith, pp. 190–215, Melbourne University Press, Melbourne.

—— 1997, 'Australia Felix Rules, Ok!', in *Race Matters*, G. Cowlishaw and B. Morris, Aboriginal Studies Press, Canberra, pp. 121–38.

Rowse, T. 1998, *White Flour, White Power: From Rations to Citizenship in Central Australia*, Cambridge University Press, Melbourne.

Sackett, L. 1991, 'Promoting Primitivism: Conservationist Depictions of Aboriginal Australians.' *The Australian Journal of Anthropology*, vol. 2, no. 2, pp. 233–46.

Williams, R. 1973, *The Country and the City*, Chatto and Windus, London,

5. Water as collaborator

Jay Arthur

It used to be a dry country out there in years gone by, but bores have changed all of it to white man's land, carrying many sheep.[1]

The yarn flowed as sluggishly as his river, with anabranches and deep waterholes of reminiscences and irrelevant snags and sandspits to check its course.[2]

Whenever I hear of an election, I feel a dam coming on.[3]

This chapter is mediated through three landscapes.

The view from Geary's Gap

Lake George is a large natural lake to the north of Canberra. Its indigenous name is *Weereewa*. The Federal Highway connecting Canberra to the Hume Freeway to Sydney runs along its western shore. As I drive from Canberra to Sydney, about half-an-hour from home the highway rises up the small elevation of Geary's Gap, the break in the line of hills that mark that western edge of the Lake. Just before the car tops the rise, I always think 'How much water will there be in the Lake?' The view may be of water that's almost lapping the edge of the highway. At other times there is an expanse of bleached paddock, with sheep grazing and fencelines stretching across to a mirage on the far side – in fact not a mirage but water on the Bungendore side of the lake. Very often I see a fenceline, which runs from making a line in the waving grass to making a gradually diminishing line in the blue-grey water.

These changes in water level in Lake George have caught the settler imagination – despite the fact that such changes are a common feature of many Australian water bodies. Since European occupation the Lake has dried up at least three times and at other periods a pleasure-steamer took Sydney tourists on excursions over the Lake. Fantastic ideas have accounted for the changes in water level: it is related to the depth of a lake in New Zealand or balances the level of the Blue Lake at Mt Gambier. When Lake Burley Griffin was formed by the damming of the Molonglo River in Canberra, some locals expressed a fear that the new lake would 'do a Lake George' and disappear. In fact, its depth is a response to rainfall in its catchments.

---

[1] *Western Champion*, 31 August 1897, p. 3, column 3.
[2] Farwell, *The Outside Track*, p. 93.
[3] Kelly, Hon C. R. 'Bert' Kelly, CMG, Minister for Public Works, 1967–68.

The view to the south of Canberra Airport

Flying to Melbourne from Canberra the plane takes to off the north. As it gains height, it turns west and from the left-hand side there's a view across the hobbyfarms and 'twelve acre block' country. The morning sun catches hundreds of farm dams, shining like coins scattered across a worn carpet. It is such an overwhelming pattern of water redistribution that one cannot help thinking about how water once moved across this landscape before the building of these multitudinous dams – each now making its offer of evaporated water to the sky. There are marks of the old hydrology – creeks, some of them dry, Lake George, the Molonglo River – but the old patterns are not visible to me as they might be to a hydrologist, geologist or geographer. Some of the creeks are probably new – formed from sheepwalks – and I cannot easily trace the marks of drained swamps or old rivercourses.

The child's drawing – the haunting landscape

The third landscape is not one I have seen myself, but seen through the eyes of someone who knew it. I saw it in 1999 in a collection of a children's coloured pencil drawings of contemporary Central Australian cattle station life and the image continues to haunt me.

In the drawing, the viewer looks across the surface of a water tank full to overflowing. Beyond the tank is a dead tree and beside the tree a cow, (her station brand drawn large and clear), which has just finished drinking from a trough. Her head is turned towards the viewer and water drips from her mouth. The water in the trough comes from the pipe leading from the tank; on the left of that is the windmill, with its feeder pipe spilling water into the tank. On the right, water runs from the overflow pipe onto the ground, where a small circle of deep green grass has formed. Otherwise the red earth is completely bare. The sky is cloudless. The colours are blue, red, metallic grey and brown, with one touch of dark green.

There are only two living things in the picture – the cow and the circle of grass.

The windmill is very carefully drawn, with its pattern of struts and the name *Southern Cross* on the vane. The mechanics of the water-machinery – the connections between the various parts – are also carefully presented.

The continuing conversation

These three landscapes are presented as part of my obsessive concern with the non-indigenous relation to water in the Australian landscape. In my previous work,[4] I looked at the way in which language operates in this interaction. I

---

[4] In various articles but at most length in my doctoral thesis: 'Writing Home: a lexical cartography of twentieth-century Australia', University of Canberra 1999.

noted that terms such as *lake* and *river* are given definitions by Australian dictionaries which fit European, not Australian, waterbodies – these definitions reflecting the discrepancy in the settler understanding of this place. I analysed the discourse surrounding drought – whereby drought, a common, expected, normal, inevitable part of the Australian climatic cycle is located with vocabularies of war, disease, disaster and death.

In this chapter, I am turning to visual images – the three landscapes – to continue this conversation.

Lake George

Looking at Lake George from Geary's Gap is like looking at a double-exposed photograph. Is it a paddock or a lake? Is it pastoral Australia or a pre-occupation landscape? The fence line marks paddocks, sheep, pastoralism on the land edging the highway. But pastoralism is filling a space that is simultaneously filled with a natural lake – an aquatic environment. The borders between the two environments are blurred, confused. They change so that water flows into the photograph of the paddock, leaving only the line of the fence as a reminder of the other way of reading the landscape. The pre- and post-occupation landscapes merge – or are they laid one on the other, incompatibly?

The drawing

In the drawing, the relation between land and water is perfectly clear. The water is contained in a script of pipes, tanks and troughs. The only slight blurring occurs where water drips from the overflow pipe, where the excess of the colonised water is allowed to move back into the indigenous landscape. The tree is dead, there is no vegetation except the grass. The pre-occupation world is absent or dead, except for the patch of (indigenous?) grass. The two living things, the cow and the grass, are both dependent on the water provided by the windmill.

Clarifying the ambiguous landscape

In pre-occupation Australia, the boundaries between land and water are dynamic. Rivers appear above ground and then disappear. They vary greatly in their widths. Anabranches, billabongs, are left as evidence of this changing pattern. *Chains of ponds*, a typical pre-occupation creek system, disrupts the European concept of a continuing watercourse. Wetlands make an indistinct border. A *floodout* is one way a river moves from being water to being land. *Banker*, invented very early in the occupation, is an Australian English term used to describe an event uncommon in English rivers but very common in Australian rivers – a river flooded to its bank. In pre-occupation Australia, the edges of 'land' as opposed to 'water' or 'water' to 'land', are ambiguous.

This ambiguity is removed in the non-indigenous landscape. Here there is a clear distinction between land and water. Water is controlled, regulated, so that the amount remains more constant and the movement of water is as even as possible. Chains of waterholes become a continuous creek. Water is also visible – not underground, or blurred by swamp. If it is underground, it is contained in a pipe. Water is dammed and piped – held in a trough, tank, reservoir. It is civilised.

Water in its pre- and post-occupation forms is described, ironically, with many of the same kinds of terms that were used until the last 50 years of Aboriginal people and their culture by the occupying culture. *Unregulated* water is either irrational and 'half-formed' or primeval and magnificent – in either case not part of the occupying world. *Regulated* water is tamed, domesticated, fruitful, predictable, rational – or debased and polluted.[5]

The flight over the landscape south of Canberra displays a civilised hydrography. Hundreds of thousands of small dams, like water-paddocks, clearly show where the water is. The swamps and chains of ponds are few. This is the occupied landscape, where the world has settled into the new culture. In the view from Geary's Gap, the new and old cultures are simultaneously present – which may be why settlers have found the place so troubling.

In the child's drawing, the change from one landscape to the other is taking place in front of your eyes. Its power lies in its (implicit) violence. All life in this picture is dependent on the introduced water. At the same time, the pre-occupation landscape is still evidenced, in the dead tree and the bare earth. The bodies are still there. Occupation is still recent; this is a frontier picture.

Water as collaborator

Before the advent of bores and the access to artesian and sub-artesian water, the occupiers' relation to the landscape was similar to that of the indigenous population, but without their cultural knowledge. They were dependent on knowledge borrowed from the indigenous people, but still subject to wandering storms and intermittent rivers. But with the development of bores, water could take them and their cattle and sheep into country they could never settle before, and allow them to remain. The new status of this relation is evidenced in the invention of the word *piosphere,* to describe the environment created around a watering point.

It is this space, a piosphere, which is rendered so acutely in the child's drawing of the windmill and the water tank; a frontier post in an occupied country, where the water holds the frontier against the shifting, ambiguous and troubling indigenous space.

[5] See my doctoral thesis, especially Chapter 13: 'A Tale of Two Rivers'.

References

Arthur, J. M. 2003, *The Default Country: A Lexical Cartography of Twentieth-Century Australia*, University of NSW Press.

Farwell, George 1951, *The Outside Track*, MUP, Melbourne.

Western Champion, Barcaldine NSW, 31 August 1897.

6. You call it desert – we used to live there

Pat Lowe

When I first went to the desert with people who come from there, we travelled by car and on foot to some very out of the way places. They had names, but were not to be found on kartiya (whitefella) maps, even under a kartiya name. Sometimes I found myself wondering whether I was the first white person to have set foot in some of these places. I had, after all, been brought up in England in the days when much of the map of the world was coloured red, and when British people were proud of the Empire. I read books such as *King Solomon's Mines*. I learnt about the great explorers of Africa: Livingstone and Burton were among my heroes. My heart swelled with pride at the age of 12 when, as I sat in the rain awaiting the Queen's coronation parade, it was announced over the loudspeakers that a British team had conquered Everest. No one mentioned that they could not have got anywhere near the summit without massive support from the local Nepalese. I thought Hilary and Tensing were both Englishmen.

Of course, digging for water in the middle of a desert plain does not cut quite the same dash as stepping onto the summit of the world's highest mountain, but I had inherited the cultural sense that to be the first white person, especially if you were of British origin, to stand anywhere is somehow significant. The Great Sandy Desert was my frontier.

But one person's frontier is another person's home. At the same time that I was experiencing the newness of the desert, a country without settlement or, nowadays, human habitation of any kind for hundreds of square miles, I was learning how differently the country appeared to the people who grew up there. In this landscape, regarded by some as so inimical to human settlement as to be a suitable receptacle for the world's radioactive waste, they were profoundly at home: indeed, far more at home in the sandhills than they were in Fitzroy Crossing, where they had spent the past thirty or forty years. Not only is Fitzroy Crossing a town with kartiya rules and expectations, but also it lies within the country of the riverside Bunuba people, where the desert people who now live there remain forever outsiders.

At first, the desert appeared to me beautiful but undifferentiated. I saw regular, long red sandhills and swales clad in spinifex, wattle and small trees. Only as I picked up some of the vocabulary of the Walmajarri people did I begin to distinguish one area from another, and start to perceive pattern instead of randomness. I learnt that one place where we used to go hunting fairly regularly was a 'tinyjilwarnti' – characterised by claypans and large numbers of *Eucalyptus victrix*. Another, to me similar, eucalypt called a yarun grew on some sandhills in stands known as kurrmalyi. A third, whose pure white bark people cut to use as disposable utensils, tended to grow in ones and twos and was called nyumpurl. Other trees that once I would have described as 'stunted' – in other words, inferior as measured against a European yardstick of height, as if there were tall, non-stunted specimens to be found somewhere else – gradually became transformed into perfectly adapted hakea and grevillea, with flowers that provide welcome mouthfuls of nectar, their curved trunks the matrix from which people draw forth pairs of boomerangs.

Of course, any botanist would have made these simple distinctions at once, without having to go through a cross-cultural learning process. But the botanist would very likely have been just as naive or blind as I was when it came to the true nature of sandhills. I challenge anyone who comes to the desert for the first time to distinguish between a jilji and a jitpari, a kurrkuminti and a larralarra: terms describing sandhill formations for which English has no words.

But words are not the only means by which different perceptions of the desert are expressed. Desert art is another. In her book, *Seeking the Centre*, Roslynn Haynes has discussed the emptiness of 19th century paintings of the desert: it is a landscape of skulls, the starvation desert of Lasseter, Burke and Wills. Today that perception is changing, artists are seeing the desert as beautiful, but more for its sweeping vistas of sameness than for its variety or its detail.

In 1996, when preparing their Native Title claim and struggling with the insuperable communication gap between themselves and the Native Title Tribunal, a group of Walmajarri people decided to present their claim visually, through a painting. About seventy artists and other claimants collaborated on a huge work, measuring eight by ten metres, depicting their country. Each artist worked on his or her own area or, under direction, on that of a non-artist claimant. The result is a vast map.

Compare this with an ordnance survey map of the same area. Here indeed is terra nullius: the empty imagination of strangers.

This blindness is not confined to the desert. Let me quote three comments about the pindan savanna country of the West Kimberley region. The first comes from a pastoralist: 'That land's only good for nuclear testing or growing cotton,' he said. Note the inadvertent equation of two environmentally disastrous uses of land.

The second comment was made by a Federal Opposition spokesman on the environment. I met him to discuss a proposal to clear 250 000 hectares of the natural pindan bush for cotton production. He looked at me quizzically. 'What do you see as the problem?' he asked. 'There's not much there, is there?'

The third is one of the cotton proponents. He is on record as saying, of the pindan bush where I go hunting and bushwalking and rejoicing in the abundance of nature every weekend, 'It's literally dead.' Dead, this country of hugely varied flora, teeming with wildlife, its air filled with birds and insects? The same country that the Karajarri people plead for so eloquently, the country that supported them and several other language groups for countless thousands of years?

How can three men of presumably reasonable intelligence get it so wrong? From where do they inherit their selective blindness?

Whether we were born in Europe or Australia, we kartiya share European archetypes, as Jay Arthur has shown so effectively through her analysis of the concepts underlying the words we use. Our ideals of nature include striking features of landscape: mountains and hills, flowing rivers, tall trees, perhaps even hedgerows. The pindan has none of these. It is flat and densely vegetated, though burnt fairly regularly. For people used to navigating by hills and valleys, it is easy to get lost in. Non-Aboriginal people, apart from pastoralists, seldom venture into it. They drive past on their way to the next town, and most never see beyond the dead wattle and the cockroach bushes near the roadside. Proposals to clear many thousands of hectares of it to grow cotton meet with barely a murmur. The qualities of the pindan are subtle, and must be lived with, learnt and understood. They reveal themselves gradually, to those who make an effort to find them. And they are known intimately by the people who truly belong there.

A 'frontier' is culturally determined. It is a concept inextricable from colonial expansionism and conquest. One never has a frontier in one's own country. It is always in someone else's country. And the other person is part of the country still to be conquered. This may seem odd to people who consider the whole of Australia their country, and even that of several generations of ancestors. But Australia, to its indigenous inhabitants, is not one country but many. And much of it is still in the process of being colonised. Large areas of it are not yet 'tamed'. And, while the rest of Australia is talking about reconciliation, the people in northern Australia are still being dispossessed.

A few years ago, a middle-aged Australian couple, driving a new four-wheel drive car, well-equipped and provisioned with food and water, broke down on a desert track. Unable to get their car started, they decided to wait for rescue. They waited for two weeks. They said afterwards that they had spent the entire two weeks sitting in their car. After a number of days of this, with no sign of rescue, they wrote their wills. Somewhat belatedly, their daughter reported them missing, a rescue party went out, and they were found. This is in country that, not so long ago, was inhabited by people who knew nothing of cars, who walked confidently from waterhole to waterhole with no more equipment than they could carry in their hands and on their heads.

I once broke down in the desert with Jimmy Pike and two dogs. We spent a day-and-a-half trying to get our car started again, but failed. After lunch on the second day, Jimmy announced that we would have to walk. Carrying the rifle and a small esky of water we set off. Where I would have had to retrace our journey along the seismic lines, Jimmy cut across country, heading as the crow flies, straight towards our camp, thereby saving us hours of foot-slogging. Even so, the journey took all afternoon and most of the night: we reached camp shortly before dawn. On the way we killed and cooked a couple of small goannas to eat and set fire to the spinifex to warm ourselves. I had no fear, because I was in the competent hands of someone who knew the country intimately and was at home there. Even if we had broken down two hundred kilometres away, I have no doubt we would have got back safely, though it would have taken a little longer.

On another occasion, I lost a key. We had driven to a particular spot, parked the car, and gone hunting on foot. After a few hours of following tracks wherever they led, we headed back to the car. When we got there, I felt in my pocket: no key. I remembered taking a packet of dried fruit out of my pocket somewhere in the course of our walk, and supposed I had pulled the key out with it. Jimmy and I looked at one another. My dismay was greater than his. 'Well,' he said, 'you'll just have to follow your tracks back and find it.' I pleaded, he relented, and we set off in a straight line back across the sandhills, Jimmy leading, me following. No need to retrace our tortuous tracks. After some time, with a slight jerk of the head and a nonchalance all his own, Jimmy indicated a spot on the ground. 'There's your key,' he said. And there it was: a single car key lying on the red sand where it had fallen.

I have just come back from a two-week journey into the Great Sandy Desert with 20 traditional owners. We were well equipped with modern vehicles and communication systems. Even so, it is hard travelling. The seismic lines are covered with several years of regrowth and, when you approach the waterholes, you make your own tracks. For hours you bump over the spinifex in the flat, then hurl your vehicle up sandhills, relying on your momentum to carry you over the humps to the crest, sometimes becoming airborne on the other side. It is hot, dry; the only water is what you carry, or what you dig. It is the sort of journey for which, if you were a tour operator, you would have an age limit and require your passengers to obtain medical clearance. Yet most of our passengers were in their sixties, seventies and eighties, suffering from all manner of ailments: diabetes, heart disease, obesity, blindness. At night they slept in their swags on the sand and got bitten by centipedes. They lived largely on tins of corned beef and kippers, with an occasional treat of goanna or feral cat. Yet the only complaint we heard from those old people was when we ran out of milk for the Weetbix. And several of them said spontaneously: 'We don't get sick out here; we only get sick in town.'

People found and dug out waterholes they hadn't seen in 45 years or more. They identified over 150 plants and, where relevant, described their uses.

These are the differences between being at the frontier and being at home.

But there were a few younger people on the trip, children and grandchildren of the happy older people, who were experiencing the desert for the first time. They complained of the heat and the bumps. They were unfamiliar with the plant life. They said they would not be able to find the waterholes again, by memory, the way the older people had done. They no longer understand their country in the way their parents or grandparents did. They attend kartiya schools and learn kartiya concepts. They learn much that is new, but in doing so they unlearn much that is not only old, but priceless.

Once, Jimmy and I were talking to a class of school children in Fitzroy Crossing. I showed them our book, *Jilji*[1] , the title of which means 'sandhill'. It is a book about Walmajarri people's country in the Great Sandy Desert, which consists almost entirely of jilji: these long, regular sandhills stretching sometimes for hundreds of kilometres across the landscape. Expecting most people in the class to know, I asked, 'What does jilji mean?' No one answered. 'Are there any Walmajarri people here?' I asked. A forest of hands flew up. 'You should be able to tell us: what is a jilji?' Not one child knew. All had been brought up as exiles in Fitzroy Crossing and had attended kartiya schools. None had ever seen a jilji, let alone walked around the waterholes in their own country. How many, when they grow up, will be able to find a key left forgotten on the sand? In a single generation, the knowledge of countless former generations will be lost. It still exists, but it is fading from the world's screen and there is no way of retaining more than a smattering of it. The Walmajarri children's map of the desert has diminished from the big painting to the ordnance survey map. The home of their parents and grandparents is becoming for them, as it has always been for us, the unknown frontier.

[1] Pat Lowe and Jimmy Pike, 1990, *Jilji*, Magabala Books, Broom.

References

Haynes, R.D. 1998, *Seeking the Centre: The Australian Desert in Literature, Art and Film*. Cambridge University Press, Cambridge, Melbourne.

Part III. Science and Nation

7. The platypus frontier: eggs, Aborigines and empire in 19th century Queensland

Libby Robin

On 19 February 1971, Professor Rick Beidleman of the Department of Biology, Colorado College, USA sent a letter to Dr Michael Hoare, Research Fellow at the Academy of Science. The letter sought advice on a sabbatical project on the 'impact of Australian historic frontiers on the development of Australian natural science'. Beidleman had undertaken a study of the relation between the American frontier and natural science in the 1950s, and saw Australia as a logical extension: 'The comparison is so similar, indeed, that one finds the same people carrying out natural science exploration in the two countries, as you appreciate', he wrote.[1]

Hoare's response to the question of 'frontier science' was to translate it as 'colonial science'. His 'futuristic dream is to do a study of the science in the old "Empire" New Zealand, Australia, Canada, S. Africa, India, etc, etc. (I guess, too, the USA before it was such!)'. He was interested in the influence of places at the margins of empire on 'ideas and the advancement of knowledge', whilst Beidleman is actually pursuing a notion of 'national science' in America itself. The idea of a 'national frontier', well-developed in the United States since the Frederick Jackson Turner era late last century, did not, in fact, translate as easily to the Australian context as Beidleman had hoped. The empire got in the way. The place of science in empire was an ongoing concern of both science and history of science well into the 20th century in Australia.[2] The land itself also got in the way. The frontier in Australia never closed.[3] Hoare was afraid for the American who claimed he wanted to take 'field trips' following explorers. '[I] must ask you whether you know just how merciless and hard the Australian interior can be even nowadays', he cautioned . In 1971 Australia was a nation that had turned back to its coasts, never closing the frontier. It was a land where the Great Australian Silence about the violence of the Aboriginal past still

---

[1] Beidleman and Hoare correspondence is held in the Australian Academy of Science Archives (AAS 352).RGB to MEH 19 February 1971; MEH to RGB 14 March 1971. The file also contains letters from Beidleman to Miss E. Newman, the AAS Librarian (20 March 1971) and a reply from J. Deeble to RGB (7 April 1971).
[2] Libby Robin, 'Ecology: A Science of Empire?'
[3] Tom Griffiths, 'Ecology and Empire: Towards an Australian History of the World', pp. 10-11.

reigned.[4] While Hoare and Beidleman have in common an interest in 'pioneering' natural science in new lands, the 'frontier' only works in America.

The cross-cultural dimensions of Australian history have exploded in the past 30 years, and the idea of 'frontiers' has taken on new meaning in the Australian context. The role of Aboriginal people in science has remained under-studied, however. The other question also remains of the relation between science and nation. The uncomfortable suspicion persists in Australia that the 'frontiers of knowledge' are somewhere else. The American Professor never had that doubt. 'National science' meant 'world science' for an American. In Australia, the attachment to Empire was essential to making an impact on the frontiers of knowledge. That attachment meant clinging to the coast and looking outward again, not resolving the issues of place and people at the heart of the continent, not using the resources of this very different land to ask different questions about the world.

The parable of the platypus, a famous moment in 19th-century Australian scientific history, was about empire, knowledge (eggs, in this case) and Aborigines. It is also about the anxiety of local science, left out of the loop. The people who lived with the exceptional material lacked the scientific institutions of the old country, and the people with the institutions carried northern hemisphere expectations and values, and tended to carry away the specimens to work on elsewhere. The silence of the frontier worked to prop up Empire and to support a long cultural cringe. The rhetoric of 'frontiers' and 'colonials' captures some of this confusion.

When the rhetoric of 'frontier' reached Australia, the frontiers were not of battles but of settlement, with implicit rather than explicit wars. Studies of the imaginative space of the settler frontier explore encounters between colonising people, indigenous inhabitants and contested land.[5] In science however, we find another frontier. The scientific frontier is perhaps about war on ignorance. The divide between civilised and savage, so important to the settlement frontier is present again in muted form: scientific knowledge civilises; to remain ignorant is savage. The imperative to *know* clearly motivated much of the exploration that made settlement/invasion possible. In this chapter, I will explore some episodes of science on the frontier, which open up the interplay between frontiers of settlement in Queensland and frontiers of science.

The complexity of mixing frontier metaphors is immediately apparent. The frontiers are different shapes and textures, if you like. The frontiers of settlement concern a (sometimes bloody) commingling on the plain. The scientific frontier

[4] W. E. H. Stanner coined this term in his Boyer lectures in 1969. See *After the Dreaming; Black and White Australians – An Anthropologist's View*.
[5] See Elizabeth Furniss, 'Imagining the Frontier: Comparative Perspectives from Canada and Australia', this volume.

is a (rarefied) mountaintop. Both are about meeting the unknown, discovery, and embracing/colonising the 'other'/unknown. Frontiers of knowledge apply in disciplines other than science. But the perceived cumulative nature of science, which builds 'up' knowledge, makes the gaining of scientific knowledge particularly rich with mountain and vertical metaphors. The most famous is Isaac Newton's statement that 'If I have seen a little further it is only because I have stood on the shoulders of giants'.[6] Science is a story of effort-laden progressive steps towards 'the' answer. There may be many slips on the way, but the goal is to gain that mountaintop. The spread of settlement, by contrast, is a horizontal metaphor, the horizontality flattening the violence and oozing with inevitability.

The central story of the chapter is the 'discovery' by British scientist W. H. Caldwell that monotremes (platypus and echidna) lay eggs. The famous telegram 'monotremes oviparous, ovum meroblastic' (monotremes lay eggs of the same sort as reptiles), sent to the British Association for the Advancement of Science meeting in Canada in 1884, resolved a long debate about whether platypus laid eggs or had live young.[7] The story reveals much about the imperial shaping of scientific knowledge – British settlers in the Australian colonies and Aboriginal informants had long asserted that platypus laid eggs, but they had been disbelieved. 'Discovery' was reserved for a British scientist of impeccable scientific lineage.[8] Only certain sorts of people are allowed to declare that the top of the mountain has been reached.

The platypus debate

The platypus debate began in the 18th century. David Collins in 1797 saw 'an amphibious animal of the mole species'. 'The most extraordinary circumstance observed in its structure', Collins wrote, 'was its having, instead of the mouth of an animal, the upper and lower mandibles of a duck'.[9] George Shaw of the British Museum described the dried specimen he had been sent in 1798 by a naturalist named Dobson as 'of all the Mammalia yet known ... the most extraordinary in its conformation; exhibiting the perfect resemblance of the beak of a Duck engrafted on the head of a quadruped'. The dried skin he received is still marked by the scissors that Shaw used to check that the beak had not

---

[6] Newton's letter to Robert Hooke, 5 February 1675/6. I am grateful to Rod Home for this reference.
[7] 'Meroblastic' actually means that the egg partly separates during development, but the significance of this is that it is like a reptile rather than a bird.
[8] The literature on this is extensive. Examples include: Jacob W. Gruber, 'Does the Platypus Lay Eggs? The History of an Event in Science'; Kathleen Dugan, 'The Zoological Exploration of the Australian Region and its impact on Biological Theory'; Roy MacLeod, 'Embryology and Empire: The Balfour Students and the Quest for Intermediate Forms in the Laboratory of the Pacific'.
[9] Charles Barrett, The Platypus, p. 12.

been stitched on by a taxidermist.[10] The British Museum could ill-afford to become the butt of a cheap hoax.

Shaw named it *Platypus anatinus* in 1799, and the German anatomist Blumenbach, *Ornithorhynchus paradoxus* in 1800.[11] A genus of beetles already carried Shaw's name, it was later discovered, so the platypus today is scientifically known as *Ornithorhynchus anatinus,* using the rules of priority. Even the vernacular naming story is not simple – why was this animal not 'mallangong', (or another Aboriginal name)?[12] The kangaroo (cunquroo) had defied description, so an Aboriginal name had been borrowed. The wallaby, koala and others had all similarly needed 'new' names. But the platypus is known by its lost (Greek) scientific name, although until the mid-twentieth century 'duckbill' (a translation of *Ornithorhynchus* – literally, bird-nosed) was also popular.[13] And the paradoxical, although lost to priority from the scientific literature, stuck in popular consciousness.

Naming and renaming are events of colonisation, but in this case the naming of the platypus did not resolve the matter of where it belonged in the citadel of knowledge. Everard Home dissected a specimen preserved in spirits sent to Sir Joseph Banks by Governor Hunter in 1802, and was able to give a full internal description. Home noted its likeness to the echidna in having a common cloaca for reproduction and excretion: 'this tribe [has] a resemblance in some respects to birds, in others to the Amphibia'.[14] Until 1824 evidence of mammary glands, the distinguishing feature of mammals, had been undiscovered.[15] But even when they were, the matter of whether the platypus and echidna gave birth to live young was unresolved, and this was seen to be critical to their place in the 'natural' world. It also became a question of nationalism. The French evolutionary thinker, Étienne Geoffroy Saint-Hilaire, ignoring the evidence of milk glands,

[10] Harriet Ritvo, *The Platypus and the Mermaid and other Figments of the Classifying Imagination*, p. 4.
[11] George Shaw, *The Naturalist's Miscellany: or Coloured Figures of Natural Objects Drawn and Described Immediately from Nature*, vol. 10, June 1799 Fascicle, near plates 385 and 386. Johann Blumenbach, *Abbildungen*, vol. 5, Part 41, April 1800.
[12] George Bennett (1860) noted that *Mallangong* and *Tambreet* are used in 'the Yas, Murrumbidgee, and Tumat countries' and '*Tohunbuck*' at Goomburra, Warwick near Darling Downs in *Gatherings of a Naturalist in Australasia*, p. 97. Neither Richard Semon nor W. H. Caldwell records the Burnett River Aboriginal name for platypus (but since it was not eaten by them, it may not have been important).
[13] The over-determined 'Duck-billed platypus' still seems popular in Britain. This was observed, for example, in captions in the Royal Scottish Museum and the British Museum of Natural History (South Kensington and the Rothschild Collection at Tring in 1999).
[14] Cited in Ritvo, p. 7.
[15] J. F. Meckel had dissected mammary glands in 1824, but it was George Bennett's account of 'actual observation that milk is secreted from it' (letter to Owen, 4 February 1833) that was the basis for Owen's account of the glands to the Zoological Society of London in 1834. See Elizabeth Dalton Newland 'Dr George Bennett and Sir Richard Owen: A Case Study of Early Australian Science' pp. 55–74, esp. p. 68.

separated the Order Monotremata, from 'true' mammals. He placed them halfway between mammals and reptiles. The British anatomist Richard Owen, disagreeing with the Frenchman's theories of evolution, saw them as definitely mammals, and therefore, he argued 'ovoviviparous' (the eggs were hatched inside the mother and the young born alive). The classification of platypus and echidnas as mammals remained a problem, and the question of egg-laying contested for nationalistic as well as scientific honour. Perhaps this was partly why neither Aboriginal nor colonial evidence had been regarded as valid. Caldwell records three letters from colonial observers: John Jamison (1818), John Nicholson (c. 1865) and George Rumby (1864), who claimed they had seen platypus eggs.[16] The nations concerned were both of the European world, far from the specimens concerned. But the bitter rivalry between the English and the French permeated the status in science of the little faraway swimming monotreme. Stephen Jay Gould has observed that the language of taxonomy still reveals to some extent the Eurocentrism of classification: Prototheria (monotremes) are 'premammals'; Metatheria (marsupials) are 'middle mammals – not quite there'; and 'Eutheria' (the warm-blooded animals of the north) are 'true mammals'.[17]

The platypus was the archetype of Australian otherness in the popular British imagination. The title of Umberto Eco's 1999 book, *Kant and the Platypus*, which has very little to say about platypuses and a great deal about enigmas, suggests that this may still hold. Although scientists were doubtful about its egg-laying habits, at least some of the general public accepted this as one among so many Antipodean oddities.[18] The anonymous illustrated poem, *The Land of Contrarieties*, published in 1860 in Britain begins with the platypus:

> *There is a land in distant seas*
> *Full of all contrarieties.*
> *There beasts have mallards' bills and legs,*
> *Have spurs like cocks, like hens lay eggs.*[19]

[16] W. H. Caldwell 'The Embryology of Monotremata and Marsupialia – Part I', pp. 463–85, esp. pp. 467-8. He does not mention here that George Bennett also initially thought monotremes were oviparous. (See note 14.)

[17] Stephen Jay Gould, 'Sticking up for Marsupials' pp. 240–5, esp. pp. 241–2. Not all the Eurocentric thinking originated in Europe. For example, see the evolutionary 'trees' in T. Thomson Flynn (Professor of the University of Tasmania) 'The Phylogenetic Significance of the Marsupial Allantoplacenta' pp. 541–4.

[18] George Bennett changed his position on the subject: in 1834 he wrote to Owen that his samples proved that the platypus was oviparous, but later writings (e.g. *Gatherings of a Naturalist*) supported Owen's position that they were 'ovoviviparous'. See Newland, 'Bennett and Owen', p. 69. The public was clearly divided on this issue. Even after eggs were discovered by science, the *Illustrated London News*, commenting on the Australian pavilion at the Colonial and Indian Exhibition in 1886, reported that 'fables were formerly told of this queer creature, as that it laid eggs'. (Cited in Ritvo, p. 15.)

[19] This theme is developed in the exhibitions at the National Museum of Australia. I have drawn here on Nick Drayson's 1999 workbook (0412-50.04 Hoax to Enigma), which provides a curatorial basis for exhibition design.

In the Australian colonies, meanwhile, people were becoming more familiar with platypus – no longer was it perceived wet – camouflaged as 'a lump of dirty weeds', but increasingly its lovely fur was noticed. George Bennett the Sydney doctor, in his *Gatherings of a Naturalist in Australia 1860*, describes the thick fur as 'a beautiful adaptation to both the burrowing and aquatic habits of the animal'.[20] Bennett celebrated the personality of the animal, speaking of the 'playfulness' of his captive platypus twins. He was also reluctant to shoot the animal, trying to capture it to watch its behaviour. But there was no money in the maturing colonial economy (gold rushes notwithstanding) for 'pure' research. Bennett's research was constantly interrupted by the need to earn money (as a medical doctor), much as he would have preferred to explore the life of the platypus and other matters of natural history.[21]

I will return to Bennett's platypuses later, in connection with W. H. Caldwell, but in order to understand the story of the platypus frontier, it is necessary to locate the particular place for this scientific and colonial encounter. The question of *whose country* yielded up the mystery of the platypus was not determined by the platypus, but by another 'missing link' in the evolutionary story.

Ceratodus (The Queensland Lungfish)

One of the last 'freaks' of Australian natural history to come to the attention of European science was Ceratodus, the Queensland lungfish (known today as *Neoceratodus forsteri*). It normally breathes through gills like other fish, but, when the oxygen levels in the water fall, it can rise to the surface and gulp air straight into its lung, an organ that other fish do not possess. The Australian lungfish is unlike lungfish in Africa and South America, in that it can live both underwater and on land. Fish with lungs were known only as fossils in the northern hemisphere at the time of the naming of Ceratodus, so the Queensland specimen was immediately dubbed a 'living fossil'.

Ceratodus had an immediate place in the history of ideas. Its relevance to debates about Darwinian evolutionary theory, debates that had been heated since the publication of *The Origin of Species* in 1859, was obvious. Natural selection depended on continuities, but the classes of animals lacked 'missing links'. Classes of fish, amphibians, reptiles, birds and mammals seemed discrete (apart from such absolute anomalies as the paradoxical platypus). Ceratodus, however, as a lung-breathing fish, was clearly halfway between fish and amphibian. It was of course, also intriguing because it was halfway between *dead* (fossilised, like its nearest relatives) and *alive* (known to science). It was also interesting

---

[20] Bennett, p. 97.
[21] Australian Museum Archives: Series 37, Papers of George Bennett; Bennett's correspondence with Owen often refers to financial stringencies. (e.g. p. 54 – 'the Museum appointment has been made only £100 per annum & therefore anything but lucrative').

because it was not unknown – only unknown to science. Not only Aboriginal people, but also the Mary River and Wide Bay district squatters ate it, calling it 'Burnett Salmon' for its pink flesh.

'Considering that the fish is not uncommon and has for some years been used as an article of food,' wrote Alex M. Thomson, Professor of Geology at Sydney University to Sir Richard Owen in 1870, 'it is surprising that it had not fallen into scientific hands much earlier'.[22] Owen, as Superintendent of the Natural History Collections at the British Museum, was in a position to dissect the fish and determine its place in the citadel of knowledge. Only at the heart of Empire were there sufficient type specimens of fish to decide where this one fitted. Gerard Krefft's independence in publishing in Australia – in the *Sydney Morning Herald,* of all places – suggested a growing bloody-minded independence in the hearts of colonial scientists at arms' length from good specimens.[23] Ronald Strahan records that Gerard Krefft, the Director of the Australian Museum, had identified the fish as interesting when seeing so-called 'Burnett Salmon' being prepared for the table at the home of Mary River squatter and later New South Wales Minister for Lands, William Forster.[24] Thomson's letter accompanied a specimen of the fish taken from a tributary of the Mary River and sent to England within months of Krefft's announcement. The specimen was chosen for Owen and his staff because it had 'not been cut in the least, so that I trust it will reach you in a fit state for dissection'.[25]

Edward Smith Hill prepared the field notes for the Australian Museum file, dated 30 June 1870. Hill was a retired wine and spirit merchant, best known for his work on flora and geology. He was also a trustee of the Museum, an anti-Darwinian and no friend of Krefft's. It was possibly he who arranged for the fish specimen to be collected for Owen at the British Museum. In his description, Hill noted that some Aboriginal people called the fish 'Barramundi'. Hill was known as a defender of Aboriginal rights and clearly had regular dealings with Aboriginal people. Aboriginal collectors may have been essential to collecting a specimen in such good condition.[26] If Aborigines were involved, then the Australian Museum's was the first of a number of significant international scientific/colonial frontier encounters in the very limited part of Queensland where Ceratodus can be found. Only certain sections of two rivers,

---

[22] Australian Museum Archives: Series 48, Thomson to Owen 6/9/1870.

[23] Gerard Krefft, *Sydney Morning Herald*, Fig. 1-3; Krefft also published the description in the *Proceedings of the Zoological Society of London*, but the *SMH* was first.

[24] Ronald Strahan, *Rare and Curious Specimens*, p. 29.

[25] AMA 48, Thomson to Owen 6/9/1870.

[26] AMA 48: Memo E. S. Hill 30/6/1870; Hill's memo identifies the Aboriginal people naming the fish as from the Fitzroy River area, but this is clearly a mistake as Ceratodus does not live that far north. 'Barramundi' may of course have applied more broadly than just to Ceratodus. The fact that Burnett River people called the fish 'Djellah' suggests that Hill's collectors, if they were Aboriginal, were from a different language group.

the Mary and the Burnett, were suitable for the fish, the temperature and balance between salt and fresh water being critical to their survival.[27]

Albert Günther undertook a full anatomical analysis of Ceratodus at the British Museum. Gerard Krefft's use of the name *Ceratodus* showed that he was well aware of the fossil fish of the northern hemisphere and recognised that the 'new' fish had an ancient lineage. Even so Günther's anatomical description of the fish as an 'intermediate form' between fish and amphibians excited Krefft very much. In July 1870 (some time before Günther's paper on the anatomy of the fish was published), he wrote 'your *Ceratodus forsteri* if true a greatest discovery …[I am] amazed at it.'[28] Krefft, an evolutionary sympathiser, wrote regularly to Günther, mostly in German. Although Krefft had given the fish its name, his use of the pronoun 'your' suggests that he was giving Günther credit for seeing additional significance in the specimen. The warm tone might have been attributable to Krefft's and Günther's common German background, but it is more likely that this correspondent allowed Krefft to sidestep the more senior anti-Darwinian, Richard Owen.

The anti-evolutionary bias of the senior scientists of the Australian colonies at the time delayed local work on the lungfish after its discovery. Mulvaney and Calaby commented of this period that: 'It was rather remarkable that the members of the Australian scientific establishment almost to a man … were vocal opponents of Darwin's ideas on the origin of species by means of natural selection.'[29] Krefft himself ran foul of anti-evolutionary forces with his trustees. In 1874, he was physically removed from the Museum from which he refused to resign – ignominiously carried out onto the footpath outside by two prizefighters employed by the Trustees.[30] The bitter battle that ensued after Krefft's dismissal put paid to further research papers from the Australian scientist most sympathetic to Darwinian evolution.[31]

I want to leave the hypothetical might-have-beens and return to the reasons for 'discovering' Ceratodus in 1870. The limitations of its habitat and the narrowness of its geographical distribution made its discovery by a scientifically-literate observer improbable. The relevant part of Queensland could hardly be said to be new to European eyes at this time, but it was probably still fair to call it frontier country. Indeed the idea of a continuing frontier in Queensland dies

---

[27] They have since been successfully introduced into the Brisbane River, the Stanley River and the North and South Pine Rivers but further south the water is too cold and further north the competition with crocodiles makes introduction impossible. See David McGonigal, 'The Lungfish: Australia's Living Fossil'.

[28] AMA 48, Krefft to Günther 13 July 1870. This is the only sentence in English in the letter.

[29] D. J. Mulvaney and J. H. Calaby, *'So Much that is New': Baldwin Spencer 1860-1929*, p. 146.

[30] Strahan, *Rare and Curious Specimens*, pp. 33–34. George Bennett and W. B. Clarke resigned from the Museum over this. E. S. Hill was the Trustee who employed the prizefighters.

[31] G. P. Whitley and Martha Rutledge, 'Johann Ludwig (Louis) Gerard Krefft (1830-1881)'.

hard. As David Trigger has observed, Queensland premiers were still talking about the state as a 'a new frontier' bound to create an 'era of prosperity' in the 1990s.[32] Wide Bay had been surveyed in 1848, and there had been 'settlement' up both rivers. This perhaps masked the area's scientific interest. Once exploration finished, good scientific observers may have had a tendency to move to other unsettled/pristine sites, leaving the settlement frontier to squatters and adventurers, who may or may not have been good natural history observers. When the squatters at the frontier did make an observation, the scientists were slow to believe them. William Forster, had described Ceratodus but had been disbelieved by Gerard Krefft until 1870, a point Krefft confessed in his letter to the *Sydney Morning Herald*. The species name *forsteri* was a belated attempt to make amends to the now important Forster.

Gold and adventure seeking

The Gympie gold rushes of 1867 attracted a large population of adventurers. 'Gold upheaves everything, and its disruptions are like that of an earthquake', wrote Anthony Trollope travelling in Queensland in 1873.[33] Trollope was as much concerned about the upheaval of morality, as of the Queensland soil. The attractions of what we might call now 'boys' own adventures', were celebrated by the Englishman, Arthur Nicols in his fictionalised account *Wild Life and Adventure in the Australian Bush: Four Years Personal Experience*. Writing eloquently of the 'noble territory of Queensland', Nicols boosted the frontier as a place for personal and financial development. 'These resources are waiting development at the hands of vigorous manhood which the upper and middle classes can contribute in abundance towards the making of this part of the Queen's realm'.[34] His natural history observations were excellent and he displayed a high level of curiosity about the platypus and echidna specimens he shot (including dissecting them, preserving the skins – and eating them). Nicols's hero, Harold, told a hunting story all about a man and his dog, Don. His prose captured the thrill of the hunt:

> what was that strong boil of water just now near the lilies? … There it is again, and a strangely shaped animal crawls over the leaves, dives in and out among them with the easy gliding motion of an otter, and disappears … suddenly, the surface breaks into a turmoil … and two long brown bodies are seen rolling over and over, playing or fighting … showing beaver-like tails and duck-like bills … The hoarse roar of the gun breaks the stillness of the scene. He is stripped in a few moments and eagerly swimming around the spot where the charge rippled along

---

[32] The Premier was Wayne Goss in 1992. Quoted in David S. Trigger 'Mining, Landscape and the Culture of Development Ideology in Australia' pp. 161–80, esp. p. 164.

[33] Quoted in J. W. McCarty, 'Gold Rushes', p. 284.

[34] Arthur Nicols, *Wild Life and Adventure*, p. vii.

the water … Don hearing the report, hurries up … [and] sees a dusky object crawling through the reeds, and secures it before it can regain the deep water; and Harold soon stands on the bank, triumphantly holding his first platypus.[35]

Because he is working within a particularly British sort of hunting ethic, Harold does not use Aboriginal collectors.[36] The heroics of catching the platypus made it a worthy 'trophy', despite the fact that its size was not as clearly respectable as a lion or an elephant. The platypus for Nicols is working as the drawcard for young men of the Empire with hunting aspirations. Australia's kangaroos and other marsupials did not generally carry the excitement of the wild animals of Africa. Nicols is suggesting that here is one that might arouse the sort of excitement where 'away flies conscience, philosophy and all such abstract considerations', in short, a manly challenge for the imperial hunter.[37]

Science and frontier life

The difficulty for scientists working in Queensland was, perhaps, to make it clear that their task was different from that of frontier-adventurers, morally more worthy and more important to the glory of empire. Whether they were visitors from Europe, or aspiring Australian scientists, they would have been largely sympathetic with the evocation of empire, class and gender portrayed by Nicols, but would have seen all of these as in service to science. The glory of Australia in empire through science was perhaps more important to locals, and the booty of Australia for a glorious scientific empire more the concern of visiting Europeans, not all of whom were British. The visitors, in particular, were clearly fearless about taking very large numbers of specimens. But the scientists' virility was tied to hunting for knowledge rather than hunting for trophies. Such hunting demanded that they tap into the best local knowledge sources, including Aboriginal ones.

The young German embryologist, Richard Semon in his popular account of his travels in Queensland, goes out of his way to make it clear that the purposes of his journey are purely scientific:

[35] ibid., pp. 347–8. The place of this platypus is probably southwest Queensland, not the Gympie area, but it is unclear, and because it is all 'fiction', conflation of places and events is possible. On the hunting ethic, see John MacKenzie, *The Empire of Nature: Hunting, Conservation and British Imperialism*, esp. pp. 25–53.

[36] The chief role of the one Aboriginal personality in Nicols' tale, Murray Jack, is to lead (and die in) a revenge battle against the Warrego people following the murder of a shepherd at an outstation. The 'cowboys and indians' stylism and the laundered clarity of the ethics of the account gives the reader clues about the purposes of fictionalising in Nicols' so-called 'adventure' writings (see pp. 315–339).

[37] Harriet Ritvo, *The Animal Estate: the English and Other Creatures in the Victorian Age*, p. 267.

In June 1891, when I set out on my scientific journey, nothing whatever had been recorded with regard to the development of Ceratodus. Concerning oviparous mammals [there were] no developmental facts but that of their laying eggs, and an interesting observation about the teeth of young Ornithorhynchus...Thus it was that I chose Australia as my first and my main field of action, and within Australia those quarters which harboured the animals chiefly exciting my interest.[38]

The book's dedication to the eminent scientists Ernst Haeckel and Paul von Ritter, alerts us to the fact that it is an account of 'an expedition' [not for mere adventure but] 'destined to bring some Phylogenetic Problems nearer their solution'. Semon's geographical research was as thorough as his zoological. Before leaving Jena, he had precisely identified the Ceratodus territory where he would make his home in Australia:

[O]nly a brother naturalist will sympathise with me, when I own that an almost solemn feeling overcame me, on starting from the little station of Maryborough on the morning of 24th August, I began my pilgrimage to land sacred to the zoologist.[39]

W. H. Caldwell had made the scientific expedition internationally famous for this region, and Semon wasted no time in directing his attentions to the area where Caldwell's collecting had been most successful.

I now want to turn to the central story of this scientific frontier, the Ceratodus-driven collecting expeditions of Caldwell and his Aboriginal companions in the 1880s, which resulted in the famous telegram to the British Association about the platypus. It is very difficult to infer the Aboriginal perspectives from Caldwell's brief account alone. The fact that Semon went to precisely the same area only seven years later, however, and was introduced to Aboriginal collectors by the same squatter (W. F. McCord), allows us to draw on his much fuller account of the Aboriginal people to supplement Caldwell's remarks.

Mr Caldwell's travels

William Hay Caldwell's Cambridge lineage was impeccable. The department he came from was leading the world in embryological research. He distanced himself from the 'early days of Darwinism' where 'it was hoped to get a pedigree for every animal'. 'Now that all biologists are Darwinists,' he declared to the Royal Society of New South Wales on 17 December 1884, (where in fact there would

---

[38] Richard Semon, *In the Australian Bush and on the Coast of the Coral Sea. Being the Experiences and Observations of a Naturalist in Australia, New Guinea and the Moluccas*, p. 2.

[39] ibid., p. 15.

have been very few Darwinian sympathisers!), 'pedigree-hunting has gone out of fashion'.[40] Perhaps he was aware of the lack of sympathy to Darwinian biology in Australia and letting the colonials know they were out of touch with the action. It is significant that he did not bother to write up this extempore talk. He left it to someone else (in all probability a colonial not sympathetic to Darwinian biology) to prepare a publication from his notes. Caldwell ultimately published so little that this account is crucial to gaining an idea of the state of his mind when in Australia. His work in morphology was to observe the minute differences between organic beings at various stages of development, in the belief that the patterns of evolution may be reflected in the patterns of individual development. His teacher at Cambridge, Professor Francis Maitland Balfour, had suggested in 1882 that Caldwell should consider travelling to Australia to work on the development of Ceratodus and 'the peculiar Australian mammalia'. Balfour, elected to a Fellowship of the Royal Society aged only 27, was taught by Professor Michael Forster (no relation to the Forster of the fish, but an active member of the British Association, and Secretary of the Royal Society). Forster in turn, was taught by T. H. Huxley, Darwin's most outspoken advocate. Caldwell benefited from the strong Darwinian lineage of Forster and Balfour at Cambridge, but it was also a burden to him.[41] In 1882, Balfour, aged only 31, was killed in a mountaineering accident, and a travelling studentship was endowed in his memory. Caldwell, Balfour's own student, working on a task assigned by Balfour, was the obvious first recipient of an 'instrument by which [Balfour's] memory was to reach beyond Cambridge and encompass the world for Darwinian biology'.[42] Caldwell's mission was well funded. In addition to a personal salary from the Balfour Trust, he brought with him grants totalling £500 from the Royal Society (of London) towards the cost of equipment. Both Cambridge University and the Royal Society eagerly awaited results.

George Bennett had studied the platypus mostly in New South Wales, and Caldwell, guided by this, determined to start in Sydney on his arrival in Australia in September 1883 and work over the platypus country inland. He had not counted on the skin-hunters. The trade in platypus skins had escalated dramatically in the two or three decades since Bennett's trips. By late in the 19th century, platypus rugs of 40 or more pelts were being stitched together.[43] 'I wasted a fortnight trying to obtain information in Sydney as to where the animals were to be found in sufficient numbers for my purpose'.[44] By mid-October,

[40] W. H. Caldwell, 'On the Development of the Monotremes and Ceratodus', pp. 117–22.
[41] MacLeod, 'Embryology and Empire'.
[42] ibid., p. 148. MacLeod records that £8,446 was subscribed to the scholarship, a phenomenal amount at the time.
[43] See Barrett, *The Platypus*, pp. 17–19. The National Historic Collection of the National Museum of Australia has such a rug.
[44] Caldwell, 'Embryology of Monotremata and Marsupialia', p. 464.

Caldwell had given up on platypus, and moved his attention to koala and wallaby, which were just beginning to breed. This material gave Caldwell new information on foetal membranes, and he sent home an account that was published in 1884 in the *Quarterly Journal of Microscopal Sciences*.

In April, Caldwell went north to the Burnett River district to find Ceratodus, and noticed when he arrived that as well as Ceratodus with ripe spermatozoa, both echidna and platypus were numerous in the area. He decided to stay there for the monotreme breeding season to try to get both Ceratodus and monotremes in the same year. 'The Burnett district', he wrote, 'presented the further advantage of possessing a considerable number of black natives. I afterwards found that without the services of these people I should have had little chance of success'.[45]

He set up under canvas out of Gayndah, realising that in order to work with Aboriginal people, he would have to create an independent camp with provisions, away from the town and stations, near the river where Ceratodus lived. This was probably on the advice of district squatters such as W. F. McCord, who gave similar advice to Semon seven years later. It was McCord who recommended 'Frank' an Aboriginal from Gayndah to Semon as 'best adapted to act as an agent between me and the blacks, to explain my wishes to them, and to be of help in my searches for the desired animals'.[46]

The curious travelling-scientist circus was appreciated by both blacks and whites in these districts where the economy was in a downward spiral. The wool industry was failing as the first good pastures had degenerated, and it was no longer possible to run sheep on the inferior regrowth pastures: 'the survival of the unfittest', wrote Semon wryly.[47] Any new industry – even a passing science industry was embraced. It was probably no coincidence that the enterprising Frank recommended by McCord turned up on Semon's coach from Biggendon to Gayndah, and became 'the first black who crossed my path'. Semon came to have reservations about Frank, however, and 'refused his services during my second stay in the Burnett.'[48] The majority of workers in the new industry were Aboriginal, because of the particular skills required, but Caldwell reports that he employed some 'white navvies' to dig up platypus burrows (because the Aboriginal team was reluctant to do so). Semon also employed one of the local German farmers of the area to accompany him in the bush.

Caldwell revealed that his purse was well filled with his opening offer of £10 to 'anyone who would show me Ceratodus spawn'. Once he had camp set up, he

---

[45] loc. cit.
[46] Semon, *In the Australian Bush*, p. 17.
[47] ibid., p. 19.
[48] ibid., p. 17.

spent 'many hours in the water' in June and July hunting everywhere for the eggs of Ceratodus. Meanwhile:

> the blacks began to collect *Echidna* and very soon I had segmenting ova from the uterus. In the second week of August I had similar stages in *Ornithorhynchus,* but it was not until the third week that I got the laid eggs from the pouch of *Echidna.* In the following week (August 24) I shot an *Ornithorhynchus* whose first egg had been laid; her second egg was in a partially dilated *os uteri'.*[49]

This he described as 'a lucky chance'.[50] To kill a female platypus (which lay eggs in twos) at the point *between* laying eggs gave him the crucial information about the stage of development at which the eggs were laid – a stage he describes as 'equal to a 36-hour chick'.[51] The capture of this specimen is so absolutely crucial to the story, that it is interesting that he claims to have shot it himself. Perhaps he did. His timing was impeccable. On 29 August he sent in the telegram 'Monotremes oviparous, ovum meriblastic' to a neighbouring station. The telegram was delivered to Professor Archibald Liversidge at the University of Sydney, who in turn sent it to the British Association at Montreal. Less than a week later, on 2 September, Dr William Haacke from the South Australian Museum was able to give evidence of egg-laying in monotremes, displaying an egg from an echidna's pouch, at a meeting of the Royal Society of South Australia.[52] The Norwegian, Carl Lumholtz also claims to have heard reports of echidna's eggs, and was in pursuit of them at the time he had to leave Australia, being convinced that 'the reports I had received from the blacks corresponded with the facts'.[53] Caldwell's ability to tap the very consciously international audience in Canada – this was the first time that the British Association for the Advancement of Science had met outside Britain – was critical to his fame. The mystery was ripe for solution, but the telegram gave Caldwell a dramatic edge.

Caldwell himself hardly celebrated this historic moment. He was still anxious about that fish, and one can read in his words the pressure and burden that the Cambridge expectations and financial support had given him 'Meanwhile I had never relaxed my efforts to find *Ceratodus;* but after four months I was beginning to despair of success'.[54]

---

[49] Caldwell, 'Embryology of Monotremata and Marsupialia', p. 464.
[50] Caldwell, 'On the Development of Monotremes and Ceratodus', p. 120.
[51] Caldwell, 'Embryology of Monotremata and Marsupialia', p. 464.
[52] William Haacke, 'Exhibits', p. 81.
[53] Carl Lumholtz, *Among Cannibals: An Account of Four Years Travels in Australia and of Camp Life with the Aborigines of Queensland,* p. 329. Lumholtz was aware of Caldwell's work, so there may be some hindsight in this observation.
[54] Caldwell, 'Embryology of Monotremata and Marsupialia', p. 464.

He finally found his Ceratodus eggs in September, and at this time employed some fifty 'black retainers'. It was the women who were given the responsibility of trawling the river weed for Ceratodus, whilst the men collected echidna, a favourite food. 'It was only occasionally, and then with great difficulty, that I persuaded them to dig for *Ornithorhynchus*. Not only the blacks, but their dogs, refused to eat the animal.'[55] It is yet another paradox of the platypus that the mystery of its egg-laying habits was solved with the assistance of Aboriginal collectors who themselves had no reason to hunt for the animal. This contrasts sharply with the earlier experience of George Bennett with Goulburn Aboriginal collectors. Bennett writes:

> The eyes of the aborigines, both young and old, glistened, and their mouths watered, when they saw the fine condition of the young Mallangongs. The exclamations of 'Cobbong fat' (large, or very fat), and 'Murry budgeree patta' (very good to eat), became so frequent and earnest, that I began to tremble for the safety of my destined favourites... But I was wrong in my calculation of the natives' power of resisting temptation, for they brought them all home safe, and were delighted with the reward of tobacco which was given for their trouble.[56]

But the Aborigines of the upper Burnett District, whose interest in platypus was minimal were the ones who assisted not only Caldwell, but also Semon in obtaining long embryological series critical to the debates in anatomy and morphology in the late 19th century.

Scientific and settlement frontiers in tension

There are two points to this story: the first is the contingency of scientific discovery. Calwell was climbing the Ceratodus mountain when he seized the solution for the platypus puzzle. Frontiers may be unexpectedly contiguous. The fact that both questions interested the Cambridge embryological school made an opportunistic leap possible – but the coincidence was not really predictable. Despite the 'pinnacle' rhetoric, the discovery of platypus eggs by an uncontestable source, was to some extent an accident of circumstance. Caldwell was almost an accidental scientist, empowered (and burdened) by a large purse and high expectations. He was essentially charged with tasks of the post-Darwinian era, but his contribution to science was a final response to the challenge issued by Everard Home in 1825 to W. S. Macleay as he left for New South Wales: 'what is principally wanted is the ova'.[57] It is interesting that when Caldwell returned to Britain in 1887 with a Sydney-born wife, he maintained his Fellowship at Caius College Cambridge only nominally, and only

---

[55] ibid., p. 465.
[56] Bennett, *Gatherings of a Naturalist in Australasia*, p. 132.
[57] Ritvo, *Platypus and the Mermaid*, p. 14.

until about 1889. He published very little and made his way as a successful Scottish paper-manufacturer in the family firm. It was left to others to undertake the anatomical work on his huge collections. Richard Semon in 1891, realising that Caldwell had barely begun this task, decided to make his own trip. Semon, by contrast, analysed all his specimens and published several important scientific papers as well as his popular book.[58] But he too had great difficulties finding Ceratodus roe, because the part of the river he had chosen lacked the weed where the spawn is found. He found plenty of full grown 'Djellah', as the local Aborigines called them, and established that Ceratodus was no vegetarian, taking happily to meat and mollusc baits.[59] Semon's published scientific work, however, focused on the monotremes and marsupials, because he had successfully collected developmental series for these. There is no evidence that he observed the stages of growth in the living lungfish. Caldwell, by contrast, bred and displayed a young lungfish to the Royal Society of New South Wales in December 1884, but wrote no more about it after he returned to Britain.

The second story relates to the emergence of an opportunistic local Aboriginal science industry that underpinned the success of both Caldwell and Semon. Aboriginal collectors assisted many other scientific travellers including George Bennett around Yass and the Norwegian, Carl Lumholtz in Coomooboolaroo further west in Queensland, but on nothing like the scale required by both Caldwell and Semon. The demand for embryological series (collections with representatives of all stages of the growing animal) meant absolute carnage. For example, in a single season Caldwell's team collected 1300-1400 echidnas 'from which a fairly complete series of stages was obtained'.[60] Such a vast exercise demanded a whole economy. Caldwell's second season required 150 Aborigines working flat out for two months: 'A skilful black, when he was hungry, generally brought in one female *Echidna* together with several males, every day … The blacks were paid half-a-crown for every female, but the price of flour, tea and sugar, which I sold to them, rose with the supply of *Echidna*. The half-crowns were, therefore, always just enough to buy food to keep the lazy blacks hungry'.[61]

Semon tried to set up a base close to Gayndah, like Caldwell, but moved further upstream to a place outside Mundubbera, to get away from the pressures of the town. By contrast to Caldwell, Semon determined to pay his Aboriginal collectors fairly in cash at the end of each week:

---

[58] Semon's studies are published in F. Romer (ed.) *Monotremate und Marsupialia*. The National Library of Australia copy is the one from the library of the *SS Discovery* of the Antarctic Expedition of 1901–4. The adventures of Semon thus went far south with other adventurers.

[59] Semon, *In the Australian Bush*, pp. 87–8.

[60] Caldwell, 'Embryology of Monotremata and Marsupialia', p. 466.

[61] ibid., p. 466.

All this brought about a very lively competition during the first week. I received material in such abundance that I had difficulty in finishing its preparation during the day, in dissecting the animals brought to me, conserving their organs, eggs and young, and preparing them for a more thorough examination which was to take place in Europe. On 10 September, I received no less than eight female Echidnas, two of which bore eggs in their oviduct, whilst two of them carried eggs, and three other young ones in their pouch. Besides this, I received a quantity of marsupials on the same day. On settling my accounts on Saturday the 12th September, I found that every black had to receive a considerable sum... and I began to consider whether my means would suffice if things went on in this style.[62]

They didn't. 'Never again in the whole of my campaign did I attain the good results of the first week'.[63] Semon had reckoned without the opportunism of the frontier settlers. Mrs Corry, in that same week, set up an illegal operation to sell the cashed-up Aboriginal collectors booze. Despite the fact that she told Semon she was 'very sorry and promised never to do it again', he felt 'ethically obliged' to prohibit intemperance 'at the cost of my own success, for I should certainly have been more prosperous had I kept to my first system of payment'.[64] But Semon's 'fear of getting involved in serious difficulties', and unwillingness to risk the 'peaceable' temperament of his Aboriginal team members, drove his decision to settle accounts at the end of the season. This was hardly humane concern for Aboriginal people, but rather a wish to protect the good name of science, to keep science on the civil side of the frontier. There is no doubt that both Caldwell and Semon were well aware that the quality of their science depended on the quality of their relations with the local Aboriginal communities. George Bennett, too, whose relations with his collectors in New South Wales were generally cordial by his own account, was conscious that 'good Aborigines' corresponded with good science. Bennett wrote in frustration to Richard Owen about the success of Caldwell, the young professional, in solving in a few months the mystery to which he had devoted half his life. 'I had only two lazy aborigines', Bennett complains 'and Caldwell succeeds ... encamped on the banks of the river ... with the aid of a large number of aborigines. It is certainly the only way to insure success'.[65] Bennett himself was not to blame for coming up with the 'wrong answer'– only his 'lazy' Aborigines.

There is almost an intriguing suggestion here that where the scientific and settler frontiers coincide, the quality of the European observer is second in importance

[62] Semon, *In the Australian Bush*, pp. 46–7.
[63] ibid., p. 56.
[64] loc. cit.
[65] Bennett to Owen 1888, quoted in Gruber, 'Does the Platypus Lay Eggs?', p. 51.

to the quality of Aboriginal assistance. This contradicts Kathleen Dugan's contention that 'the system of colonial science left scientists unable to collect biological information from the people best qualified to provide it'.[66] The system veritably depended upon such people. The problem was the credibility of the brokers of the information, the settler naturalists. European science before Caldwell disbelieved Aboriginal and settler Australian voices alike. Settler Australian naturalists were deeply discomfited to find that their observations were worth no more than an Aboriginal's. Indeed, the fact that Caldwell fresh from Cambridge with his well-paid Aboriginal team had established the 'right answer' without assistance from colonial scientists must have added to settler anxiety. This anxiety is manifest in the strategy of blaming Aboriginal assistants for wrong answers; settler naturalists wanted to be with civilization, on the side of empire and new knowledge, not with the colony, in error, and degenerating.

The telegram that closed a frontier

Not all settler scientists shared Bennett's angst. Liversidge, the chemistry professor who had aligned himself with the 'right answer' by mediating the famous telegram's successful transmission to Canada, immediately seized on its value in attracting the attention of British science to Australia. In a letter published in the Sydney papers on 16 September 1884, and reproduced soon after in England and other colonial papers, Liversidge wrote:

> During the past fortnight we have received several telegrams from London, respecting the late meeting of the British Association, at Montreal, and in some of them references are made to suggestions that a future meeting be held in Australia.
>
> As far as one can judge, the idea seems to have been thrown out when Professor Moseley, FRS, announced Mr Caldwell's discovery of the oviparous nature of the platypus and Australian porcupine. [footnote: sent from Sydney by cable]. The news seems to have created or rather reawakened interest in the peculiarities of Australian Natural History, and on the spur of the moment some of the more enthusiastic members appear to have proposed that a subsequent meeting of the British Association should be held in Australia.

The text of this letter was also reproduced in the proceedings of the first meeting of the Australasian Association for the Advancement of Science (AAAS), held in Sydney in 1888. It was the first salvo in Liversidge's energetic campaign to bring the British Association to Australia, a campaign that was finally successful some thirty years later.[67] Perhaps the telegram's most immediate contribution

---

[66] Dugan, 'The Zoological Exploration of the Australian Region', p. 92.
[67] Archibald Liversidge, appendix to President's Address, *Proceedings AAAS*, Sydney, 1888, p. 15. The BAAS came to Australia finally in 1914.

was to draw the leading evolutionist Walter Baldwin Spencer to Australia. Spencer, whilst in Britain in 1884, wrote the note in *Nature* about the significance of Caldwell's work. Three years later he took up the Chair in Biology at the University of Melbourne.[68] Liversidge and Spencer, promoters of the monotreme mountain, both went on to be very significant in scientific affairs in Australia, especially the AAAS. But they also created closure – a sense that the platypus frontier had closed, and moved Australian science to focus on other things.

Postscript

After the Caldwell era, the platypus was neglected for many decades by mainstream science. It was energetic natural history amateurs of independent means who pressed on with platypus studies – the most notable being Harry Burrell, whose twenty years' research resulted in the publication of *The Platypus* in 1927, in which he speculated that the platypus had a 'sixth sense'. Burrell was known affectionately as 'Duckbill Dave'. He was responsible for designing the platypussary that took five platypuses to the New York Zoo in 1922. Charles Barrett's popular book of 1944, also titled *The Platypus*, included summaries of Burrell's work and the work of the other Platypus Man, Robert Eadie, who kept platypuses at Healesville, near Melbourne. Perhaps it was Barrett who kept alive the 'platypus frontier', by reminding scientists that the 'cairn of knowledge that they commenced to build with small pebbles [was] ... still uncompleted, but high and firm now, because of the work of such patient, masterly observers as Robert Eadie and Harry Burrell'.[69] Science did return to the platypus, in the 1960s, with some CSIRO studies of their milk glands confirming the similarity of the monotremes to other marsupials.[70] In the 1980s and 1990s, confirmation was found for Burrell's 'sixth' – electromagnetic – sense.[71]

The local Aboriginal communities were not the only beneficiaries of scientific (later eco-) tourism. In the upper Burnett River area over a hundred years later, there is great pride in the local curiosity and active conservation work towards the preservation of the slow-moving lungfish.[72] In a quaint tribute to the old scientific frontier, there is still a railway siding called 'Ceratodus'.

[68] 'Walter Baldwin Spencer, 'The Eggs of Monotremes', pp. 132–5. See also Mulvaney and Calaby, *'So Much that is New'*, esp. pp. 143–5.
[69] Barrett, *The Platypus*, p. 16; Harry Burrell, *The Platypus: Its Discovery, Zoological Position, Form and Characteristics, Habits, Life History, etc.*
[70] A film: 'The Comparative Biology of Lactation' was also made through CSIRO and The Australian National University. See CSIRO Division of Wildlife and Ecology, *Biannual Report*, pp. 36–7.
[71] Ian Anderson, 'Sixth Sense is the Platypus's Secret (sensors for electrical signals)', p. 39. K. H. Andres and M. Von Duerning, Two types of electrosensory organs of the platypus, p. 745.
[72] McGonigal, 'The Lungfish'.

References

Anderson, Ian 1988, 'Sixth Sense is the Platypus's Secret (Sensors for Electrical Signals)', *New Scientist*, vol. 118, no. 1612, p. 39.

Andres, K. H. and M. Von Duerning 1993, 'Two Types of Electrosensory Organs of the Platypus', *Ornithorhynchus paradoxus*. [sic] *Journal of Comparative Physiology*, vol. 173, no. 6, p. 745.

Barrett, Charles 1944, *The Platypus*, Robertson and Mullins, Melbourne.

Bennett, George 1860, *Gatherings of a Naturalist in Australasia*, London (republished 1982. Milson's Point: Currawong).

Burrell, Harry 1927, *The Platypus: Its Discovery, Zoological Position, Form and Characteristics, Habits, Life History, etc.*, Angus & Robertson, Sydney.

Caldwell, W. H. 1884. 'On the Development of the Monotremes and Ceratodus', *Proceedings of the Royal Society of New South Wales*, vol. 18, pp. 117–22.

Caldwell, W. H. 1887, 'The Embryology of Monotremata and Marsupialia – Part I', *Philosophical Transactions of the Royal Society (B)*, vol. 178, pp. 463–85.

Dugan, Kathleen 1987, 'The Zoological Exploration of the Australian Region and its Impact on Biological Theory' in Nathan Reingold and Marc Rothenberg (eds) *Scientific Colonialism*, pp. 79–100, Smithsonian Institution Press, Washington.

Flynn, T. Thomson 1922, 'The Phylogenetic Significance of the Marsupial Allantoplacenta' *Proc. Linnean Soc. NSW*, vol. 47, pp. 541–4.

Gould, Stephen Jay 1980, 'Sticking up for Marsupials' in *The Panda's Thumb More Reflections in Natural History*, pp. 240–5, Norton, New York.

Griffiths, Tom 1997, 'Ecology and Empire: Towards an Australian History of the World', in Griffiths and Robin (eds) *Ecology and Empire*, pp. 1–16.

Griffiths, Tom and Libby Robin (eds) 1997, *Ecology and Empire: Environmental History of Settler Societies*, Keele University Press, Edinburgh.

Gruber, Jacob W. 1991, 'Does the Platypus Lay Eggs? The History of an Event in Science', *Archives of Natural History*, vol. 18, no. 1, pp. 51–123.

Haacke, William 1884-4, 'Exhibits', *Transactions of the Royal Society of South Australia*, vol. 7, p. 81.

Home, R. W. and S. G. Kohlstedt (eds) 1991, *International Science and National Scientific Identity: Australia between Britain and America*, Kluewer Academic Publishers, Holland.

Liversidge, Archibald 1888, 'Appendix' to President's Address, *Proceedings Australasian Association for the Advancement of Science*, p. 15, AAAS, Sydney.

Lumholtz, Carl 1889, *Among Cannibals: An Account of Four Years Travels in Australia and of Camp Life with the Aborigines of Queensland*, John Murray, London.

Krefft, Gerard 1870, in *Sydney Morning Herald*, 18 January, no. 65, col. 5.

— 1870, description in *Proceedings of the Zoological Society of London*, pp. 221–4.

MacKenzie, John 1988, *The Empire of Nature: Hunting, Conservation and British Imperialism*, Manchester University Press, Manchester.

MacLeod, Roy 1994,'Embryology and Empire: The Balfour Students and the Quest for Intermediate Forms in the Laboratory of the Pacific', in MacLeod and Rehbock, *Darwin's Laboratory*, pp. 40–165.

MacLeod, Roy and Philip Rehbock (eds) 1994, *Darwin's Laboratory: Evolutionary Thought and Natural History in the Pacific*, University of Hawa'ii Press, Honolulu.

McCarty, J. W. 1998, 'Gold Rushes', in Graeme Davison, John Hirst and Stuart Macintyre (eds), *The Oxford Companion to Australian History*, p. 284, Oxford University Press, Melbourne.

McGonigal, David 1987, 'The Lungfish: Australia's Living Fossil', *Australian Geographic*, no. 6 April-June, pp. 46–57.

Mulvaney, D. J. and J. H. Calaby 1984, *'So Much that is New': Baldwin Spencer 1860-1929*, Melbourne University Press, Melbourne.

Newland, Elizabeth Dalton 1991, 'Dr George Bennett and Sir Richard Owen: A Case Study of Early Australian Science' in Home and Kohlstedt (eds) *International Science and National Scientific Identity*, pp. 55–74

Nicols, Arthur 1887, *Wild Life and Adventure in the Australian Bush: Four Years Personal Experience*. Richard Bentley, London.

Reingold, Nathan and Marc Rothenberg (eds) 1987, *Scientific Colonialism: A Cross-Cultural Comparison*, Smithsonian, Washington DC.

Ritvo, Harriet 1987, *The Animal Estate: The English and Other Creatures in the Victorian Age*, Harvard University Press, Cambridge, Mass.

— 1997, *The Platypus and the Mermaid and Other Figments of the Classifying Imagination*, Harvard University Press, Cambridge Mass.

Robin, Libby 1997, 'Ecology: A Science of Empire?' in Tom Griffiths and Libby Robin (eds) *Ecology and Empire: Environmental History of Settler Societies,* pp. 63–75.

Romer, R (ed.) 1894, *Monotremate und Marsupialia*, Gustav Fischer, Jena.

Semon, Richard 1899, *In the Australian Bush and on the Coast of the Coral Sea. Being the Experiences and Observations of a Naturalist in Australia, New Guinea and the Moluccas*, Macmillan & Co., London.

Shaw, George 1799-1800, *The Naturalist's Miscellany: or Coloured Figures of Natural Objects Drawn and Described Immediately from Nature*, F. P. Nodder, London:

Spencer, Walter Baldwin 1884, 'The Eggs of Monotremes', *Nature*, vol. 31, pp. 132–5.

Stanner, W. E. H. 1969, *After the Dreaming; Black and White Australians – An Anthropologist's View*, Australian Broadcasting Commission, Sydney.

Strahan, Ronald 1979, *Rare and Curious Specimens*, The Australian Museum, Sydney.

Trigger, David S. 1997, 'Mining, Landscape and the Culture of Development Ideology in Australia', *Ecumene*, vol. 4, no. 2, pp. 161–80.

Whitley, G. P. and Martha Rutledge 1974, 'Johann Ludwig (Louis) Gerard Krefft (1830-1881)' in Douglas Pike (ed.) *Australian Dictionary of Biography*, vol. 5, K-Q, pp. 42–4, 1851–1890, Melbourne University Press, Melbourne.

Unpublished sources

Australian Academy of Science Archives (AAS 352):
R. G. Beidleman and M. E. Hoare correspondence

Australian Museum Archives:
Series 37, Papers of George Bennett. Series 48, Gerard Krefft
Correspondence 1861–78

CSIRO Division of Wildlife and Ecology: Film:
'The Comparative Biology of Lactation' (as reported in Biannual Report, 1972–4, pp. 36–7)

National Museum of Australia – Curatorial Workbooks (1999): Nick Drayson
Nick Drayson 0412-50.04 *Hoax to Enigma*

8. Frontiers of the future: science and progress in 20th-century Australia

Tim Sherratt

A hymn of the future

The glow of his campfire framed a simple tableau of pioneer life. Across this 'untenanted land', Edwin Brady mused, 'little companies', such as his own, sat by their 'solitary fires'. 'They smoked pipes and talked, or watched the coals reflectively'. Around them, the 'shadowy outlines' of the bush merged into the dark northern night, and 'the whispers' of this 'unknown' land gathered about. It seemed to Brady that this camp, this night, represented the 'actual life' of the Northern Territory as he had known it. But the future weighed heavily upon that quiet, nostalgic scene. The moment would soon fade, Brady reflected, as the 'cinematograph of Time' rolled on. It was 1912, and something new was coming.[1]

Staring into the flames of the campfire, Brady imagined he heard 'the whistle of the Trans-continental Express'. The 'rumble of freight trains' followed, and the sound of water churning in the wake of 'fast coastal steamers'. The night was filled with movement as Brady perceived an end to the north's crippling isolation, the conquest of its 'lonesome distances'. New industries too! The 'chug-chug' of sugar mills, 'the buzzing of cotton jinnys', 'the clinking of harvesters', 'the hissing of refrigerators'—as Brady listened, 'the thousand homely sounds of human progress' joined in a triumphant 'hymn of the Future'. The night's subtle whispers were lost amidst the clamour of technology on the move. Not mere campfires, but 'young cities', electric lit and alive with enterprise', would soon arise to defeat the darkness.[2] This was Brady's dream. This was progress.

Edwin James Brady, poet and journalist, visited the Northern Territory in September 1912, gathering material for his ambitious compendium of Australian developmental opportunities, *Australia Unlimited*.[3] Brady was travelling the country, charting the outlines of Australia's future with his typical optimistic zeal. His trip north was drawing to a close and, as he relaxed by his last campfire, he began to ponder the transformation of the Territory. The sounds and images conjured from the night reveal much about the spirit that invigorated his work. He imagined an end to isolation and emptiness, the growth of both population and production. The future was rising like a flood, lapping at the frontiers of

[1] Edwin James Brady, *Australia Unlimited*, p. 570.
[2] ibid., pp. 570–1.
[3] ibid., p. 515ff.; Some details of Brady's travel arrangements, facilitated by the Commonwealth, are contained in National Archives of Australia (NAA): A659/1, 1943/1/3907.

settlement, ready to redeem Australia's waste lands with the regenerative flow of human ingenuity and enthusiasm. Australia's unlimited prospects lay both in the conquest of space and the fulfillment of time. Plotted against these two axes, the upward course of progress was clear.

The 'cinematograph of Time' was an apt metaphor. It portrayed the unfolding story of Australia's national progress as a product of the latest technology, presented with an assured sense of inevitability – frame follows frame follows frame. In the early years of the century, confidence in the transforming power of science and technology was high. 'The wealth of today', Brady argued, 'is but a beggar's moiety of the unlimited wealth of the future which will be won by the application of modern knowledge to local conditions'.[4] His optimism is echoed still in the slogans of 'knowledge nation' and 'new economy'. Science and technology remain as engines for change, cascading revolution upon revolution. The weight of inevitability that threatened to extinguish Brady's isolated campfire continues to press upon our visions of the future –invigorating our hopes and intensifying our fears. We are all familiar with the story of progress, a compelling tale of growth and improvement that entwines national ambition with individual longing. But how are our journeys through life framed within this unrolling narrative? What choices do we have, and how do we make them?

For Brady, progress was measured in miles and acres, a story of continental conquest. Land figures less prominently in contemporary calculations of achievement, nonetheless, we continue to imagine progress in terms of distance travelled, as a journey, ever onwards through time. In a landscape of metaphors, amidst metaphors of landscape, the meaning of progress eludes easy analysis. Our future is constructed within the shifting space of time. This essay imagines an alternate journey, one that explores the terrain that separates the life of an individual from the destiny of Australia Unlimited; a journey that carries us from science, to nation, to citizen, venturing unsteadily along the boundary between hope and fear. If the topography remains unclear, the scale awry, we might at least hope to chart a few reference points along the frontiers of the future.

All this paraphernalia

In July 1909, the Minister for External Affairs, Littleton Groom, introduced legislation for the Commonwealth takeover of the Northern Territory. Groom, a methodical and well-educated liberal MP from Queensland, briefly surveyed the history of the Territory and presented to the House 'a few opinions of practical men', all of whom were optimistic about the region's potential. '[W]e have there', Groom concluded, 'some of the finest land in Australia'. Nonetheless,

---

[4] ibid., p. 53.

122

it was clear that the Territory's 'latent resources' would not be extracted without effort. The investment of capital and a dramatic increase in population were essential, but so too was an increase in knowledge. 'We are every year acquiring a better knowledge of our natural conditions and a better understanding of the laws of production', Groom argued. It was through such an understanding, he continued, that 'much of the land which is now despised will ultimately become very productive'. Where would this knowledge come from? Groom looked to a scientific agency whose establishment he had advocated since his entry into politics—a Federal Bureau of Agriculture.[5]

Littleton Groom embodied much of the spirit of 'new liberalism', or 'progressive liberalism' as he termed it.[6] By the late 19th century, traditional laissez faire policies seemed increasingly impotent in the face of growing threats to social cohesion and unparalleled opportunities for accelerated development. Responding to this challenge, new liberals sought to wield the power of the state to claim progress as their own, to enrich the character of their citizens, and to ensure the prosperity of their nation.[7] 'I want to see the individual and individuality developed to the full', Groom argued, and wherever the state 'can be used for the purpose of doing good for the people as a whole, then I believe in the State exercising its powers accordingly'.[8] It was a creed carried into the first federal parliament under the banner of protectionism, defended most eloquently by Groom's friend and colleague, Alfred Deakin.

The idea of a federal bureau to foster agricultural improvement was emblematic of the new liberals' cause, a clear example of how government could employ 'direct agencies' in the manufacture of progress.[9] Fashioned after the US Department of Agriculture, the proposed Australian bureau was expected to coordinate scientific investigations and collect 'the very best and latest information' for dissemination to primary producers.[10] Such 'intelligent legislation', Groom maintained, brought 'greater liberty' to the farmer, while

[5] *Commonwealth Parliamentary Debates* (CPD), vol. 50, 30 July 1909, pp. 1878–1891. For more on Groom see: Jessie Groom, *Nation Building in Australia : The Life and Work of Sir Littleton Ernest Groom*; David Carment, 'Groom, Sir Littleton Ernest'.
[6] *Toowoomba Chronicle*, 21 Nov. 1906. For an examination of Groom's liberalism see David Carment, 'The Making of an Australian Liberal: The Political Education of Littleton Groom, 1867–1905'.
[7] Rather than a comprehensive political doctrine, 'new liberalism' represented a constellation of ideas that also appeared under banners such as 'progressivism' and 'national efficiency'. See: Michael Roe, *Nine Australian Progressives: Vitalism in Bourgeois Social Thought, 1890–1960*, pp. 1–20; Tim Rowse, *Australian Liberalism and National Character*, pp. 38–9; John Docker, *The Nervous Nineties: Australian Cultural Life in the 1890s*, pp. xvii-xx. For more on the relationship with science, see Roy MacLeod, 'Science, Progressivism and Practical Idealism: Reflections on Efficient Imperialism and Federal Science in Australia 1895–1915'.
[8] *Toowoomba Chronicle*, 21 Nov. 1906.
[9] *Toowoomba Chronicle*, 29 August 1901.
[10] *CPD*, vol. 2, 28 June 1901, pp. 1827–31.

also boosting the country's productive capacity.[11] Both individual and nation would grow. Deakin, who himself had made a special study of irrigation, was a keen supporter of the measure, as were a number of other prominent protectionists.[12] Isaac Isaacs argued passionately: 'All this paraphernalia ... is only the gold lace of the Constitution, unless we can make of it an engine for the promotion of the material, moral, and social welfare of the people'.[13]

The Bureau of Agriculture was invested with many of the attributes of an ideal, progressive society. Scientist and farmer would work together, melding knowledge and practice, intellect and endeavour. Their cooperative efforts promised both an enlightened citizenry and a wealthy nation. This presumed interdependence and its implicit sense of balance was at the core of Groom's liberalism. He quoted approvingly the Victorian Director of Education's assessment that an 'ideal education' concerned itself with 'physical fitness', 'mental fitness' and 'moral fitness'. 'So it was with national life', Groom added, 'Industrial and intellectual capacity must be developed'. The nation's greatest resources, he argued, lay in 'the hand power, the brain power and the heart power of our manhood and womanhood'.[14] There was no simple formula for progress. It was a property both of individuals and of nations. In a good society the two were closely linked, proceeding apace. But this could be achieved only through a complex set of balancing acts, by constantly tweaking the levels of authority and freedom, duty and reward, ideals and practice, knowledge and control.

The modern hayseed

The life and work of Littleton Groom was memorialised by his widow Jessie, in a biography she compiled under the title, *Nation Building in Australia*.[15] A tad grandiose, but the title perhaps speaks more of Groom's compelling sense of duty than it does of posthumous puffery. 'Nation building' was a commitment, an act of service, a life to be lived, not a victory to be won. However, the title also makes reference to one of the most significant periods in Groom's political life. From 1905–8, he served as a minister in Alfred Deakin's protectionist government. Although they were a parliamentary minority with a fragile hold on power, Deakin's protectionists nonetheless embarked upon an ambitious legislative program that did much to define the nature of Australian federalism.[16]

[11] Quoted in Groom, *Nation Building*, p. 56.
[12] For Deakin's interest in irrigation see: J. A. La Nauze, *Alfred Deakin – A Biography*, vol. 1, pp. 84–6; Walter Murdoch, *Alfred Deakin – A Sketch*, pp. 92–7. In 1901, John Quick noted that beside himself, William Groom (Littleton's father), Alfred Deakin (Ballarat), Hugh McColl (Echuca) and Allan McLean (Gippsland) had all campaigned on the issue, *CPD*, vol. 2, 28 June 1901, pp. 1827–8.
[13] *CPD*, vol. 2, 12 July 1901, p. 2507.
[14] *Toowoomba Chronicle*, 5 November 1906.
[15] Groom, *Nation Building*.
[16] J. A. La Nauze, *Alfred Deakin – A Biography*, vol. 2, pp. 407–8.

The achievements of this administration were eulogised by Groom himself in a pamphlet also entitled 'Nation Building in Australia'. It was a phrase that linked the personal and the political, a citizen's duty and a country's destiny.

As Minister for Home Affairs, and later Attorney-General, Groom contributed significantly to the government's tally of 'practical legislation'. But his achievements in areas such as meteorology, statistics and bounties were intended as part of a broader system of institutions and legislation, designed to manage Australia's productive resources through the rational application of scientific knowledge. At the heart of this system he imagined his Bureau of Agriculture.[17] With Australia's economy heavily dependent upon primary industry, Groom argued that the establishment of such a bureau could 'be justified on financial considerations alone'.[18] Not only would existing farms be made more efficient, the frontiers of land settlement would be advanced. Immigrants would be rallied to Australia's great nation-building crusade, inspired by the government's support for small landholders.[19]

But there was also a moral dimension to the promise of agricultural improvement. 'We may trust the cupidity of mankind to develop our mineral resources', Deakin remarked pointedly, 'but agricultural, pastoral, and kindred pursuits need the superintending and assisting help of the States and of the Commonwealth'.[20] Agriculture was not just about profit. Isaac Isaacs had argued for the need to 'liberalise' agriculture, 'to raise it to a level higher than it has ever occupied before, to give it a dignity, a worth and a profit which may raise the Australian nation in the whole scale of civilization'.[21] The application of science promised to 'elevate' agriculture and its practitioners.[22] No more would the farmer be figure of ridicule, a 'clodhopper', a 'hayseed'.[23] On the contrary, Deakin argued, 'The modern "Hayseed" is an up-to-date, keenly alive businessman, whose study is how to make the best of a small area with limited means but unlimited intelligence'.[24]

Science was a potent addition to the regenerative elixir of frontier life. The idea that a new 'type' of man was being created at the nexus of European civilisation and Australian environment had gained considerable currency, infused by progressive assumptions about the benefits of rural living and the role of the

---

[17] For example, see Groom's speech on the Bounties Bill, *CPD*, vol. 36, 23 July 1907, p. 776.
[18] *CPD*, vol. 50, 3 August 1909, p. 1928.
[19] For example: Rodgers (Wannon), *CPD*, vol. 70, 16 September 1913, p. 1261; Patten (Hume), *CPD*, vol. 72, 12 December 1913, p. 4249.
[20] *CPD*, vol. 58, 6 October 1910, p. 4215.
[21] *CPD*, vol. 2, 12 July 1901, p. 2507.
[22] For example: Senator McColl, *CPD*, vol. 52, 15 October 1909, p. 4603.
[23] *CPD*, vol. 52, 14 October 1909, p. 4521.
[24] *CPD*, vol. 59, 23 November 1910, p. 6589.

frontier in the formation of national character.[25] Edwin Brady warned that the land's 'ancient lineage forbids the familiarity of the unworthy', and welcomed its 'paradoxes and difficulties' as a test of Australia's physical and mental prowess.[26] The establishment of a Bureau of Agriculture was a response to this continental challenge, offering further improvement of the Australian type through a reinvigorated assault on the vicissitudes of frontier existence. Groom quoted approvingly US President Roosevelt's assessment, that as well as creating wealth, his own department must aim 'to foster agriculture for its social results … to assist in bringing about the best kind of life on the farm for the sake of producing the best kind of men'.[27]

But in the transfigurative furnace of frontier life, both man and land were forged anew. Just as Groom had looked to a future when the 'despised' lands of the Northern Territory would be revealed in their true productive glory, so other supporters of the Bureau of Agriculture believed that the accumulation of knowledge would ultimately redeem lands now defamed as 'desert'.[28] Deakin described the transformation wrought upon the desert plains of the United States, arguing that the answer was not simply irrigation, but intelligence: 'Brains pay better than water, and brains are making farming pay to-day'. Australia's 'hope', he continued, 'lies in those enormous tracts which have yet to be brought into the service of man and made productive of wealth for the whole community'.[29] Australia's 'Dead Heart', Brady proclaimed memorably, was in fact a 'Red Heart' destined to 'pulsate with life'.[30] Brain and heart, mind and matter, man and nature – the golem of progress would arise, moulded from the continent's red soil, in the image of the 'modern hayseed'.

Groom imagined a nation made strong through the accumulation of knowledge and the occupation of land. The frontiers of science and of settlement would be brought into alignment by his Bureau of Agriculture, thence to move forward in their inexorable conquest of the continent. Australia's 'emptiness' was no longer simply a location for scientific research, it was itself an object for study and transformation. 'Altogether, a great realm of exploration lies open to us', proclaimed Prime Minister Joseph Cook, introducing legislation for the Bureau in 1913: 'A whole vista of duties and potentialities opens up when inquiry is

[25] Richard White, *Inventing Australia*, pp. 63–84; Graeme Davison, 'Frontier', pp. 269–70. See also: Roe, *Nine Australian Progressives: Vitalism in Bourgeois Social Thought, 1890–1960*, pp. 68–70; Brigid Hains, 'Mawson of the Antarctic, Flynn of the Inland: Progressive Heroes on Australia's Ecological Frontiers'.
[26] Brady, *Australia Unlimited*, p. 636.
[27] *CPD*, vol. 50, 3 August 1909, p. 1929.
[28] For example: Fenton (Maribyrnong), *CPD*, vol. 58, 6 October 1910, p. 4217; Patten (Hume), *CPD*, vol. 72, 12 December 1913, p. 4251.
[29] *CPD*, vol. 59, 23 November 1910, p. 6590.
[30] Brady, *Australia Unlimited*, p. 630.

made as to what there is to be done in Australia'.[31] A new wave of discovery and possession was gathering momentum. 'Little now remains for the geographical explorer to do', Brady argued, 'but for the scientific investigator there is still an almost limitless field in Australia'.[32] Time and space were traded along the frontiers of the future. Science gained space, a 'vista of potentialities' to explore and conquer. The land, in return, won a sense of inevitable fulfilment – the gift of time, the power of destiny.

The battle of Australia

The campfire was slowly dying, as was the dream. Edwin Brady continued to ponder the Northern Territory's future, but the sounds of progress filling his thoughts gradually yielded to the insistent 'tramp of young Australian feet at drill'. Instead of 'clinking' harvesters, he now heard 'the wireless keeping watch by night and day'; instead of rumbling freight trains there was the sound of 'scouting aeroplanes coming home to their military hangars'. As the embers crumbled to ash, Brady concluded his campfire devotions, looking up at the stars 'glittering like bayonet points' and offering a prayer to the 'God of Nations and of Battles' that 'this Northern State-to-be might put her young feet upon the paths of Destiny … in peace'.[33] Brady's hymn of the future was scored to a martial beat; Australia's unlimited future could be assured only through determined vigilance and resolute defence.

Australia Unlimited was a 'Book with a Mission', not merely to sell Australia, but to save it. 'A mere handful of White People', perched uncomfortably near Asia's 'teeming centres of population', could not expect to maintain unchallenged ownership of the continent and its potential riches, the book's prospectus warned.[34] Even as Australia was beginning to enjoy the first fruits of nationhood, its legitimacy, its very existence, seemed imperilled. Australia's 'empty north' was widely perceived as an open door to potential Asian aggressors.[35] The Deakin government was keen to remedy this vulnerability, and its move to assume control of the Northern Territory was justified both in terms of development and security. 'We have in the north a rich, fertile country', Groom argued, introducing the legislation, 'and … that Territory, as it is to-day, especially in relation to other nations, is a menace to the Commonwealth'.[36]

Offering both the promise of riches and the threat of invasion, northern Australia revealed the complexities of nation building – development and defence were closely entwined. The problem with the Northern Territory, Groom explained,

[31] *CPD*, vol. 70, 5 September 1913, pp. 933, 935.
[32] Brady, *Australia Unlimited*, p. 53.
[33] ibid., p. 571.
[34] Copy of prospectus (undated) contained in NAA: A659/1, 1943/1/3907.
[35] David Walker, *Anxious Nation: Australia and the Rise of Asia 1850–1939*, pp. 113–126.
[36] *CPD*, vol. 50, 30 July 1909, p. 1880.

was that it remained 'unmanned'.[37] But 'manning' the country was not simply a matter of numbers. What was required was 'effective' occupation, 'by a people who are applying their energies and industry to developing the resources of the country'.[38] Only when settled by sturdy, hardworking landholders would the north be made both productive and secure. With its promise to improve the quality and efficiency of rural life, science appeared ready and able to bulwark the nation's defensive frontiers. The Bureau of Agriculture was an essential part of a system aimed at developing a strong, self-contained nation. Moreover, as part of a well-balanced civic education, science rounded out the armoury of Australia's 'citizen soldiery'. The nation's best defence, Groom argued, lay in 'the ideal of the intelligent proprietor of the land defending his own country'.[39]

But defence meant more than just preparedness. Australia's progress had to be won in an ongoing contest of legitimacy, with battles raging along the frontiers of race, land, identity and occupation. Groom's 1901 election campaign was energised by his detailed and passionate advocacy of the principle of 'White Australia'. Quoting C. H. Pearson on the dangers of Asian immigration and the threat of racial degeneracy, he warned his electors 'we are not fighting the battle of Australia alone, ...we are fighting the battle of civilised Europe'.[40] Australia was seeking to defend, not only its land, but its integrity as a civilised nation. Fears of infiltration, contamination and degeneration constantly pricked at the confidence of White Australia, reflected in Commonwealth action to enforce quarantine and eradicate topical diseases.[41] Groom's Bureau of Agriculture was justified as a means of defence against the pests and diseases, which 'have no respect for the border lines marked on our maps'.[42] It was in the denial of borders, the negation of boundaries, that Australia's dissolution threatened. The battle for racial integrity was both personal and national, moral and martial. 'Can you allow your children to blend their blood with that of the alien races?', Groom asked, 'Can you imagine anything more pathetic than sad-looking almond eyes peeping out of the Caucasian faces?'[43]

But the very notion of integrity, the fearfully imagined borders of White Australia, were themselves a denial of Aboriginal presence. The 'waste' and the 'emptiness' that Groom hoped to dispel through the application of science, were

[37] *CPD*, vol. 50, 30 July 1909, p. 1880.
[38] ibid.
[39] *Toowoomba Chronicle*, 21 November 1906.
[40] *Toowoomba Chronicle*, 29 August 1901. For more on the influence of Pearson, see: Walker, *Anxious Nation: Australia and the Rise of Asia 1850–1939*, pp. 45–9; Roe, *Nine Australian Progressives: Vitalism in Bourgeois Social Thought, 1890–1960*, pp. 17–18.
[41] Alison Bashford, 'Quarantine and the Imagining of the Australian Nation'; see also Walker, *Anxious Nation: Australia and the Rise of Asia 1850–1939*, pp. 141–153.
[42] *Toowoomba Chronicle*, 10 December 1903.
[43] *Toowoomba Chronicle*, 29 August 1901. On fears of miscegenation, see: Walker, *Anxious Nation: Australia and the Rise of Asia 1850–1939*, pp. 181–193.

constructed out of a lingering sense of unease and illegitimacy.[44] With its offer of life and renewal, science helped to legitimate possession, demonstrating the inevitability of civilised conquest. There was a place for Aboriginal people in this modern world, but it was not on the land. Opening the science section of the Austral Festival in Toowoomba, Groom noted that while the region's 'native tribes' were virtually extinct, some of their weapons remained. He suggested that 'out of love and respect for the black races that were passing away' such implements should be preserved 'as an historical lesson ... as to the weapons of those who preceded civilisation' and as a 'permanent memorial'.[45] With Aboriginal people apparently consigned to the museum showcase, it was the land itself that had to be subdued. Brady imagined the coming breed of farmers, 'with library and laboratory behind them', as a 'silent conquering army': 'Led by the shining spirit of William Farrer, this Army of Invasion is preparing its assaults upon the outstanding citadels of Nature'.[46]

Frontiers are uneasy places, juxtaposing the known and the unknown, civilisation and nature, us and them. Around and through the markers of geography, the imagined borders of knowledge and possession create place from race, gender and time. The splendour of nation is revealed against the dark, looming shadow of otherness. Unthinkingly we talk about the future in terms of our fears and our hopes, rarely pausing to consider how the two are related. Groom's vision of progress, his mission to create a prosperous and fulfilling future through the application of science, encompassed both development and denial. Progress was both a triumphant quest for improvement and a fearful battle against the spectre of degeneration and dissolution. It is this tension that gives progress its power. The oppositions and dichotomies of frontier imagining energised the process of nation building, expanding the bubble of time to create a space into which the future could unfold.[47] But this act of creation proceeds by destruction, obliterating alternatives. For Groom and Deakin the development of the north was both a fulfillment of destiny, and a vital necessity. There was no choice. Progress uses its own internal tensions to make itself seem natural, necessary, inevitable.

Blast the bush

Len Beadell was leading a survey party through the mulga scrub of central South Australia, when he came across something unusual, even unnerving. 'It was

[44] Tom Griffiths, *Hunters and Collectors: The Antiquarian Imagination in Australia*, p. 187; Walker, *Anxious Nation: Australia and the Rise of Asia 1850–1939*, pp. 12, 113ff.
[45] *Toowoomba Chronicle*, 7 November 1906.
[46] Brady, *Australia Unlimited*, pp. 286–7.
[47] Deborah Bird Rose describes the 'hand of destruction' and the 'hand of civilisation' that shape the space-time of the frontier, see Deborah Rose, 'The Year Zero and the North Australian Frontier', pp. 19–20; Deborah Bird Rose, 'Hard Times: An Australian Study', pp. 12–15.

almost like a picket fence', he described, with posts made from 'slivers of shale'. Being in such an isolated location, he decided 'it was obviously an ancient Aboriginal ceremonial ground built by those primitive, stone-age nomads in some distant dreamtime' – an Aboriginal 'Stonehenge'. As he scrabbled in the dust, searching for a piece of charcoal that might be used to fix this eerie structure in time, Beadell pondered the 'ironic clash of old and new': 'only a few short miles away the first mighty atomic bomb ever to be brought to the mainland of Australia was to be blasted into immediate oblivion … and it was by-products of this very weapon which could be used for determining the age of the charcoal from these prehistoric fires'.[48] Beadell's expedition had set out from the British atomic test site at Emu Field, searching for a permanent testing range – one that would become known as 'Maralinga'.[49] It was 1953, and something new was coming.

The 'clash of old and new', the sense of disjunction, was a familiar characteristic of frontier experience. But with the coming of the atomic bomb, the sense of 'newness' seemed to have become more acute. The destruction of Hiroshima was revealed unto a shocked world as the harbinger of a new age – the 'atomic age'. Media reports talked about 'new vistas', a 'new era' in world affairs, a 'revolution' in daily life.[50] The atomic bomb, Clem Christesen wrote in *Meanjin*, had 'severed the old world from the new with guillotine-like decisiveness'.[51] Most importantly, the world faced new challenges, for the atomic age carried grave implications for the future of humanity. It was a 'turning point', 'perhaps the most solemn turning point of all history', Rev. Dr C. N. Button warned his Ballarat congregation: 'Humanity is at the crossroads'.[52]

The *Sydney Morning Herald* relayed the news from Hiroshima under a pair of significant subheadings: 'Terrifying New Weapon' and 'Big Possibilities In Peace'.[53] The 'good' atom/'bad' atom routine dominated much public understanding of this mysterious technology.[54] It was a formula popularly represented in the image of the atomic crossroads, placing humanity at a fork

---

[48] Len Beadell, *Blast the Bush*, pp. 173–6. Radiocarbon dating was one of the products of the atomic age, see: Griffiths, *Hunters and Collectors: The Antiquarian Imagination in Australia*, pp. 86–94.

[49] Twelve full-scale atomic tests were conducted at three sites – the Monte Bello Islands, Emu Field and Maralinga – between 1952 and 1957. For an official history (with all that entails) see: Lorna Arnold, *A Very Special Relationship: British Atomic Weapon Trials in Australia*. For more critical appraisals see: Robert Milliken, *No Conceivable Injury: The Story of Britain and Australia's Atomic Cover-Up*; Tim Sherratt, 'A Political Inconvenience: Australian Scientists at the British Atomic Weapons Test, 1952–3'.

[50] *Argus*, 5 June 1946, p. 7; *SMH & Argus*, 8 August 1945, p. 1.

[51] Clem Christesen, 'Editorial'.

[52] C. N. Button, *God, Man, and The Bomb*, p. 8.

[53] *SMH*, 8 August 1945, p. 1.

[54] For US experience, see: Paul Boyer, *By the Bomb's Early Light: American Thought and Culture at the Dawn of the Atomic Age*, pp. 109–30; Spencer Weart, *Nuclear Fear: A History of Images*, pp. 170–182.

in the road of destiny, with a signpost pointing one way to destruction and the other to progress. Which was it to be, apocalypse or utopia? There was no escaping; it was time to choose. The assumed imminence of the crossroads, the disjunctive dynamic of the atomic age, obscured much of its familiarity. Like the frontier, the crossroads gained its metaphorical power from the conjunction of opposites. The wonders of a techno-utopia shone invitingly amidst the menacing gloom of atomic obliteration. But there was no choice. The signpost to destruction was a warning, a lesson to be learnt. Just as it had in Groom's plans for northern development, progress in the atomic age used the threat of dissolution to charge itself with the force of destiny. Both imagined a future fulfilled through the accumulation of space, whether by the inexorable expansion of Australia's frontiers, or by a continuing march along the road to atomic nirvana. Both offered a journey from which there was no turning back.

In the glare of an atomic explosion, Len Beadell imagined, the mulga scrub around him would instantly 'come to life'.[55] At the dawn of this 'new' age, the image of vast expanses of idle and wasted land, silently awaiting the transforming power of science, continued to evoke enthusiasm. As Britain's readied its big bang at Emu Field, the *Sunday Herald* keenly anticipated the moment when the 'inland silence that remained unbroken for ages' would be 'shattered' by the bomb. Australia's desert lands had found a new destiny, for 'the very poverty of these areas in surface resources made them valuable in the atomic field, either as a storehouse of uranium riches or as the kind of waste land where experiments can be most safely conducted'.[56] Ivan Southall described the Woomera rocket range, established some years earlier, as an 'open-air laboratory': 'one of the greatest stretches of uninhabited wasteland on earth, created by God specifically for rockets'.[57]

Even as rockets were being propelled into 'space' (the final frontier), science presented the land with yet another chance for renewal. Woomera and the atomic tests brought science and land together with a familiar mix of imperial loyalties and national self-interest, development and defence. The Minister for Supply, Howard Beale, sought to justify the establishment of the Maralinga range by portraying it as 'a challenge to Australian men to show that the pioneering spirit of their forefathers who developed our country is still the driving force of achievement'.[58] These new pioneers had the opportunity to contribute to the deterrent power of the free world, while possibly winning Australia access to

[55] Beadell, *Blast the Bush*, p. 8.
[56] *Sunday Herald*, 4 October 1953.
[57] Ivan Southall, *Woomera*, p. 3. For the history of Woomera, see: Peter Morton, *Fire Across the Desert: Woomera and the Anglo-Australian Joint Project 1946–1980*.
[58] Quoted in Milliken, *No Conceivable Injury: The Story of Britain and Australia's Atomic Cover-Up*, p. 93.

the secrets of the atomic age. Distorted echoes of Deakin's 'citizen soldiery' rang down the years, charged with imminence of the crossroads challenge.

Australia Unlimited Ltd

In June 1957, the *Sydney Morning Herald* published the first in an annual series of supplements surveying 'the great endeavours and achievement of Australian commerce and industry in the postwar years and the fabulous promise of future national development'. The supplements were titled *Australia Unlimited*. Edwin Brady would have been pleased by the overwhelming sense of optimism that suffused every page. 'Confidence', the supplement declared, was the 'theme for the future'.[59] It was a confidence born of postwar reconstruction, economic expansion, and a rise in the standard of living, but it was nourished also by a belief in the generative power of science and technology. The Chairman of CSIRO, Ian Clunies Ross, provided something of a keynote in his observation that 'there are no problems so great that they cannot be solved once we marshal our resources for a resolute and sustained attack on them'.[60] Clunies Ross's 'faith', the supplement concluded, 'articulates the endeavours of the planners and makers of Australia's future'.[61]

The Minister for Primary Industry, Billy McMahon, praised the work of Australia's 'modern explorers', the 'scientists and scientifically minded farmers', who were 'rolling back our farm horizons' and revealing our 'unlimited' opportunities.[62] He invoked a familiar catalogue of hopes, but one that was charged with an increasingly powerful sense of expectation. Attempting to define the 'newness' of the atomic age, the nuclear physicist Ernest Titterton suggested that 'the funeral pyre of Hiroshima' was 'the symbol of an era in which science has become so important in our lives that all decisions, including political ones, must be made with scientific considerations in mind'.[63] No nation, it seemed, could afford to ignore the implications of science. The power of science was the power of the bomb, the ability to change the world, to bring down the guillotine on the past, to erect the signposts at the crossroads of destiny. Progress, science and atomic energy were virtual analogues, each brought the promise of a future transformed.

Old dreams were invested with new hope. Atomic energy would power the reclamation of Australia's 'great spaces'.[64] The Chairman of the Australian Atomic Energy Commission, J. P. Baxter, described the possibility of 'package power stations' to serve 'the remoter parts of the continent', particularly those

[59] 'Australia Unlimited Supplement', *SMH*, 19 June 1957, p. 1.
[60] ibid., p. 28.
[61] ibid., p. 1.
[62] ibid., p. 24.
[63] E W Titterton, *Facing the Atomic Future*, p. 4.
[64] 'Australia Unlimited Supplement', *SMH*, 19 June 1957, p. 16.

whose mineral wealth 'will demand exploitation'.[65] Uranium offered a solution at last to Australia's 'empty north', propelling the nation into a new phase of 'pioneering'.[66] The mining and processing of this mysterious metal, it was argued, would give 'the economic life of the Territory the transfusion of new blood it needs'.[67] Progress was represented not only by the Rum Jungle uranium mine, but by the modern town of Batchelor, created specifically for miners and their families. Opening the project, Prime Minister Menzies declared it 'something of a miracle'. 'Not long ago', he continued, the Northern Territory had seemed 'almost worthless': 'But the history of Australia is the history of converting people from despair to hope and from hope to achievement'. With the discovery of uranium, the north seemed destined to host 'one of the great communities of Australia'.[68]

Edwin Brady always intended to write a sequel to *Australia Unlimited*, and if he had lived a few years longer, one could imagine him poring over accounts of the Rum Jungle project, thinking back to that campfire and his dreams of progress.[69] But there was something rather different about this new style of pioneering. The town of Batchelor, with its individually styled family homes and its remarkable range of 'comforts and amenities', had brought suburban living to the frontier.[70] More importantly, its inhabitants were not sturdy landholders working their properties, but wage earners, employees of Consolidated Zinc Pty Ltd. *The Sydney Morning Herald*'s version of *Australia Unlimited* was not the story of hardworking individuals creating national progress out of their own instinctive drive for improvement. In the wake of the Manhattan Project, the scale of progress had changed dramatically, represented now by huge developmental projects that married government-supplied infrastructure with foreign investment and expertise.[71] Progress was measured not in the sweat of the yeoman farmer, but in the profits of large multinational companies.

The Liberal Party went before the electors in 1958 emphasising its achievements in national development and its success in attracting foreign capital.[72] 'Our slogan is "Australia Unlimited"', Menzies asserted, 'and we pronounce it with

---

[65] ibid.
[66] 'Australia Unlimited Supplement', *SMH*, 19 June 1957, p. 10. See also: Alice Cawte, *Atomic Australia: 1944–1990*, pp. 64–95; Noel Saunders, 'The Hot Rock in the Cold War: Uranium in the 1950s'.
[67] *National Development*, no. 1, October 1952, p. 13.
[68] *SMH*, 18 September 1954, p. 3.
[69] Brady's hopes for further volumes and revisions of *Australia Unlimited* are documented in Series 10, Brady Papers, NLA MS 206.
[70] D. E. Burchill, 'Rum Jungle Uranium Field – Building the Township of Batchelor'; *SMH*, 23 September 1954, Womens Section p. 7. See also: Noel Saunders, 'The Hot Rock in the Cold War: Uranium in the 1950s', pp. 155–69.
[71] Lenore Layman, 'Development Ideology in Western Australia, 1933–1965', pp. 235, 258–60; Lenore Layman, 'Development'.
[72] Marian Simms, *A Liberal Nation: the Liberal Party & Australian Politics*, p. 58.

confidence'.[73] The campaign theme was highlighted by a tour of key projects and facilities, including the opening of Australia's first nuclear reactor at Lucas Heights.[74] But behind the confidence of 'Australia Unlimited' lurked a new fear. Electors were urged, not to make, but 'to conserve the forces of progress'.[75] As the security enclosures at Rum Jungle and Lucas Heights demonstrated, while individuals had seemingly lost the power to create progress, they had somehow gained the ability to threaten it.

A change of heart

The war, when it came, only lasted for a month, but that was long enough. All life was quickly extinguished in the northern hemisphere, and the clouds of deadly radioactive fallout gradually diffused to shroud the whole globe. For the people of Australia, it was a lingering, drawn out journey to oblivion. Nevil Shute's apocalyptic novel *On the Beach* was published the same year as the first *Australia Unlimited* supplement. Its theme was not confidence, but fear, resignation and confusion. There was a new threat from the north, invisible and unstoppable. 'It's going to go on spreading down here, southwards, till it gets to us?', Moira asks, 'And they can't do anything about it?' 'Not a thing', replies Commander Dwight Towers, 'It's just too big a matter for mankind to tackle. We've just got to take it'.[76] All they can do is wait helplessly for their own death. In this final act of surrender the people of Australia are united with the rest of humanity: one world or none.

Just as atomic power promised to conquer Australia's vast spaces, so the bomb seemed poised to obliterate national boundaries. There would be no winners in an atomic war. G. V. Portus from the University of Adelaide argued that the 'only defence of the world against the threat of atomic warfare is political defence', and called for the 'abandonment' of the 'out-of-date' concept of national sovereignty.[77] Some looked with hope to the newly formed United Nations and its attempts to negotiate a system of control, but the UN Atomic Energy Commission soon descended into deadlock.[78] Others sought more radical solutions, inspired by Einstein and his declaration in favour of world government.[79] But the political fallout from our atom-bombed world soon settled,

---

[73] *Australian Liberal*, vol. 2, no. 1, November 1958, p. 1.

[74] An occasion celebrated by the *SMH* with yet another supplement, the 'Australian Nuclear Research Establishment Feature', 18 April 1958.

[75] Liberal Party of Australia, *Australia Unlimited! A Nation on the March*.

[76] Nevil Shute, *On the Beach*, pp. 39–40.

[77] Kerr Grant and G. V. Portus, *The Atomic Age*, pp. 16, 23–4.

[78] Joseph I. Lieberman, *The Scorpion and the Tarantula: The Struggle to Control Atomic Weapons, 1945–1949*. For Australian involvement see: Tim Sherratt, 'A Physicist Would Be Best Out of It: George Briggs and the United Nations Atomic Energy Commission'.

[79] *SMH*, 29 October 1945. See also: Boyer, *By the Bomb's Early Light: American Thought and Culture at the Dawn of the Atomic Age*, pp. 33–45.

and the divisions became clear again. In this new age of oxymorons, war was cold, and the bomb was a weapon of peace.

The Cold War pushed Australia's defensive frontiers ever northward, as the concept of 'forward defence' emerged to contain the threat of communism.[80] 'We must, by peaceful means extend the frontiers of the human spirit', Menzies proclaimed, 'We must, by armed strength, defend the geographical frontiers of those nations whose self-government is based upon the freedom of the spirit'.[81] Menzies invoked the prospect of a looming third world war to justify his government's defence preparation program, but increasingly Australia sought security in treaties and alliances, rather than men and guns.[82] The nation's defence was to be assured through the graces of its powerful friends, rather than the character of its citizen soldiery. Just like the characters in *On the Beach*, Australians were left to ponder a threat that they barely understood, and against which they could do very little.

But even as the frontiers of Australian security expanded, so they rebounded inwards, enclosing hearts and minds in an ever tighter grip. Long-held fears of infiltration were revived, with communism identified as a domestic as well as an international threat. Agents of the enemy were amongst us. The circumstances of the bomb's creation and use focused much of this anxiety on the myth of the 'atomic secret'.[83] The CSIR, with its modest atomic energy program, proved a favourite target for political opportunists.[84] Not only was it believed to be harbouring communists, its Chairman, David Rivett, had the temerity to suggest that good science entailed the free and open interchange of information.[85] To prove their security credentials at home and abroad, both Labor and Liberal governments cranked up the legislative apparatus, providing new levels of protection for defence 'secrets', and creating new agencies to monitor the threat within.[86] The common citizen was no longer the nation's guarantee of security, but a potential weak link in its defensive perimeter.

It was, perhaps, human weakness that was most glaringly exposed by the bomb blast over Hiroshima. Even as the world marvelled at this new conquest of the forces of nature, they wondered if humanity had the maturity and wisdom to control it. 'It is a challenge to the conscience of man', the *Argus* considered, 'to

[80] Lachlan Strahan, 'The Dread Frontier in Australian Defence Thinking'.
[81] Quoted in ibid., p. 162.
[82] Geoffrey Bolton, *The Middle Way*, pp. 79–80.
[83] For some cultural antecedents, see: Weart, *Nuclear Fear: A History of Images*, pp. 55–74. See also: Saunders, 'The Hot Rock in the Cold War: Uranium in the 1950s'.
[84] Phillip Deery, 'Scientific Freedom and Postwar Politics: Australia, 1945–55'; Jean Buckley-Moran, 'Australian Scientists and the Cold War'.
[85] Rohan Rivett, *David Rivett: Fighter for Australian Science*, pp. 1–14.
[86] Frank Cain, 'An Aspect of Postwar Australian Relations with the United Kingdom and the United States: Missiles, Spies and Disharmony'; Frank Cain, *The Australian Security Intelligence Organization: An Unofficial History*, p. 30ff.; David McKnight, *Australia's Spies and their Secrets*, pp. 6–48.

ponder gravely whether his intellectual achievements have not outrun his moral perceptions'.[87] The 'crossroads of destiny' had brought a 'moral test' upon the world; science demanded 'a change of heart'.[88] And there was no time to get your breath back. Bomb tests followed bomb tests, and then the Russians had it, and so the Americans built the H-bomb, and there were more tests ... The frontiers of science were running ahead, pushing ever deeper into unknown territory, leaving the world gasping, trying to catch up. In April 1954 a distinguished panel of speakers considered the latest menace under the title 'The H-Bomb – A Challenge to Humanity'. Canon E. J. Davidson proclaimed: 'Our civilisation stands at the point of decision ... It must conform to the moral order of the universe or perish'.[89]

Each new challenge brought its own sense of urgency, its own restatement of the crossroads choice – change or die. There was no 'turning point', no critical juncture on the road to progress, only constant reminders of our own fallibility and the apparent disconnection of science from the ethical life of humanity. The crossroads offered not the chance to change the future, but to conform to it. We were the 'other', able to occupy the future only through the courtesy of science. The destructive sense of inevitability that the frontier wreaked upon the land and its original inhabitants was turned upon us all. It was humanity itself that threatened progress.

A hapless mess of wreckage and misunderstanding

In May 1999, *The Australian* invited a range of 'well-informed and influential' speakers to examine the question: 'How can we continue to build an open, competitive international economy while ensuring we develop a progressive society?'[90] The resulting conference was entitled – yes, you guessed it –'Australia Unlimited', and focused on the dangers and opportunities wrought by the latest in revolutionary forces – globalisation. Something new was here. The forum's major sponsors provided a convenient summary of its themes in their half-page advertisements. Ansett offered 'a world of destinations', Foxtel brought the news of the world to you 24 hours a day, while IBM described the 'treasure trove of products' available on the Web. 'Now it really is a small world', they told us.[91] But globalisation is simply progress rebadged, measured still in the conquest of distance, the colonisation of space. Science and technology continue to bolster its imagined momentum, pushing time beyond its limits, creating the fault-lines of the new.

---

[87] *Argus*, 8 August 1945, p. 2.
[88] *Age*, 1 July 1946, p. 2; *Argus*, 6 July 1946, p. 2.
[89] ibid., p. 19.
[90] 'Australia Unlimited' Liftout, *The Australian*, 8–9 May 1999, p. 2; Articles and reports from 1–8 May in the *Australian*.
[91] *The Australian*, 1–2 May 1999, p. 17; 3 May 1999, p. 12; 4 May 1999, p. 16.

Within each Australia Unlimited, there was an attempt to articulate the balance of forces that will ensure continued progress: the interplay of nation and citizen, knowledge and capital, freedom and control. In the latest version it was the balance between the 'two competing imperatives' of 'economic growth and social harmony' that most concerned the movers and shakers.[92] Stuart Macintyre was the only contributor to comment on the link to Brady and Deakin, noting that 'the principal object of Australian policy in the early years of the century was not the economy or social justice but the nation'.[93] It was a point lost on most forum participants, who imagined progress to be found in the maintenance of a healthy, global economy. Nations are not built; they grow in the rich and fertile environment of globalisation – just keep piling on the manure. But all is not well in this garden of plenty, for the disintegration of social cohesion threatens continued reform. 'Even at a terrible cost to themselves', Dennis Shanahan wrote in his summary of the forum, 'individuals and single nations have the potential to turn the advantages and underpinnings of globalisation against globalisation itself'. Unless governments and corporations can persuade individuals of the benefits of this new age, their 'resistance … has the potential to … set off a chain reaction threat to general progress'. The danger is not ideological, resistance derives not from political commitment, but from 'a sense of alienation, envy and resentment'.[94] The problem is in being human.

In traversing these three versions of Australia Unlimited, it is tempting to imagine a linear narrative, to trace the progress of progress. That is the lie at the heart of this paper. Concepts such as the individual, the nation, even science, are never simple, and are always contested. There is no single stream of progress meandering through time, there are many countercurrents, eddies, backwaters and divergences. The point is not what progress has become, but that it *has* become, and is becoming still. Progress is not a belief, a hope, a naïve aspiration; one that we can in our supposed sophistication simply reject or deny. Within the meaning of progress there are many balances to be negotiated and boundaries to be drawn: a continuing process of accumulation and disjunction that shapes our perceptions of time and our awareness of change.

The process of future-making leaves its traces, and this brief, inconclusive sortie has tried to find the chisel marks in the smooth, worked surface of the new. *Who makes the future?* Groom's idealised citizen seems to have been overtaken by the scientist, and both by the forces of global change, but all are fictions drawn from the battlefields of identity and authority. *Where is the future made?* Spatial metaphors are commonly invoked to illuminate the meaning of time, and so it is that progress is seen to be forged at the frontier, the crossroads, or in the

---

[92] *The Australian*, 1–2 May 1999, p. 16.
[93] ibid.
[94] 'Australia Unlimited' Liftout, *The Australian*, 8–9 May 1999, pp. 1–2.

networks of globalisation. Movement is taken for granted, we are on a journey, ever onwards. *Is there a choice?* Images of a future under threat, of a menacing otherness, of the imminent danger of annihilation, all work to deny alternatives. We are warned to keep to the main road for our own safety, for the safety of the future. But to understand our options, we have to explore the meaning of our journey, to chart its origins, to look again at the signposts. We have to find the frontiers of our future in our past.

In one of his last journal entries, Alfred Deakin struggled to stay within time: 'Why babble more ... I have shed, once and for all, my past as a whole – my present fruitless – my future a hapless mess of wreckage and misunderstanding'.[95] His memory was almost gone, so too his words, his life. Groom lived on, but also battled to keep pace with progress. So thoroughly modern in his nation-building enthusiasm, he suffered the ultimate humiliation of being remembered by Robert Menzies as 'old fashioned'.[96] And Brady? Edwin Brady died in 1952, just short of his 83rd birthday. He spent most of his later years at his camp in Mallacoota, sandwiched between the bush and the sea. He was, he reflected 'perhaps the most successful failure in literary history'. Barely able to make a living, he nonetheless persisted 'in asserting that Australia is the best country in the world'.[97] Most of his plans had come to nothing. There was no sequel to *Australia Unlimited*, no film version, his hopes for the economic development of East Gippsland had been thwarted, his utopian farming community had failed. 'Should I end up, therefore, on a melancholy note?', he asked. Brady's journey along 'Life's Highway' was coming to an end, but he would not submit to the inevitable, he would not surrender to time. 'I decline to become mournful', he answered, 'I refuse to grow old'.[98] There is no turning back. Is there?

[95] Quoted in Murdoch, *Alfred Deakin – A Sketch*, p. 284.
[96] 'Foreword' in Groom, *Nation Building*, p. vi.
[97] Edwin James Brady, 'E.J. Brady, by Himself'.
[98] Edwin James Brady, 'Life's Highway'; extracts from 'Life's Highway' were published in *Southerly* from no. 4, 1954 until no. 4, 1955.

References

Arnold, Lorna 1987, *A Very Special Relationship: British Atomic Weapon Trials in Australia*, London : H.M.S.O: Available from HMSO Publications Centre.

Bashford, Alison 1998, 'Quarantine and the Imagining of the Australian Nation', *Health*, vol. 2, no. 4, October 1998.

Beadell, Len 1976, *Blast the Bush*, Rigby, Adelaide.

Bolton, Geoffrey 1990, *The Middle Way*, vol. 5, *The Oxford History of Australia*, Oxford University Press, Melbourne.

Boyer, Paul 1985, *By the Bomb's Early Light: American Thought and Culture at the Dawn of the Atomic Age*, Pantheon Books, New York

Brady, Edwin James 1918, *Australia Unlimited*, George Robertson and Company, Melbourne.

—— 1949, 'E.J. Brady, by Himself', *Life Digest*, vol. 3, no. 3, June 1949, p. 23.

—— 1955, 'Life's Highway', *Southerly*, vol. 16, no. 4, p. 201.

Buckley-Moran, Jean 1986, 'Australian Scientists and the Cold War', in Brian Martin, et al. (eds), *Intellectual Suppression: Australian Case Histories, Analysis and Responses*, Angus & Robertson, Sydney, pp. 11–23.

Burchill, D. E. 1955, 'Rum Jungle Uranium Field – Building the Township of Batchelor', *Walkabout*, vol. 21, no. 1, January, pp. 29–33.

Button, C.N. 1945, *God, Man, and The Bomb*, St Andrews Kirk, Ballarat.

Cain, Frank 1989, 'An Aspect of Postwar Australian Relations with the United Kingdom and the United States: Missiles, Spies and Disharmony', *Australian Historical Studies*, vol. 23, no. 92, April, pp. 106–202.

—— 1994, *The Australian Security Intelligence Organization: An Unofficial History*, Spectrum Publications, Richmond, Vic.

Carment, David 1977, 'The Making of an Australian Liberal: The Political Education of Littleton Groom, 1867–1905', *Journal of the Royal Australian Historical Society*, vol. 62, no. 4, March, pp. 232–50.

—— 1983, 'Groom, Sir Lilttleton Ernest', in Bede Nairn and Geoffrey Serle (eds), *Australian Dictionary of Biography*, Melbourne University Press, Melbourne, pp. 130–1.

Cawte, Alice 1992, *Atomic Australia: 1944–1990*, New South Wales University Press, Sydney.

Christesen, Clem 1945, 'Editorial', *Meanjin*, vol. 4, no. 3, Spring 1945, p. 149.

Currie, Sir George, and John Graham 1966, *The Origins of CSIRO: Science and the Commonwealth Government 1901–1926*, CSIRO, Melbourne.

Davison, Graeme 1998, 'Frontier', in Graeme Davison, John Hirst and Stuart Macintyre (eds), *The Oxford Companion to Australian History*, Oxford University Press, Melbourne, pp. 269–70.

Deery, Phillip 2000, 'Scientific Freedom and Postwar Politics: Australia, 1945–55', *Historical Records of Australian Science*, vol. 13, no. 1, June, pp. 1–18.

Docker, John 1991, *The Nervous Nineties: Australian Cultural Life in the 1890s*, Oxford University Press, Melbourne.

Grant, Kerr and G. V. Portus 1946, *The Atomic Age*, United Nations Association, SA Division, Adelaide.

Griffiths, Tom 1996, *Hunters and Collectors: The Antiquarian Imagination in Australia*, Cambridge University Press, Cambridge.

Groom, Jessie (ed.) 1941, *Nation Building in Australia: The Life and Work of Sir Littleton Ernest Groom*, Angus and Robertson, Sydney.

Hains, Brigid 1997, 'Mawson of the Antarctic, Flynn of the Inland: Progressive Heroes on Australia's Ecological Frontiers', in Tom Griffiths and Libby Robin (eds), *Ecology and Empire: Environmental History of Settler Societies*, Melbourne University Press, Melbourne, pp. 154–66.

La Nauze, J.A. 1965, *Alfred Deakin – A Biography*, 2 vols., vol. 1, Melbourne University Press, Melbourne.

Layman, Lenore 1982, 'Development Ideology in Western Australia, 1933–1965', *Historical Studies*, vol. 20, no. 79, pp. 234–60.

—— 1998, 'Development', in Graeme Davison, John Hirst, and Stuart Macintyre (eds), *The Oxford Companion to Australian History*, Oxford University Press, Melbourne, pp. 184–6.

Liberal Party of Australia 1958, *Australia Unlimited: A Nation on the March*, Liberal Party of Australia, Canberra.

Lieberman, Joseph I. 1970, *The Scorpion and the Tarantula: The Struggle to Control Atomic Weapons, 1945–1949*, Houghton Mifflin Company, Boston, 1970.

MacLeod, Roy 1994, 'Science, Progressivism and Practical Idealism: Reflections on Efficient Imperialism and Federal Science in Australia 1895–1915', *Scientia Canadensis*, vol. 13, no. 1, pp. 7–26.

McKnight, David 1994, *Australia's Spies and their Secrets*, Allen & Unwin, Sydney.

Milliken, Robert 1986, *No Conceivable Injury: The Story of Britain and Australia's Atomic Cover-Up*, Penguin, Melbourne.

Morton, Peter 1989, *Fire Across the Desert: Woomera and the Anglo-Australian Joint Project 1946–1980*, AGPS, Canberra.

Murdoch, Walter 1999, *Alfred Deakin – A Sketch,* Bookman, Melbourne.

Reynolds, Wayne 2000, *Australia's Bid for the Atomic Bomb*, Melbourne University Press, Melbourne.

Rivett, Rohan 1972, *David Rivett: Fighter for Australian Science*, R D Rivett, Melbourne.

Roe, Michael 1984, *Nine Australian Progressives: Vitalism in Bourgeois Social Thought, 1890–1960*, University of Queensland Press, St. Lucia.

Rose, Deborah 1977, 'The Year Zero and the North Australian Frontier', in Deborah Rose and Anne Clarke (eds), *Tracking Knowledge in North Australian Landscapes*, NARU, Darwin, pp. 19–36.

—— 1999, 'Hard Times: An Australian Study', in Klaus Neumann, Nicholas Thomas and Hilary Ericksen (eds), *Quicksands: Foundational Histories in Australia & Aotearoa New Zealand,* University of NSW Press, Sydney, pp. 2–19.

Rowse, Tim 1978, *Australian Liberalism and National Character*, Kibble Books, Malmsbury, Victoria.

Saunders, Noel 1986, 'The Hot Rock in the Cold War: Uranium in the 1950s' in Ann Curthoys and John Merritt (eds), *Better Dead than Red,* Allen & Unwin, Sydney, pp. 159–65.

Sherratt, Tim 1985, 'A Political Inconvenience: Australian Scientists at the British Atomic Weapons Test, 1952–3', *Historical Records of Australian Science*, vol. 6, no. 2, pp. 137–52.

—— 1993, 'A Physicist Would Be Best Out of It: George Briggs and the United Nations Atomic Energy Commission', *Voices*, vol. 3, no. 1, pp. 17–30.

Shute, Neville 1957, *On the Beach*, Heinemann, London.

Simms, Marian 1982, *A Liberal Nation: the Liberal Party & Australian Politics*, Hale & Iremonger, Sydney.

Southall, Ivan 1962, *Woomera*, Angus & Robertson, Sydney.

Strahan, Lachlan 1996, 'The Dread Frontier in Australian Defence Thinking', in Graeme Cheeseman and Robert H. Bruce (eds), *Discourses of Danger & Dread Frontiers: Australian Defence and Security Thinking After the Cold War*, Allen & Unwin, Canberra, pp. 157–65.

Titterton, Ernest William 1956, *Facing the Atomic Future*, F. W. Cheshire, Melbourne.

Walker, David 1999, *Anxious Nation: Australia and the Rise of Asia 1850–1939*, University of Queensland Press, St Lucia.

Weart, Spencer 1988, *Nuclear Fear: A History of Images*, Harvard University Press, Cambridge, Massachusetts.

White, Richard 1981, *Inventing Australia*, George Allen & Unwin, Sydney.

Part IV. Interrupting the frontier

9. Eight seconds: style, performance and crisis in Aboriginal rodeo

Richard Davis

One Sunday late in August 1999 I was in a car travelling to Koongie Park station, just outside of Halls Creek in the Kimberley, with Quentin and Aaron, two Aboriginal cowboys just finished competing at the Broome Rodeo. They had not won a buckle or taken home a cheque, but they were, despite a couple of misgivings, reasonably happy with their participation in the bull-ride, one of the three, with saddle bronc riding and bareback bronc riding, basic rough stock events at any rodeo. One of their reservations concerned the quality of the stock, both the bulls and the bucking horses, as they did not buck high or fast enough for their liking. They also regarded the judges as less than impartial in their scoring, giving out point scores that were sometimes hard to fathom.

In their opinion the judges showed a partiality towards contestants based on station affiliation. That is, they felt the non-Aboriginal judges favoured riders who worked on particular stations over other riders. This was a criticism of judges that cropped up at most rodeos but at this particular rodeo there was also the accusation made by some Aboriginal onlookers that a particularly good bull-ride by a young Aboriginal boy was not recognised in the score he was awarded. A subsequent ride by a non-Aboriginal cowboy from another station was awarded higher points from the judges and it was felt by some that judging consistency was not maintained between the two riders. Quentin and Aaron put the inconsistent scoring down to the judges favouring contestants from particular stations and firmly rejected my suggestion that race was an issue, but other Aboriginal people felt that it was a clear matter of racial prejudice. One Aboriginal woman succinctly expressed her frustration at the perceived prejudice when she said that the next time that he rode, 'we should make him white', to ensure impartiality in the point scoring. In contrast her Aboriginal husband said that the non-Aboriginal rider had mastered a particularly difficult set of manoeuvers by the bull and deserved his high points.

While there was disagreement about the points awarded to different riders in Broome, it was similar sentiments expressed by this Aboriginal couple that led them to organise a rodeo in 1992 in the town of Fitzroy Crossing that was unique in Kimberley rodeo history. In this rodeo the participants, organisers and judges were exclusively Aboriginal, the first Kimberley rodeo to exclude non-Aborigines. As the principal organiser told me, his staging of this rodeo allowed the Aboriginal contestants the freedom to compete without the scoring bias that they regarded as being so prevalent in previous non-Aboriginal organised and judged rodeos. Rodeos had been an annual event since the mid-1960s in the Kimberley, but none had been organised by Aborigines or held on their stations. Prior to this time, rodeos were not an organised event in their own right in the Kimberley, although rodeo events occurred in race meets around the region, the most well known occurring at the Negri River during the 1940s and 1950s and organised by the Vesteys firm. So, some 30 years after the first independent rodeo in the Kimberley, the situation was reversed, not because the organisers did not like white people or regard them as tainting the sanctity of their rodeo, but simply so that they could compete amongst themselves and be assured that they would receive equitable scores. The following year, 1993, the same Aboriginal man organised an open rodeo, but this time held it in yards on the Aboriginal-owned station that he manages. He has not organised a rodeo since that time, but it is now commonplace for one rodeo a year to be organised by Aborigines in either Broome, Fitzroy Crossing, Halls Creek or Kununnurra, which together comprise the yearly rodeo circuit in the Kimberley.

On the face of it this situation looks no more than Aboriginal people struggling to have their presence felt in an event that they have participated in for many years, but had little say in. However, there are two specific features of Aboriginal organised rodeos and Aboriginal participation in rodeos that reveal more consequential aspects of this struggle. The first feature is that the participation in, and particularly organisation of, rodeos by Aborigines reflects the rapidly changing place of Aborigines within the Kimberley pastoral industry. The organisers of rodeos in the Kimberley are almost always those who own and manage stations or are involved in the service sector of the beef industry. Unlike the large American and Canadian rodeos written about by Frederick Errington and Elizabeth Furniss, Kimberley rodeos are highly localised affairs and rarely draw contestants, spectators, or sponsors outside of the Kimberley. Local stations provide the horses, cattle and rodeo labourers such as chute bosses, judges and clowns and no Kimberley rodeo committee registers rodeo results with any of the regional or national governing bodies for professional rodeo.[1] Station organisers value their independence too highly to submit themselves to the regulations these organisations require, so have nurtured their own regional rodeo circuit independent of the central Australian, eastern and western state circuits. Since the first purchase of four stations in 1976 for traditional owners, there has been a rapid increase of Aboriginal-owned stations in the Kimberley. Today there are 26 Aboriginal-owned stations with a further three in the process of being handed over to the traditional owners. This is slightly more than 28% of all Kimberley pastoral leases which effectively places grazing rights, pastoral

---

[1] The two national rodeo associations, the Australian Professional Rodeo Association and the National Rodeo Council of Australia, are independent organisations with responsibility for seperate rodeo events around Australia. Other regionally based organisations tend to be affiliated with these two national bodies.

designated lands and cattle in their hands for the first time since sheep and cattle entered the Kimberley in the 1880s at the hands of Queenslander pastoralists.[2] If the frontier in the Kimberley has been largely defined by a century of pastoralists taking Aboriginal lands and utilising cheap and at times, slave Aboriginal labour, then the current state of affairs with regards to lease-land ownership represents a shift in frontier relations.[3]

The second aspect of Aboriginal rodeos that is worth highlighting is the challenge that Aborigines and rodeos make to general tenets of frontier theory, that biography of settler-colonial nations that enlists the environment and indigenes to the historical project of defining a distinctive national ethos. The frontier thesis offers an interpretation of national genesis and development in which Aborigines are usually posited as being subject to the violence of colonisation, itself an object and process in Australia that provides for a pragmatic and energetic national character to emerge. Further, rodeo has generally been interpreted as performatively expressing the importance of the frontier of colonisation to the development of nationhood.[4] As a historiographical interpretation of colonialism, the frontier is generally defined by the distinctive causative roles granted to the environment and indigenes. Their generative status derives from the consistent interpretation of a defining 'otherness' that is attached to them in frontier analysis, not in their particular distinctiveness, which could conceivably contribute to different national scenarios. To make only one international comparison of environments – the celebrated chronicler of American settler history, Frederick Jackson Turner regarded the open and empty expanses of American wilderness as contributing to self-reliance, restless individualism and the distinctiveness of New World democratic ideals.[5] By contrast, across a number of genres the Australian environment, as bush, outback and desert, revealed itself to contribute not only to the conditions for the development of laconic, anti-authoritarian virtues in white male pioneers, the local equivalent of Turner's frontiersman, but also a more somber, tragic timbre to national culture.[6] In both historical cases though, the wild, anti-civilised status of the environment and indigenes are often regarded as providing the

---

[2] J. S. Battye and Matt J. Fox, *The History of the North West of Australia, Embracing Kimberley, Gascoyne and Murchison Districts*; G. C. Bolton, *A Survey of the Kimberley Pastoral Industry from 1885 to the Present.*
[3] See D. B. Rose, *Hidden Histories.*
[4] E. A. Lawrence, *Rodeo. An Anthropologist Looks at the Wild and the Tame.*
[5] F. J. Turner, *The Significance of the Frontier in American History*, p. 27; F. J. Turner, *The Frontier in American History.*
[6] The contrasting themes of the relationship of the Australian environment to grandeur and heroic failure, finding significant voice in the last decades of the 19th century, have been explored by a number of Australian writers. While that period fostered attention away from the influence of a British heritage, later considerations of the influence of the environment on nationhood were no less concerned to chart the particular impression of landscapes on culture. See Blainey 1992; Griffiths and Robin 1997; Haynes 1998; Schaffer 1988; Smith 1989.

flashpoints by which the nation can define itself, implicating them as the compulsory other in the process of civilising, racialising and gendering a continually emergent nation as well as idealising them as the necessary sources for national crises. To restate this in more succinct terms, the frontier conceptually links the environment and indigenes to the nation through the tense medium of crisis. The most noticeable feature of this ideology is that the undifferentiated nature of indigenous peoples and the environment allows for a mutable national identity to develop. It is at this point that I wish to suggest that Aboriginal rodeos and contestants call into question the validity of locating mutability with the nation, while immutability resides in Aborigines.

Ideology of indigenes

In her discussion of the schools of Old and New Western History in American historical scholarship, Furniss (this volume) notes that both the analytic and descriptive uses of the term 'frontier' are so varied as to make any integrative theory about it almost impossible. Further, following Patricia Limerick's[7] and Richard Slotkin's[8] critique of the ethnocentric bias of frontier theory, frontier scholars ignorance of other critical factors in settlement, and its own status as triumphalist myth, there is considerable difficulty in using any notion of the frontier to discuss the relationships between power, settlement and invasion. Limerick's trenchant critique takes aim at the triumphalist nationalism assigned to racial conflict in the Turnerian thesis. Turner's reflections on the American frontier, which dominated interpretations of American history for the first half of last century and has been influential in the analysis of other national histories in liberal democracies despite its embodiment of a particular type of American progressivist ideology, used the geographical and racial frontier to define 'national self-consciousness'.[9] As 'an unsubtle concept in a subtle world'[10] Limerick regards it at once too monolithic, ethnocentric, racist and masculinist to be usefully employed. However, amongst American as well as Australian scholars, the conceptual flexibility of the term has led to alternative conceptions of the frontier imagination than dispossession, that describe cultural boundaries, intercultural processes, interlocking practices, and the formation of subjects in their relations to each other.[11] Some of these developments continued aspects of the Turner thesis while others introduced new ideas about the asymmetrical relations of power operating between social groups as well as introducing concepts of culture into the analysis of frontiers. As Kerwin Klein has noted,

[7] P. Limerick, *The Legacy of Conquest: The Unbroken Past of the American West.*
[8] R. Slotkin, *The Fatal Environment: The Myth of the Frontier in the Age of Industrialization 1800–1890.*
[9] F. J. Turner, 'Problems in American History', p. 72.
[10] P. Limerick, *The Legacy of Conquest*, p. 25.
[11] K. L. Klein, 'Reclaiming the "F" Word, or Being and Becoming Postwestern'.

anthropological uses of culture, at least in a relativistic sense, are not synonymous with the social evolutionist ideas of social groups that were common in Turner's day and so the meanings and usages of the frontier tend to be different when different theoretical tools are applied.[12] The multiple uses of the frontier led Limerick to reluctantly accept its continuing usage even if she continued to object to the placement of celebratory conquest at the heart of defining nationhood and civil society.

I want to continue this revisionist strain and return to the notion of the primitive that Turner developed, especially with regard to the question of its importance to defining the distinctiveness of settler-colonisers and nationhood in general. I wish to suggest that notwithstanding their transformation as political subjects from natives to original citizens, as Beckett describes it,[13] in terms of a frontier imagination Australia's indigenous peoples continue to be defined against settlers and are critical to creating a settler identity. Here, I think, the weight Turner gave to the colonised in defining the frontier is worth considering. Mark Bassin elucidates the character of Turner's quest for a defining national story as one which draws on 19th century European ideas of scientific history, in which society is regarded as an evolving organism.[14] Social development, in Turner's thinking, was predicated on a struggle with wildness and its peculiar features in any particular geographic and territorial setting. Nature consisted of, broadly speaking, environment and indigenous, both characteristically wild, in the sense of '…awaiting discovery, and that it would be the antidote for the poisons of industrial society'.[15] Where human society (which excluded indigenous peoples) interacted with nature was the frontier, and the character of that interaction defined the settler nation's central characteristics. By constantly testing the margins of what constitutes national character it reinforces those very attributes that are regarded as central such as institutions (jural), political types (democracy) and characteristics (entrepreneurial individuality). The frontier is also, said Turner, that place away from the central communities of national life where settler society returns to be reborn and renewed. There at the frontier, resides the primitive, immutable and constant, to provide the conditions by which the character of the nation might recreate itself before it succumbs to the hubris of civilised life. In regards to this process in America he says,

> American social development has been continually beginning over again
> on the frontier. This perennial rebirth, this fluidity of American life, this
> expansion westward with its new opportunities, its continuous touch

[12] ibid., p. 186.
[13] J. Beckett, *Torres Strait Islanders: Custom and Colonialism*, p. 17.
[14] M. Bassin, 'Turner, Solov'ev, and the 'Frontier Hypothesis': the Nationalist Significance of Open Spaces', p. 477.
[15] S. Schama, *Landscape and Memory*, p. 7.

with the simplicity of primitive society, furnishes the forces dominating American character.[16]

The primitive, the nation's indigenous companion, is the antithesis of civil order. It is both the conditions of wilderness and the primitive condition, 'our untamed selves ... in tune with nature',[17] an empty expanse and a presence to be subjugated. Where the environment is concerned there is recognition by Turner that it undergoes transformation as it is subject to the frontiersman's developmental urges. By contrast, Turner never imagines the indigenous as being affected by its interactions with the settler nation except in a deleterious sense. Neither its violence, nor its subtle promptings invigorates positive change there. In Turner's recapitulationist frame of thinking, a return to barbarism brings about individual and social rebirth and a consciousness of the progress modern man has taken from indigenous hunter to urban manufacturer.[18] All of these types are expressive of increasing social complexity, but at the moment the ideology of the natural development of social complexity reaches its apex, it is in crisis. Without recourse to the earliest mode of social being, which is predicated on direct and unimpeded reliance on the environment, the nation is in danger of losing itself. In a colourful passage from his original 1893 lecture, Turner describes the decivilising process:

> The wilderness masters the colonist. It finds him a European in dress, industries, tools, modes of travel, and thought. It takes him from the railroad car and puts him in the birch canoe. It strips off the garments of civilisation and arrays him in the hunting shirt and moccasin. It puts him in the log cabin of the Cherokee and Iriquois and runs an Indian palisade around him. Before long he has gone to planting Indian corn and plowing with a sharp stick; he shouts the war cry and takes the scalp in orthodox Indian fashion. In short, at the frontier the environment is at first too strong for the man. He must accept the conditions which it furnishes, and so he fits himself into the Indian clearings and follows the Indian trails.[19]

In this moral economy of a continually beginning nation, the frontier defines necessary and ongoing crises. Paradoxically, these crises are predicated on a struggle ('its continuous touch') with the wilderness and the Aboriginal, both fabricated as interior peripheries. The causative logic that bound these components of settler nation-building rested on the maintenance of fundamental differences between settler-colonists, indigenous inhabitants and the environment

---

[16] F. J. Turner, *The Significance of the Frontier in American History*, p. 28.
[17] M. Torgovnich, *Gone Primitive: Savage Intellects, Modern Lives*, p. 8.
[18] F. J. Turner, *The Significance of the Frontier in Amercian History*, p. 28; Mark Bassin, 'Turner, Solov'ev, and the "Frontier Hypothesis": the Nationalist Significance of Open Spaces', p. 506.
[19] F. J. Turner, *The Significance of the Frontier in American History*, p. 29.

in which there is transfer of creative energy from indigene and environment to settler-colonist. The frontier is that discourse, that active struggle, which does not recede as long as the settler nation consists of a set of relationships and principles that are predicated on the ever-continual transfer of those energies.

Performance

The frontier's distinctive annexation of nature, it has been argued by Elizabeth Lawrence, has its performative expression in rodeo. In Lawrence's words, 'rodeo embodies the frontier spirit as manifested through the aggressive conquest of the West, and deals with nature and the reordering of nature according to this ethos. It supports the value of subjugating nature, and re-enacts the taming process where the wild is brought under control'.[20] While the rural pageantry of Australian rodeos undoubtedly lends itself to this analysis, there is significantly more occurring in rodeos in both performative and social terms than the symbolic control of an abstract 'Nature by Culture'. At a symbolic level the riding, catching and roping of cattle and horses performatively expresses the resolution of the crisis of national anxiety that is implicit in the frontier. These eight second events then, within the ludic structure of rodeo, are also crisis events. As I have suggested, the wild in this instance is simultaneous with the Aboriginal and the environment. Within frontier theory there is little room to consider what constitutes relationships between these two as they are fundamentally differentiated from settler-colonists and their nation-forming activities. If the function of rodeo is to performatively resolve national crisis and replay the colonial venture then how does one explain what is occurring in Kimberley rodeos, where Aborigines compete in and organise rodeos which are sometimes exclusive, but tend to be inclusive? A general answer to this is that Lawrence's argument rests on a series of presumptions about the categorical separation of humans and nature that she regards as uniquely Western. A more substantial response though is possible if rodeo competition is regarded as more than human dominance over animals, as many riders experience a relationship to the animal they ride where the boundaries between animal and human are fluid, and that distinctive Aboriginal perceptions of land, that underlie their participation in rodeo events, further erode this classical opposition.

Rodeos and stations

As a total performance Kimberley rodeos have a recognisable, often repeated structure. All events take place within a single open ring around which yards and chutes holding stock are located. Opening events usually involve all or some of team roping, rope and tie, steer wrestling, campdraft and barrel racing events, after which come the roughstock events. The early events have a mixture of

[20] E. A. Lawrence, *Rodeo. An Anthropologist Looks at the Wild and the Tame*, p. 7.

women and men competing whereas the roughtstock events are almost completely devoid of women competitors. Another distinction between the two groups of events lies in the preparation of the stock and contestants. In the non-roughstock events the stock are usually held in an open yard separated from the rodeo ring by a gate around which contestants, friends and assistants assemble to prepare. From this yard, out into the rodeo ring, come the calves and steers for roping and campdraft as well the riders and their horses that chase them. The preparation of contestants and release of stock are different in the roughstock events. After departing from family and friends around the rodeo ring the usually male contestants gather in a secluded area adjacent to the rodeo ring where they put on their contest apparel: chaps, padded vest, riding boots, gloves, etc. While they are visible through the surrounding fence, theirs is a public seclusion and noticeably fewer friends gather round them than the non-roughstock events. When their ride comes near, they move over to the chute area where their ride will be guided into a small area barely larger than animal itself. After they lower themselves on to the back of the animal, secure themselves to the rope that is wrapped around the bovine or horse, the chute gate is opened and within specific rules about body placement and self-support, they have to stay on for eight seconds, after which they will receive a score and relative ranking.

Kimberley rodeos are complex social events in terms of prestige, gender and race relations. They create a social space in which people involved in the commercial cattle industry come together and socialise on the basis of their shared cattle-based activities. Managers, stockhands and their families mingle together in the public space around the rodeo yards and those Aboriginal people who have come into the rodeo off the stations set up camp around the perimeter of the rodeo ring on the basis of family affiliation. These are independent groupings, and stockhands may or may not have a separate camp to their manager, moving between groupings as it suits them. As people move around the ring, conversations are struck up between people who may not have seen and talked to each other for months or years. Race rarely informs the overt structure or content of these interactions, mirroring the ideal of competitive egalitarianism informing the rodeo events. Rather, status is determined through the prestige achieved in contesting rodeo events as well as being determined by the success of a station in achieving monetary profit, independent of government intervention, through successful grazing, stock-handling, labour recruitment, infrastructure maintenance and other aspects of station management. Aboriginal-owned stations have historically been less likely to have achieved this position, and it is usually those families which are associated with commercially viable stations that involve themselves in the attendance and organisation of rodeos. Men who attend rodeos and work on a station that is in severe financial difficulties can avoid the implied detrimental status implications by emphasising the quality of their technical work on the stations[21] as well as their rodeo prowess, both of which are interconnected. These are matters between men as stock workers and managers on Aboriginal cattle station are always male, women are rarely afforded the opportunity to acquire the skills to negotiate such technicalities. The exclusive gendering of the Aboriginal station workforce is not as common in non-Aboriginal stations, but they nevertheless employ far greater numbers of men than women. Some of this gender exclusivity and status achievement is evident in the rodeo events themselves. Apart from those events in which young children compete, adult events are usually defined by their gender inclusiveness or exclusivity. The prestige of an event can be gleaned by reference to the amount of prize money attached to it, the size and ostentatiousness of the buckle and trophy that goes with the prize money and the corresponding levels of personal danger that each event poses to a contestant. Men and women compete in roping, bulldogging and barrel-racing events, which are regarded as involving a low degree of risk, whereas the roughstock events – bronc and bovine (steer, bullock and bull respectively) rides – are almost always contested by men. The men-only events carry the highest cash prizes and the largest trophies and buckles, the latter worn with great pride whenever possible.

In Kimberley rodeos most of the contestants are directly involved in Kimberley located cattle stations. Few contestants are permanent or semi-professional rodeo competitors, contributing to the localism of Kimberley rodeos. The prestige gained in these events circulates around the cattle community, generating a rodeo history that is rarely touched by outsider interventions. While Aboriginal people have been present as audience and as event contestants for as long as rodeo has been performed in the Kimberley, their ownership of stations is a relatively recent affair. Since the mid-1970s various Commonwealth government departments (Department of Aboriginal Affairs, the Aboriginal Land Fund Commission [ALFC], and Indigenous Land Fund) have purchased pastoral leases on behalf of Kimberley Aborigines. In each of the Aboriginal leases the reaction to their acquisition has differed with some caring little for the cattle they have obtained and others regarding the cattle as an opportunity to establish commercial cattle operations for their own benefit. Those leases where a congruence of good quality land, desire by traditional landowners and capacity to run a business exists, structure their stations in a similar manner to non-Aboriginal Kimberley stations. Historically, Kimberley stations have been owned by absentee landlords, companies or the more common resident owner-managers. In some stations the management team is a family where decision-making powers rest with the male manager and his wife, a continuation of pre-transfer station management styles.[22]

[21] cf. G. McLaren, *Big Mobs: The Story of Australian Cattlemen.*
[22] A. McGrath, *Born in the Cattle: Aborigines in Cattle Country*, p. 27.

In this centralised management system the manager, sometimes called 'boss', takes operational responsibility for the herding of cattle and establishes himself and his family in a homestead around which mechanical workshops, plant machines and stockhand quarters are located. On those stations where the manager makes his decisions after discussion with a group of experienced Aboriginal stockmen and landowners, he is still accorded high status as manager and is credited with responsibility for making sure the decisions are carried out effectively. All cattle handlers on stations are men and their preponderance in the industry is reflected in roughstock events where it is rare for more than a single woman to compete amongst up to forty competitors. The economic returns to managers and stockhands are typically low, but the high social status and corresponding levels of self-worth are often cited by both as compensating for a meagre pay packet. Cattle movement is controlled by the use of water points, paddocks and stockyards. The life-production cycle of a commercial bovine, in station terms, ends in the stockyard, no matter their age or sex. They are primarily reared for their commercial potential and their exit from a station almost always occurs on the back of a cattle truck as it speeds away from a stockyard from which it has just picked up its livestock load. The only other use for cattle is as meat for the station and Aboriginal communities that are established nearby or on the leases.

Landed cowboys

Scratch an Aboriginal man long enough in the Fitzroy Valley region of the Kimberley and you will undoubtedly find he was or is a cowboy. Even those men who no longer are fit enough to handle the rigours of long hours of station work, will express their cowboy experience and pride in their dress: a large hat with upturned brim, press-stud shirt, blue jeans and riding boots. This gear says that he is able to handle himself in the saddle and with cattle, is conversant with a stoic work ethic, and likely he also has a cosmological knowledge and experience of land that cattle are moved across. For such an Aboriginal man his personal identification with land is entwined. It derives from the ability to physically survive in the land and ensure the good health of his cattle with a cosmological geography in which the physical environment manifests the actions of ancestral beings and their continual and ever-present palpability.[23] The twining most often appears at water holes where those holding ancestral beings and exuding power are learnt of through song and ceremony. The knowledge of their whereabouts also allows a cowboy immersed in these traditions to guide cattle to them in times of drought. It is notable though that cattle are rarely

---

[23] D. B. Rose, *Dingo Makes us Human; Life and Land in an Aboriginal Australian Culture*, pp. 40–45; H. Morphy, *Ancestral Connections: Art and an Aboriginal System of Knowledge*; N. Munn, *Walbiri Iconography: Graphic Representation and Cultural Symbolism in a Central Australian Society*.

accorded a place in that cosmological geography and the social correlation to this is that some young Aboriginal cowboys actively seek to identify their relationships to land as cowboys, rather than through the mythico-ritual aspects associated with initiation.

There is considerable variability amongst Aboriginal cowboys as to why this is the case. While no one person outlined to me the full range of reasons as to why station-based cowboys choose rodeo over initiation or participated in both, a number cited their own reasons that were shared by others. For some, rodeo offers the chance to meet female partners, foster friendships and through the rides display their competence as good stockmen. Attached to the latter capacity is the opportunity afforded by rodeos for young men to participate in highly visible, prestige-granting festivals that offer a land-based alternative to initiation ceremonies, cults and other collective ceremonial activities in which locality based knowledge and candidature is controlled by senior men or prompted by territorial organisation. This is particularly so for men who are residentially town and station based and find admission into that field of ritualistic activity complicated by their own parents' or appropriate relatives' lack of involvement in ceremonial or cult activities, issues of locality, and concerns of relatedness beyond the Aboriginal domain. This is not always the case though and some, who judged themselves suitable for candidature, stated that they just did not want to go through initiation, although they did not clearly articulate rodeo as the alternative ritualised domain. The most elaborate rejection of initiation candidature was expressed to me by a 19-year-old cowboy who said that despite his mother's father being a senior custodian for the country his station leased and in a position to advance his candidature, he had no desire to go through the circumcision aspects of initiation as it amounted to an unwelcome violence being visited upon him. He did not clearly state that rodeo was a land-based alternative or a domain in which his identity could be publicly regarded, instead he narrated an alternative career path that envisaged rodeos and responsibility for land generated from cattle related activities. He planned a long-term career in rodeo, hoped that financial sponsorships, prize monies and monies earned as a station hand would sustain him for the foreseeable future and eventually saw himself inheriting the managerial responsibilities from his father for running the cattle station. Station managership was often mentioned by Aboriginal cowboys as a desirable personal goal but not as often as the almost universal aim, informally granted by others in the cattle community, of recognition as a ringer, a cowboy fully versed in cattle-based land knowledge and horse riding skills, an aim that was also shared by non-Aboriginal cowboys. It is in this context of personal recognition and prestige that rodeo participation can be regarded as producing social persons in a most public arena. As rodeos draw participants and spectators from across the Kimberley region they can also be said to produce a wider regional sociality based on egalitarian, non-residential principles between

Aborigines and between Aborigines and non-Aboriginal persons resident in the region. From an Aboriginal perspective commensurate relations with non-Aboriginal stockmen and across the Aboriginal domain would be one outcome of Eric Kolig's series of observations that changes in the religious life of the Kimberley region during the 1970s would result in increased egalitarianism within the religious community, individuation on the basis of personal assessment rather than classificatory positioning and expansive, non-localised connections forming the basis of ceremonial activity.[24]

Many Aboriginal cattlemen refer to themselves in day-to-day conversation as 'cowboys', rather than 'stockhands', 'stockworkers' or 'stockmen'. The compound 'stock' has historically been the self-reference of station workers' choice throughout Australia, differentiated from the use of 'cowboys', which has a more populist or American inflection. The difference is more than country based though. Some of the flavour of this difference is evident in the work of Glen McLaren who emphasises technology as an indicator of competency amongst white northern Australian cattlemen as much as land-based skills.[25] As the 'stock' compounds suggest, station-based labour is emphasised, where technical proficiency is summarised in an informal tradework designation. The use of the term 'cowboy' does not diminish the fundamental importance of competency with respect to land traversal and animal handling but it introduces a more self-conscious stylistic and performative sense to station work. Australian stockmen have certainly been aware of screen cowboys independent of television broadcast as American films were shown on stations at least as far back as the 1950s. The American actor John Wayne is still remembered fondly by older Aboriginal cowboys as they saw him pass across the station screen in the evenings in his cowboy guise. Indeed, the powerful depictions of stylishly dressed, gun-toting cowboys had an indelible effect on dress sense and resonated strongly with the use of force and guns on the Australian stations that Aborigines laboured on. Attention to style, an expression of a vigorous independent filmic masculinity, flowed from the screen into Aboriginal sensibilities. Alternate racial subjectivities and associations could be made in this imaginative space that offered more to race relations than the model of white mens' capture and possession of Aborigines that Aboriginal stations workers laboured under. From the point of view of some Aboriginal men who worked on stations in the decades after the Second World War, film cowboys spoke to them about independence, power and vigour. Were they not also cowboys, as was John Wayne, did they not work for a boss, fight, drink, work together, chase women and drove as did their filmic companions? The critical eye that Cowlishaw knew to be cast on white bosses by Aborigines expanded to include commensurability with white

---

[24] E. Kolig, *The Silent Revolution: The Effects of Modernization on Australian Aboriginal Religion*, p. 182.
[25] G. McLaren, *Big Mobs: The Story of Australian Cattlemen*.

men whether they were aware of it or not.[26] Film did not alleviate the power of station bosses over station Aborigines but it did provide alternative imaginative spaces for expression by Aboriginal men. Knowing what it was that powerful independent white men wore meant that wearing a pair of recognisable riding boots or cowboy hat, or a particular style of clothing allowed for a vital, if small, reclamation of an integrity that was so often denied on stations.

More recently, the sensual immediacy of filmic social engagement has found renewed life through television. The ability to scrutinise film and television for its prompts to style has taken a new twist as many cowboys are aware that being a cowboy is itself an iconic exercise in a nation that has embedded pastoralism and the romantic traditions of stockwork deep within its national psyche. Their awareness of their public iconicity is exacerbated by the many documentaries, films, newspaper and magazine articles and photos that are produced about them and their lifestyle.[27] The preponderance of such media is linked to the increased consumption of the cowboy as a commodity and a national figure that can be draped in fashion, itself tightly circumscribed amongst cowboys in terms of association with specific commercial brands. Rodeos are an important aspect of the circulation and exchange of commodity, representation and person, allowing as they do the creation of an audience (anywhere between 50 and 500 people at any given moment) comprised of industry regulars and others to witness the exchange. An unwritten rule of rodeos requires that contestants personally supply and wear appropriate dress, which does not mean safety clothing, but clothes that are recognisably cowboy clothes in pattern and cut.

To a large extent rodeos express station skills and the particular knowledge of cattle handling that mustering entails in a sporting dance between rider and beast. The bronc events mimic the breaking in of horses for the mustering season, the roping, bulldogging and campdraft events reproduce the separation of calves around the muster herd and the barrel races display an all-round horse riding proficiency. The only events that do not have a direct correlation to cattle and horse handling are the poddy, steer, bull and bullock rides. On the property they may be ridden for fun but there is nothing gained from riding a bovine. Nevertheless, riding on the back of a bull in a Kimberley rodeo usually denotes

---

[26] G. Cowlishaw, *Rednecks, Eggheads and Blackfellas: A Study of Racial Power and Intimacy in Australia*, p. 57.

[27] It is not possible to do justice to the vast amount of print and film media that has been produced about Austalian cowboys, but let me make brief mention of a few works. Most recently the magazine *Outback* has devoted itself to maintaining the importance of cattle for binding people, land and the nation. Regular features are devoted to land, stations, individuals, including Aboriginal people and properties (cf. Dunn 2000). A recent publication by Jenny Hicks (2000) on Australian rodeo has already reached a second publication run due to its popularity. Made-for-television works specifically relating to rodeo include director David Batty's Kimberley-based documentary *Rodeo Road*, televised on the ABC on June 7, 2000 and the Queensland-based documentary 'Born to Buck', televised on the ABC July 15, 2000 as part of *Australian Story* series.

that the competitor works on a station, because the general skills needed to do so are often only acquired by working with cattle and horses on stations. Competitors in Kimberley rodeos come in off the stations to the towns and often are announced to the onlooking crowd by personal name and station affiliation. The latter is immensely important and announces an association to the activities of that station and the land it encompasses, Aboriginal or otherwise. It is rare for an Aboriginal competitor or onlooker to express an identity that is not station related. The only time I saw otherwise was when the Aboriginal station hands of the Mt Pierre station, Gooniyandi country, wore a padded vest with a Rainbow Snake painted along the spine every time they competed in an event. Even then the snake was crested by the name of a cattle-trucking company, so that the two associations with land lay across their backs. These symbolic expressions of identity show that Aboriginal cowboys are not readily amenable to the dominance of nature argument that Lawrence[28] holds, which uncritically assigns whiteness as the racial identity of the rider. Indeed, as I will show, this inconsistency about symbolic categories also applies for beasts, but for quite different reasons.

Despite the dangers involved, all of the crisis events are expressed by riders as a playful contest with chance: 'too much fun', as one cowboy running to the fence after being thrown sky-high by a bull, shouted out at the Broome crowd. But as to dominance, that is less clear. Indeed, to ride a horse or bull successfully, the rider must give themselves up to extreme velocities in the steep, jerking, manic movements of the animal. There is no pretence of affect before the onlooking eyes, only the solitary becoming with the beast: to blend the edges of the body, to freely dissolve the surfaces of beast and man, to find a series of moments amongst incredible speeds and forces when one's centre of gravity is a point and not a weight to be repudiated by the animal. It is constantly said by all riders that successfully riding a bucking beast is about a state of mind (calmness and clarity) and a physical concurrence with the beast so that, 'There is a reality of becoming-animal, even though one does not in reality become animal'.[29]

That other supposed aspect of nature in the frontier, the beast, is also shown to be more than the function it has been assigned; that of a vigorous masculine wildness to be tamed. This is because all bovine in rodeos are wards of capital and to a certain extent, the state. In the system of capital to which they belong, their value is monetary as their identity is primarily assessed in terms of cash for weight units (kilograms). They are continuously classified with characteristics pertaining to this system by the state as it seeks to tailor their growth to market forces. At the beginning of each calendar year, Department of Agriculture officials

[28] E. A. Lawrence, *Rodeo*.
[29] G. Deleuze and F. Guattari, *A Thousand Plateaus: Capitalism and Schizophrenia*, translated by Brian Massumi, p. 273.

advise station owners to produce bovine with particular characteristics: meat with distinct marbling qualities; to breed cattle with single colour skins; encourage weight types; to remove horns and to regulate teeth numbers. They are told each year new characteristics to promote or avoid in congruence with market expectations and are given regular updates through widely distributed departmental newsletters (Kimberley Pastoral Memo). Far from the beast being a wild animal, it is already produced by the twins of capital and the state the moment it enters the rodeo ring. Remember Aaron and Quentin's complaint about the torpidity of the bulls. This was because they had been mustered for sale and had been waiting for a few days in uncovered yards for a truck to remove them, not because it was their natural state in rodeos. In my abstractions, this repudiates the distinctions needed between non-Aboriginal and bovine in order to generate the conditions for taming as both are, in symbolic terms, expressive of far more than civil society and wilderness. This situation would seem less an issue of the dominance of one over the other, than the both expressing different aspects of money, state and nation.

At a symbolic level then we see that Aborigines and animals frustrate the place assigned to them in frontier theory. While the masculine and sexual associations in rodeo are undiminished in Aboriginal rodeo, Aboriginal participation in and organisation of rodeos display a mélange of expressions beyond dominance. At a political level, Aboriginal-organised rodeos show how important Aboriginal people are to regional society in general and the cattle industry in particular. This is congruent with what Liz Furniss[30] has said regarding Canadian Rodeos where Canadian Indians organised cultural displays to raise the profile of Indians in Canadian regional society. In the Kimberley, Aboriginal rodeos strategically display cattle competence and knowledge of the land that is comparable to their non-Aboriginal neighbours and challenge the racism and pessimistic stereotypes of Aboriginality that are still common there. Also, I argue there is a subterranean knowledge of land displayed by Aborigines in rodeos that is never openly mentioned in rodeo grounds but is often talked on outside of the arena. The landscape for all Kimberley Aborigines, whether within the ceremonial tradition or not, is imbued with a personal, collective and cosmological history that very few non-Aborigines can claim. In this experience of the land, personal movement is oriented by '…ways of talking, seeing, of knowing, and a set of practices …'.[31] This experience maps totemic ancestral presence in the landscape as both enduring and negotiable.[32] As one Aboriginal station manager said to me, 'I will always listen to the advice of the oldfellas for this country when I am working out where to put a bore. They know the land because they have walked

[30] E. Furniss, 'Cultural Performance as Strategic Essentialism: Negotiating Indianness in a Western Canadian Rodeo Festival', p. 36.
[31] K. Benterrak, S. Muecke and P. Roe, *Reading the Country: Introduction to Nomadology*, p. 14.
[32] A. Rumsey, 'The Dreaming, Human Agency and Inscriptive Practice'.

it, not like these consultants, they don't know the land, the way the water flows under the ground'. The walking he refers to is the walking done during the wet months after the cattle season was over and people visited each other, went to sacred sites and gathered for ceremony. An even clearer account of the dual experiences of land an Aboriginal cowboy can have is expressed by Morndi Munro.[33] When he recounts his entrance onto the earth he describes it in two different ways. In one account he says, 'My name is Morndi, it's a saltwater name in Ungummi and Worrora. I'm just about saltwater myself. I'm Morndi, the saltwater mirage. I came to my father as a vision. He caught sight of me out of the corner of his eye'. In the second account he says: 'I was born raw in the bush at Hawkestone Peak, in the cattle yards between Kimberley Downs and Napier. Right in the middle of those two stations. My bush name is Morndi and my whiteman name is Billy Munro'.[34] The different place names and conception stimulant, in both accounts, suggest a dual consciousness of orientation to place that registers Morndi as the outcome of two creative fields of agency, a process Alan Rumsey,[35] Francesca Merlan,[36] Jeremy Beckett[37] and Deborah Bird Rose,[38] amongst others, have noted in other locations across Aboriginal Australia. In Morndi's case his articulation of two different aspects of identity based on distinctive and conjoined social references generates modes of articulation and relatedness across Aboriginal and pastoral domains that looks for simultaneous identification, although it could well lend itself to a blended and possibly hybrid formulation in the intentional and agentive sense Homi Bhabha grants the term.[39]

To return to Broome and the two Aboriginal men, Aaron and Quentin, I shared company with on our drive to Koongie Park. As I said, they were not amongst the placegetters there but Aboriginal men were first and third in the bull ride and first in the other roughstock events. Indeed in the five rodeos held throughout 1999 in the Kimberley, Aboriginal men won the crisis events and took out the overall cowboy award at each rodeo. If rodeos play out themes about the relationship between settler-colonists, Aborigines and the environment implicit in the constitution of nationhood then far from rodeos recreating the settler-colonist taming of the wild, Aboriginal participation in and organistion of rodeos in the Kimberley performatively express an Aboriginal repossession of the nation.

[33] M. Munro, *Emerarra: A Man of Merarra/Morndi Munro Talks with Daisy Angajit, Weeda Nyanulla, Campbell Allenbar and Banjo Woorunmurra.*
[34] ibid., pp. 1, 3.
[35] A. Rumsey, 'The Dreaming, Human Agency and Inscriptive Practice'.
[36] F. Merlan, 'Narratives of Survival in the Post-Colonial North'.
[37] Jeremy Beckett, 'Aboriginal Histories, Aboriginal Myths: An Introduction'.
[38] D. B. Rose, 'Ned Kelly Died for Our Sins'.
[39] H. Bhabha, 'Signs Taken for Wonders: Questions of Ambivalence and Authority Under a Tree Outside Delhi', p. 173.

References

Bassin, Mark 1933,'Turner, Solov'ev, and the 'Frontier Hypothesis': the Nationalist Significance of Open Spaces', *Journal of Modern History*, 65 (3), pp. 473–511.

Battye, J. S., and Matt J. Fox 1985, *The History of the North West of Australia, Embracing Kimberley, Gascoyne and Murchison Districts*, Hesperian Press, arlisle, Western Australia.

Beckett, Jeremy 1989, *Torres Strait Islanders: Custom and Colonialism*, Cambridge University Press, Cambridge.

—— 1994, 'Aboriginal Histories, Aboriginal Myths: An Introduction'. *Oceania* 65(2):97–115.

Benterrak, K. S. Muecke and P. Roe 1984, *Reading the Country: Introduction to Nomadology, Fremantle Arts Centre Press, Fremantle, WA*.

Bhabha, Homi 1986, 'Signs Taken for Wonders: Questions of Ambivalence and Authority Under a Tree Outside Delhi, May 1817', pp. 163–84 in *'Race', Writing and Difference*, edited by H. L. Gates, The University of Chicago, Chicago and London Press, Chicago and London.

Blainey, Geoffrey 1992, *Spoils and Spoilers: A History of Australians Shaping Their Environment*, Allen and Unwin, Sydney.

Bolton, Geoffrey Curgenven. 1953, *A Survey of the Kimberley Pastoral Industry from 1885 to the Present*. Western Australia.

Cowlishaw, Gillian 1999, *Rednecks, Eggheads and Blackfellas: A Study of Racial Power and Intimacy in Australia*, Allen and Unwin, Sydney.

Deleuze, G. and F. Guattari 1987, *A Thousand Plateaus: Capitalism and Schizophrenia*, translated by Brian Massumi, University of Minnesota Press, Minneapolis.

Dunn, John 2000, 'The Determined Dolbys', *Outback* vol. 10 (April-May).

Errington, Frederick 1990, 'Rock Creek Rodeo: Excess and Constraint in Men's Lives', *American Ethnologist* vol. 14, pp. 628–45.

Furniss, Elizabeth 1998, 'Cultural Performance as Strategic Essentialism: Negotiating Indianness in a Western Canadian Rodeo Festival', *Humanities Research,* pp. 25–40.

—— 1999, 'Imagining the Frontier: Comparative Perspectives from Canada and Australia', unpublished paper delivered at the symposium 'Frontier Australia: Contact Geographies in Northern Australia', North Australia Research Unit, Darwin, September 23/24.

Griffiths, Tom and Libby Robin (eds) 1997, *Ecology and Empire: Environmental History of Settler Societies*, Melbourne University Press, Melbourne.

Haynes, Roslynn 1998, *Seeking the Centre: The Australian Desert in Literature, Art and Film*, Cambridge University Press, Cambridge, Melbourne.

Hicks, Jenny 2000, *Australian Cowboys Roughriders and Rodeos*, Angus and Robertson, .Sydney,

Klein, Kerwin Lee 1996, 'Reclaiming the "F" Word, or Being and Becoming Postwestern', *Pacific Historical Review*, vol. 65, no. 2, pp. 179–215.

Kolig, Eric 1981, *The Silent Revolution: The Effects of Modernization on Australian Aboriginal Religion*, ISHI, Philadelphia.

Lawrence, Elizabeth Atwood 1982, *Rodeo. An Anthropologist Looks at the Wild and the Tame*, University of Tennessee Press, Knoxville.

Limerick, Patricia 1987, *The Legacy Of Conquest: The Unbroken Past of the American West*, Norton, New York.

McGrath, Ann 1987, *Born in the Cattle : Aborigines in Cattle Country*, Allen & Unwin, Sydney..

McLaren, Glen 2000, *Big Mobs: The Story of Australian Cattlemen*, Fremantle Arts Centre Press, Fremantle.

Merlan, F. 1994, 'Narratives of Survival in the Post-Colonial North', *Oceania* 65(2):151–175.

Morphy, Howard 1991, *Ancestral Connections: Art and an Aboriginal System of Knowledge* . Chicago University Press, Chicago.

Munn, Nancy 1973, *Walbiri Iconography: Graphic Representation and Cultural Symbolism in a Central Australian Society*, Cornell University Press, Ithaca, N.Y.

Munro, Morndi 1996, *Emerarra: A Man of Merarra/ Morndi Munro Talks with Daisy Angajit, Weeda Nyanulla, Campbell Allenbar and Banjo Woorunmurra*, Magabala Books, Broome, Western Australia.

Rose, Deborah Bird 1991, *Hidden Histories: Black Stories from Victoria River Downs, Humbert River and Wave Hill Stations*. Aboriginal Studies Press, Canberra.

—— 2000 [1992], *Dingo Makes us Human: Life and Land in an Aboriginal Australian Culture*, Cambridge University Press, Cambridge.

—— 1994, 'Ned Kelly Died for Our Sins', *Oceania* 65(2):175–86.

Rumsey, A 1994, 'The Dreaming, Human Agency and Inscriptive Practice'. *Oceania* 65(2):116–30.

Schaffer, Kay 1988, *Women and the Bush: Forces of Desire in the Australian Cultural Tradition*, Cambridge University Press, Melbourne.

Schama, Simon 1995, *Landscape and Memory*, Harper Collins Publishers, London.

Slotkin, Richard 1994, *The Fatal Environment: The Myth of the Frontier in the Age of Industrialization 1800-1890*. New York: HarperPerennial.

Smith, Bernard 1989, *European Vision and the South Pacific*, second edition, Oxford University Press, Melbourne.

Torgovnich, M. 1990, *Gone Primitive: Savage Intellects, Modern Lives*, University of Chicago Press, Chicago.

Turner, Frederick Jackson 1948, *The Frontier in American History*.

http://xroads.virginia.edu/~HYPER/TURNER/home.html , accessed 15 February 2000.

—— 1965 (1892), 'Problems in American History', in *Frederick Jackson Turner's Legacy: Unpublished Writings in American History*, ed. W. R. Jacobs, San Marino, California, Huntington Library.

—— 1969 (1893), *The Significance of the Frontier in American History*, Frederick Ungar Publishing Co., New York.

Filmography

Battye, David 1998, *Rodeo Road*, Australian Broadcasting Commission.

Various 2000, 'Born to Buck'. *Australian Story*, Australian Broadcasting Commission.

10. Boxer deconstructionist

Stephen Muecke[1]

A ghost is haunting Australian politics, the ghost of Aboriginal power. Perhaps in the way that Marxism has been a 'critical factor' in the articulation of world politics, Aboriginal power has been a spectre in white Australian history. And despite all the struggles, the regular announcements of victory, assimilation, 'reform' or ten point plans, Aboriginal power persists. Marxism, too, continues to haunt the languages we use to analyse politics and history.[2] How does one explain the persistence, even the growth of Aboriginal power; the power it uses to unravel those often-held certainties of politics and history?

In order to attempt to answer this I shall have to avoid that language which seems to aim towards certainty and closure (history and politics) and stray into philosophy, a mode of activity that rarely engages with Aboriginal knowledges (or is indeed rarely seen as a kind of Aboriginal knowledge; you have religion, but not philosophy, why is this?[3]).

My discussion will centre around a famous Kalkatungu man, who lived with the Duracks in the East Kimberley when they started their pastoral empire. 'And on the more benign stations,' says Tony Swain, 'there was room for the creative philosophic thought of people like Boxer.'[4] What kind of philosopher was he? Mary Durack also mentions philosophy, in a book talking a lot about Boxer, *All-about*, 1935, in which the dedication, the most significant encapsulation of the book, ends by saying: 'Yours is the gift of laughter and human kindliness and true philosophy. Were you ever savages?'[5] .

'Were you ever savages?' is the question picked up by Tim Rowse for his significant article, his historical and political analysis of the turn-of-the century frontier in the East Kimberley, '"Were you ever savages?" Aboriginal Insiders and Pastoralists' Patronage'. Why this interrogation about savages, from Durack in 1935 and then Rowse 50 years later, when the thrust of the question is that you can no longer be considered savages? We know this from the change of tense in Durack: 'Yours *is* the gift of laughter ...' becomes '*Were* you ever ...'

---

[1] Thanks to Stephanie Bishop for research assistance, the delegates at *Frontier Australia*, Darwin, September 23rd and 24th, ANU, NARU, for their generous comments, and John W Durack for his generous reading of the paper and suggestions for improvement.
[2] Jacques Derrida, *Specters of Marx*.
[3] For Kierkegaard, according to Zizek, '*religion is eminently modern*: the traditional universe is ethical, while the Religious involves a radical disruption of the Old Ways – true religion is a crazy wager on the Impossible we have to make once we lose support in the tradition.' *The Ticklish Subject*, p. 115.
[4] Tony Swain, *A Place for Strangers*, p. 233.
[5] Mary and Elizabeth Durack, *All-About*.

But 50 years later Tim still asks the same question, and I will ask why again later.

Now I want to ask about that gift, that precondition for not being savages. 'Yours is the gift of laughter and human kindliness and true philosophy.' Unlike Tim I want to begin with what Durack asserts in that present of 1935; *true* philosophy (and *laughter*, not many jokes in historical and political analysis, these are no laughing matter); and *kindliness*, which is of course about kinship – knowledge and kinship, kith and kin, go together in the philosophies I am speaking about. Laughter, human kindliness and true philosophy are of course the opposite of savagery, as Durack implies, questioning the assumptions of her readers (just as Bruno Latour was to do in 1993, telling his European readers, 'We Have Never Been Modern'[6]), so my interrogation of the analysis of certainty might just have to pop the question, might your analysis not be getting a little bit savage, or at least a bit blunt, to the extent that it does *not* incorporate laughter, human kindliness and true philosophy?

So I am going to tell the story of the philosophy of Boxer, an 'insider black', a 'magic', a *maban*, and how his *work* made Aboriginal power persist. I am going to re-read the available texts, which give us just about all we know about Boxer. I am going to make these texts work a little bit harder – this is deconstructive method – find the words in them which have given up and, it seems, can go no further on the road to truth. Exhausted words which fall back on our old assumptions.[7] Tim Rowse, for instance, knows that the arrival of the Europeans

---

[6] Latour, 1993, *We Have Never Been Modern*, Harvard University Press, Cambridge Mass.

[7] Critics of deconstruction say that it is apolitical, that it is all negativity and has nothing positive to offer, that it denies the existence of reality. Keith Windschuttle, for instance, says: 'Because we are locked within a system of language, Derrida argues, we have no grounds for knowing anything that exists outside this system. "What one calls real life," according to Derrida, is itself a text. Hence it follows that all we have access to are texts. "There is nothing outside the text", he has claimed in a famous aphorism (Windschuttle, *The Killing of History*, p. 24).

Derrida would never make such arguments, and the quotations are not referenced. For a book that is supposed to take questions of history and truth seriously, it is very shortsighted and self-serving. It aims only to create a skirmish in a little academic field. However, I want to take some of the accusations on, to correct them and reveal more of the method I am using. The thrust of 'there is nothing outside of the text' *il n'y a pas d'hors texte*—better translated as 'there is no outside position on a text' is not to deny the existence of objects in the world, but to argue that a philosophical project, like deconstruction, does not consist in bringing a theory to a situation, or text, as if the theory would enlighten it, but rather to scrutinise what is being said in order to 'articulate the problematic foundations of our currently conceived political programs' (Elizabeth Wilson, *Neural Geographies*, p. 22). In other words there is no outside in the sense of a stable, overarching or common sense position from which all things can be examined for their truth values. If deconstruction works from the inside, then its aim is to question the most basic assumptions and concepts underpinning a project. To neglect them is to acquiesce to political stasis. Elizabeth Wilson states the problem for feminism:

'Feminism's complicity with patriarchy, for example, is the structure of violence that is the 'origin' of feminist politics in general. An examination of this 'origin' is neither a disinterested pursuit nor a leeching [parasitic] one; on the contrary it is the hard political work of feminism itself. Without such (self) scrutiny, that is without an examination of how this violent origin enables feminism in general, feminism may be tempted to declare itself a sanitized and sanitizing political practice' (p. 22).

on the Kimberley frontier was a massive disruption of the old way of life: 'a world in such ferment'[8] and, 'the unprecedented nature of the phenomena confronting Aborigines'[9] are phrases he uses. And before too long he divides the frontier between 'insider' station people and 'outsider' wild blackfellas – which is pretty convincing – yet he uses too quickly, for my liking, the word 'order' to describe station life: '... the universe of Kimberley Aborigines came to be divided between the pastoral *order* and its dangerous exterior'[10], and, 'to be lost, as in Jack Bohemia's police tracker stories, is 'to be in a state of moral *disorder*''.[11] The crucial question is, whose life was more ordered? Whose law is wilder, the cattle spearers or the blackfella-shooters (and there is evidence that the Duracks as well as their insider blacks like Boxer, were among the shooters, though almost surely not the worst of them). Old Bulla (from Kununurra) puts the same question, talking about magic: 'Who's the powerful? Who's the strongest? The white man or the blackfeller, see, out of those two?'[12]

Now, having posed those questions, I am not going to be in a position to answer them here and it is not my place to do so. I have simply woken up a sleepy word, 'order', which was happy to go along with the assumption that the whitefella world was taking over on this frontier, that this would be the new world order, so to speak, what Rowse calls the *Pax Durackia,* and others have called the 'golden age' in Northern frontier history:

> Here is a lasting ideology of paternal responsibility – timeless compared to the shifting government philosophies of protection, assimilation, land rights and self-management ... It is this ideology, as much as Durack's books themselves, which enjoys classical status in Euro-Australian culture. An ideology as secure as this must have reason to be so. Jack Sullivan's memoirs have shown us one reason: he and his fellow stockmen

Now, this can be argued for Aboriginal political situations, and the notion of inside and outside is most relevant to the frontier as reality and as metaphor. There is indeed a founding violence in the colonial or frontier situation. Many have experienced that this violence can be perpetuated by the words used in the analysis of it, and that another kind of critical or symbolic violence has to be performed on those words to open up a space for new political conception and action. This is deconstruction. It works from the inside, it does not bring ready-made concepts from somewhere else and 'apply' them. And if we agree that there is no Aboriginal politics which is not complicit with the colonial violence which created the need for them in the first place, then there will be no pure Aboriginal position *outside* to provide a critique of what is going on *inside* Aboriginal politics Those doing these politics are working within and continually on the symbolic violence of colonial history, where that history can never be purely a whitefella imposition, nor a pure blackfella revolution from the other side. So, for this paper, Boxer is the enigmatic figure of frontier ambivalence whose work should be able to cast some light on how we think about Aboriginal politics and power.

[8] Rowse, 'Were You ever Savages?' p. 93.
[9] ibid., p. 94.
[10] ibid., p. 88, my emphasis.
[11] ibid., p. 89, my emphasis.
[12] Bulla, in Shaw, *Countrymen*, p. 181.

were able to expound their good fortune as subjects of the Durack's peace.[13]

After many thousands of years of Aboriginal reign in the Kimberley, we have a picture of a 'lasting' new peace, a 'timeless' and classical ideology installed at Argyle under the benevolent patronage of the Duracks. But what happened? Charlie Court had grander plans for the Kimberley, and in 1971 the lands around Argyle were submerged by the waters of the Ord, a veritable biblical flood. This new order hadn't lasted too long, on the scale of Kimberley history.

But yet it lives. The Duracks transformed this pastoral order into books, and *All-about* is a fine pastoral classic. Boxer, for his part, transformed it into a new cult, *Djanba*, the ceremonial boards of which are disintegrating along with the remains of the station (the homestead itself was relocated) under all that water. Whose magic is the more powerful? I can only keep asking that question, but I am an *outsider* critic, a group Rowse perceptively included. Who *were* the enemies of the Duracks' order?

> From the Durack point of view there were two sets of outsiders to be dealt with: the urban critics of pastoralists' apparent enslavement of local Aborigines; and those local Aborigines who distanced themselves from the homestead's regime of rationed work and remained a danger to people and to cattle. For the Duracks and their contemporaries 'the insiders, both black and white' enjoyed an accord that neither the critics with pens nor those with spears could share.[14]

The critic with the pen is wild in the sense of being out of line. What would those city folk know? For instance, there is a profound accord, a loving trust, which makes Mary Durack able to write in the following way about the housekeeper who comes up from the camp to wake up the people in the homestead each morning:

> Nubbadah's coming marks the beginning of the day for the white community. She pads noiselessly, from one to the other, and upon the sounder sleepers lays a firm black hand. 'Cub-a-dee!' she says, thrusts a cup and saucer into half-dazed hands and disappears.[15]

Do a bit more work on the text. There are two sorts of hands; 'firm black' ones and 'half-dazed' [white] ones. Each day her coming 'marks the beginning'. Who is running this show? And already on the previous page we have met Boxer for the first time, as a young boy, insisting that a boab tree be planted in the garden against the wishes of the gardener who found them

[13] Rowse, 'Were You ever Savages?' p. 97.
[14] ibid., pp. 81–2.
[15] Durack, *All-About*, p. 14.

hideous ungainly things; but Boxer the ten-year-old rascal, had brought
it in to be planted in the garden and called after himself. Boxer thought
very highly of boab-trees (particularly boab nuts), and what Boxer said,
even in those days, went. 'Boxer' the boab tree is nearing its forty-fifth
year.[16]

Where did this powerful boy come from, who could boss around the white
gardener? Mary Durack tells us that he was

> ... from the Mt Isa area ... the eight year-old Boxer had come across from
> Queensland with his mother and a man called Wesley Lyttleton, then
> on their way to the Halls Creek goldfields. Pumpkin, so the story goes,
> took a fancy to the boy and acquired him in exchange for a good
> packhorse and a tin of jam.[17]

This boy grew up to be so trusted by the Duracks that he virtually ran the cattle
camp, as did Jack Sullivan who followed in his footsteps and left his oral history
with Bruce Shaw. As a Queenslander, raised by another Queenslander (Pumpkin),
he had some conflict with the locals, but at the same time learned the local
languages and mediated strongly between 'inside' and 'outside': 'Boxer was a
man who flowed around like the wind,' said Bulla.[18] He was always turning up
just as he was needed, the whitefella and blackfella testimonies agree on this.

Most importantly, for my argument, he was a cultural innovator. Was he happy
with the 'order' the Duracks had installed, or rather the order that his peoples'
cooperative effort had installed *with* the Duracks, which was only to last a little
more than his lifetime? There was obviously such a huge disparity between
these two ways of life that he could not help but have his intelligence challenged
in making sense of it all. Not totally unlike Mary Durack writing *All-about* to
make sense of it all, from her point of view. But while Mary Durack's text was
sent off to the *Bulletin* to be published far away from its source ('You will never
read this, for to learning you have no pretensions ...' she says in her dedication
to her 'all-about' mob, 'You cannot sue us for libel'), what Boxer did was
performative: he created a new cult, called *Djanba,* which would have been quite
opaque to the Duracks (they too, had no pretensions to learning):[19] This *Djanba,*
that Boxer created, really took off:

> Old Daylight ran that *Djunba* from down near the jetty road at Wyndham.
> He just flew around like that , all over, like this *Mulalai* who started
> from that way too. *Djunba* flew in the sky, Mulali went on the ground.

---

[16] ibid., p. 13, the dating puts Boxer's birth date in 1880.
[17] Durack, *Sons in the Saddle*, p. 379.
[18] Bulla, in Shaw, *Countrymen*, p. 170. *Djanba* is variously spelt and appears as *Djunba* and *Tjanba*.
[19] 'You wanna come down see'm corroboree to-night?' Nubbandah asks the white community. "Im
properly good one, all right.' 'Different kind?' we ask sceptically, being fully acquainted with the
usual somewhat monotonous procedure. (Durack, *All-About*, p. 60).

Djunba started from Wyndham and came this way past to Argyle right back this way to Darwin. The corroboree belonged in Queensland to those Kaukadunga, in mixed English … They were really clever men and flew over just like the wind.[20]

Tim Rowse quotes the full text from Lommel, who observed the cult in the 1930s:

In the myth of *Tjanba*, some of the characteristics of this ghost are borrowed from modern culture: his house is of corrugated iron and behind it grow poisonous weeds. *Tjanba* is able to impart the hitherto unknown diseases of leprosy and syphilis by means of little sticks which have lain in those weeds overnight. Men who possess [name deleted, but incised boards thought to have circulated from the desert Aborigines] are able to infect other people. *Tjanba* hunts with a rifle and ornaments his slabs with iron tools. To distribute his slabs to men (some of his slabs are stolen, others he himself sends out) he uses aeroplanes, motor cars and steamers. When showing the slabs to fellow ghosts, he asks them for tea, sugar and bread. Following the myth, the modern cult demands exuberant feasts with tea, sugar, bread and as much beef as possible but no meat from any indigenous animal. The cult places have to be in the vicinity of farms and stations. The cult language is Pidgin-English. The cult is directed by a 'boss', the slabs are stored away be a 'clerk', the feasts are announced by a 'mailman', and order and discipline during them is maintained by some specially appointed 'pickybas' (from police-boys). [21]

Now Tony Swain has written about this cult, and others like it, in interesting ways. Swain's habit, when citing these Aboriginal innovations is to talk of the 'cosmic marriage' of two laws: '… having of necessity allowed White Law to impose itself on them, they have sought their salvation partially by employing its representations, but pre-eminently by conjoining it with the law of the lands and their spirits.' [22]

To which one has to ask, is 'salvation' what cultural innovators, even philosophers, seek? Are these two laws 'conjoined', 'married'? All of these metaphors suggest closure, the pious end of the story. But Djanba, like Boxer knows how to flow around, and put himself *inside* every ceremony: As Swain says:

Jack Sullivan [says] … Djanba 'was a wild human' … The multifaceted Djanba has a chameleon-like capacity to conceal himself within ceremonies; 'he puts himself in every corroboree; just fits himself in'.

[20] Bulla, in Shaw, *Countrymen*, p. 180
[21] Lommel, 1950, p. 23, cited in Rowse, 'Were You ever Savages?' p. 96.
[22] Swain, *A Place for Strangers*, pp. 238–9

His ability to appropriate perhaps reached its height when, at the request of the Catholic priest who asked that traditional songs accompany mass, Djanba entered holy communion: 'he goes through the white fellers now that Djanba'.[23]

Swain makes a strong case for power coming from the East, not only the colonisation by the Durack mob, but also a tradition of new cults emerging from Arnhem land. Coming on that wave Boxer seemed to have brought, from his own country around Mt Isa, a way of thinking which coupled fierce loyalty to the whites with a culture, which according to Swain, was 'more subtle and dangerous' than the millennial cult of *Mulunga*, born about the same time as Boxer, in the late 1880s, and spreading right down through the centre to South Australia. This was a millennial cult, with a compelling reason for people to participate in it. If you didn't, you would die, along with all the white people. It thus proposes a magical solution to white power, and a possible return to the way things were before. Swain argues for its historical source in the famous Kalkatungu battle of 1884 where 600 warriors died. Boxer would have been about three at the time, though we don't know if he was anywhere near there.

Now, unlike *Mulungu*, the argument goes, *Djanba*, Boxer's cult, does not promise as its outcome a return to homelands free of whites. It does three rather new things. It articulates Aboriginal power with white objects like cars and aeroplanes, giving it speed of transmission. The second is insider work, 'he puts himself in every corroboree; just fits himself in'. The third innovation opens up time by proposing a future; personal immortality in the form of stories about Boxer's resurrection after death, the introduction of the subsection system (by Boxer) and Moon stories which involve recycling of individual bodies rather than places, and possibly also the promise of equal co-existence with whites. Swain is assertive ('Time is central to the innovations of Boxer ...'[24]), but not entirely convincing on these questions, he lacks evidence.

Now let me consider these with a deconstructive attitude which is attentive to the persistence of Aboriginal power in the face of the opposing power of white philosophies. Take an innovative object for instance, as described by Tonkinson in Swain:

> Crayon drawings made by Aborigines of *badundjari* [dream-spirits] sometimes resemble aircraft, and vehicles said to be used by *badundjari* to transport others are depicted as aeroplanes, complete with wings, tail, windows and headlights, but with sacred boards, not propellers or jets, supplying the power source.

Swain concludes:

[23] ibid., p. 236
[24] ibid., p. 240.

In other words, these spirit aircraft were propelled to their lands by icons manifesting the potentiality of place. Beyond dreams filled with invading places are visions of place-planes offering a ride home.[25]

This innovation, which articulates Aboriginal power with white objects of power, speed and travel, has a poetic resonance in the very shape of the propeller boards and the sound they make. But we all know those guys must be quite wrong to think *that* is what gives these machines power, it is of course the engines, the petrol ... unless we make one little shift, which is to humanise the object, not fetishise its technology. The plane articulates with the bodies which use it, the seats and controls are made for bodies to occupy, it cannot function without them. The object has emerged out of human invention, out of bird-dreams, and how far is it from them in the ways we enjoy it? The power is ultimately human. Whether the humanism is relevant or not, understanding the plane from this perspective makes the Aboriginal version no longer primitive. It sees it from what we might call Aboriginal connectivist (relation-based) thinking, rather than thinking in terms of discrete objects and beings. We can ask once again, with Bulla: 'Who's the powerful? Who's the strongest?' – not to decide that contest, but to deconstruct notions of strength, and explain the paradoxical power of weakness.

Tim Rowse supports his history of the stability of insider station life, *opposed to* the 'landscape of terror'[26] on the outside, with narratives in the 'police tracker genre', as documented by Bill McGregor. In these narratives, understandably because told by a police tracker, there is no safe return for outlaws, people would generally die out there.

> The safe return of the lost is a non-event in Bohemia's narratives because, in the moral order that gave rise to police tracker narrative, people had no business being out of place.[27]

But there is another genre which contradicts this one, one which suggests to me that people like Boxer who had no terror of the outside,[28] might just have soon been *inside on the outside,* so to speak, flowing around, getting in with the locals. So when Boxer is put in gaol, he can escape at will with his magic:

> They put the poor bugger in the jail house in Wyndham, locked him in. He'd done nothing. They just put him in the jail, that's all, and he came

---

[25] ibid., p. 238.

[26] Rowse, 'Were You ever Savages?' p. 82.

[27] ibid., 'Were You ever Savages?' p. 89.

[28] Mary Durack writes that Boxer was usually M. P. Durack's travelling companion because, 'unlike the Kimberley-born Aborigines, he did not mind how far afield he rode, or among what potentially hostile tribespeople. It could hardly be said that he was without fear, or had no reason for it, but he prided himself on being alert to every native wile and strategy, sleeping at all times 'with one eye open' and a hand on the revolver on his belt.' (*Sons in the Saddle*, p. 63.)

out and went away. After a while they saw Boxer walking round in the pub out there. 'Oh blimey', the policeman said, 'There Boxer outside walkin around.' 'Oh well', old M. P. Durack said to him, 'You can getim and putim in jail if you wantim.' They went up. The policeman caught him and took him back and locked him up in the jail house. As soon as they walked away, two or three hours after, they saw Boxer again walking about outside. 'Ah well, give him another go.' The third time they tried again and saw Boxer sitting down in the store in a chair, the old bastard. They didn't know what to do. The policeman couldn't do anything.[29]

This escape narrative has exactly the same structure as Paddy Roe's 'Mirdinan', even down to the three-part structure.[30] Mirdinan goes further afield, down to Fremantle, to dramatically escape from the noose as he is hanged, transforming into an eaglehawk and flying back to his country. Boxer's magic persona shares some of these features of freedom of movement; self transformation (changing into an emu, also in Paddy Roe's stories); letting his guts spill out and putting them back; creating songs and stories, all in explicit assertion of blackfella power.[31] This, I would argue is inside work on the representations of both black and white culture. It is less the mediation of the clever man, creating a syncretic culture by going backwards and forwards, and it is certainly not the culture of a radical outside, as in the Mulunga cult (or Pigeon's guerilla warfare in the central Kimberley) which would bring whitefella rule to an end and take things back to the old ways.

Boxer's infiltration and conceptual change of both laws is open-ended. As Swain says, it incorporates time, perhaps for the first time, in a significant way in Kimberley cultures. We don't know what happened to Boxer in the end. Unlike Paddy Roe's Mirdinan, who was defeated by a whitefella power, alcohol, and dumped in the deep water off Broome (another source of ceremonial power according to Swain), Boxer, in a way, still lives. One source says he was 'in our

---

[29] Bulla, in Shaw, *Countrymen*, p. 181–2 (see note in Shaw).

[30] Paddy Roe, 'Mirdinan', in *Gularabulu*, pp. 1–17.

[31] He'd open his guts just to show a trick and they'd all go back the same way again, with all the guts sewed up again ... That fella was wide open like when you kill a killer. You could see his guts hanging right down to the ground, his heart, liver, and everything (*Countrymen*, pp. 180-81).

(...)

At Ivanhoe they'd say, 'Ah, look out look out, emu comin through the ration camp', the old people's camp, 'sendim up dog'. There was no more emu, only Boxer. The next minute when they went out along a little bit you saw him. Well, where's that emu gone?

(...)

Same as the white man doctor the blackfellers are just the same. Who's the powerful? Who's the strongest? The white man or the blackfeller, see, out of those two? To tell the truth the white man doctor didn't know what to say. I saw this done, you know, and I knew that. That's fair dinkum (*Countrymen*, p. 181).

cemetery down at Argyle.'[32] Jack Sullivan says he was buried in Darwin, but then years later seen in a pub in Hughenden, North Queensland, by a white station manager, who returned to Darwin to find his grave split open.[33] 'I don't think magic people die,' concludes Bulla.[34]

And it's my turn to conclude. In my experiment of inflecting deconstructive method with the changing stories of Aboriginal power, leading up to the radical challenge to historiography posed by Boxer, I am left with further questions: What is the most appropriate method for understanding that frontier history? As Tim Rowse says, 'The most difficult part of frontier history for Europeans is the history of Aboriginal understanding: how did they make sense of the invaders … ?'[35]

My feeling is that we have to go further than the opposition of inside and outside, that the method will also involve simultaneous inquiry of how the invaders understood the Aborigines. I also think that it is not just a question of getting the words right, for if the Boxer story has taught us anything, it is about the importance of performance. The stations and the country of the East Kimberley were the *theatre* of his life as 'a magic'. I haven't been able to reproduce any of that drama in my poor performance today (maybe I should make an excuse, like old Bulla: 'I could dance it but my knee's buggered'[36]). But that is the question: what forces does history writing mobilise which reach truths other than, or as well as, the factual? What will be their poetry, their magic?

And in deconstructing the insider/outsider opposition, let me recall that spectre of communism with which I began. Tim Rowse, quite rightly warns against 'city' outsiders, who are too quick to condemn exploitation on the stations, armed as they are with a Marxist theory insensitive to the more 'human' relations of affection on the Durack stations which enabled survival and cultural innovation for the station Aborigines, pretty much on their own terms, running the stations almost as much as they were run by them. Now what is curious is that Swain's book concludes with another infiltration of that Marxist philosophy, but one which works its way up from the Pilbara, becomes known as Don McLeod law, infiltrates ceremonies like *Djuluru*, and perhaps culminates at Wave Hill with the revival of the lands rights campaigns. This is the law of the 'fair go', of the historical, future-oriented promise of equality and moral rights. Was it Boxer, perhaps the first Aboriginal modernist, who paved the way along this frontier for the passage of these ideas?

---

[32] Mandi, in Shaw, *Countrymen*, p. 39.
[33] Durack, *Sons in the Saddle*, pp. 158–66.
[34] Shaw, *Countrymen*, p. 183.
[35] Rowse, 'Were You ever Savages?' p. 93.
[36] Bulla, in Shaw, *Countrymen*, p. 80.

How can it be, that communism, now dead as a social system (capitalism is triumphant on the world stage) came both inappropriately from the city as European theory, and from the bush as insider knowledge, to produce, in conjunction with local cultures which I have been unable to expand upon, a radical transformative cult which still lives in the name of Boxer. Boxer's story has the power that is often attributed to European theories, stories with the power to change our understandings of things. Boxer is dead, we are pretty sure[37] (maybe we should check that grave again), but as the Algerian-French philosopher says 'the dead can often be more powerful than the living.'[38]

[37] Deborah Bird Rose says that Boxer may not have been born, a story she has from the Yaralin says that he came out of a hole in the Pinkerton Ranges. Personal communication.
[38] Derrida, *Specters of Marx*, p. 48.

References

Derrida, Jacques 1994, *Specters of Marx: The State of the Debt, The Work of Mourning, and the New International*, translated by Peggy Kamuf (with an introduction by Bernd Magnus and Stephen Cullenberg), Routledge, New York.

Durack, Mary and Elizabeth Durack 1935, *All-About: The Story of a Black Community on Argyle Station, Kimberley*, The Bulletin, Sydney.

Durack, Mary 1983, *Sons in the Saddle*, Constable, London.

Latour, Bruno 1993, *We Have Never Been Modern*, translated by Catherine Porter, Harvard University Press, Cambridge, Mass.

Lommel, Andreas 1950, 'Modern Cultural Influences on the Aborigines', *Oceania*, vol. 21.

Roe, Paddy 1983, 'Mirdinan', *Gularabulu: Stories from the West Kimberley*, edited with an introduction by Stephen Muecke, Fremantle Arts Centre Press, Fremantle.

Rowse, Tim 1987, '"Were You Ever Savages?" Aboriginal Insiders and Pastoralists' Patronage,' *Oceania*, vol. 58, no 2, December, pp. 81–99.

Shaw, Bruce 1986, *Countrymen: The Life Histories of Four Aboriginal Men as Told to Bruce Shaw*, Australian Institute of Aboriginal Studies, Canberra.

Swain, Tony 1993, *A Place for Strangers: Towards a History of Australian Aboriginal Being*, Cambridge University Press, Melbourne.

Wilson, Elizabeth A. 1998, *Neural Geographies: Feminism and the Microstructure of Cognition*, Routledge, New York.

Windschuttle, Keith 1994, *The Killing of History: How a Discipline is being Murdered by Literary Critics and Social Theorists*, Macleay, Paddington, NSW.

Žižek, Slavoj 1999, *The Ticklish Subject: The Absent Centre of Political Ontology*, Verso, London.

11. Absence and plenitude: appropriating the Fitzmaurice River frontier

Andrew McWilliam

Introduction

The concept of the frontier has been an enduring one over the course of European colonisation and settlement in Australia. In its classical form, it may be defined as an expanding boundary of conflict created in the process of colonial settlement and associated with coercive appropriation of land and landscape from its indigenous residents.[1] In Northern Australia the frontier was contested comparatively recently under the guise of 19th century pastoralism, prospecting and missionisation. The impacts differed in character but the results were more or less the same. Writer Ernestine Hill, renowned for her heroic prose puts the issue succinctly;

> To form a station you brought a few thousand cattle and swung them clear of the world to new waters. If there were blacks around the waters you moved them over with a gun[2]

As elsewhere, Aboriginal resistance to the appropriation of their land dissipated under the pressure of these dispersals, the ravages of disease and demographic decline. Pastoralism, by necessity, also held out the prospects of a 'taming' process whereby 'wild or bush blackfellows' were incorporated into pastoral settlements and mustering camps as ringers, cooks, sexual partners and dependents. Physical resistance tended to be sporadic, contained and ultimately, untenable.

A second order definition of the frontier in Australia, one which also has its counterparts in other colonised indigenous landscapes, is the notion of the frontier as a physical unknown or environmental wilderness.[3] Reflecting on this idea Rose has commented that, 'frontier mythology depends upon the creation of a vast emptiness in which the new nation forms itself'.[4] In Australia the frontier was found at a conceptual level through the doctrine of terra nullius (i.e. land belonging to no one), and its supporting legislative apparatus, which denied and subsumed Aboriginal rights, and cultural identity. At the same time

---

[1] R. White, 'Frederick Jackson Turner and Buffalo Bill'; R. Slotkin, *The Fatal Environment*.
[2] E. Hill, *The Territory*, p. 175.
[3] F. Turner, 'The Significance of the Frontier in American History 1893'.
[4] D. Rose, 'The Year Zero and the North Australian Frontier', p. 22.

the 'advancing' frontier of colonial settlement also needed to actively create this perceptual fiction because of the uncomfortable reality of large numbers of resident Aboriginal populations all over the country. Proactive erasure of the Aboriginal presence was therefore also an inherently complicit component of the Australian nation building project and the image of an open unpeopled environment.

In some cases however, these emptied regions remained beyond or outside the subsequent settlement process. In other words, the frontier was 'conquered' and de-populated of its indigenous identity but it remained unsettled, undomesticated so to speak. This continuing emptiness of certain frontier regions has come to be viewed in terms of an environmental otherness, one that lies both physically and imaginatively beyond the familiar and settled social landscape. In other words the qualities of the empty frontier in contemporary Australia have been transformed and positively revalued in terms of environmental and conservation significance. Thus we arrive at the notion of the 'untouched wilderness' and the so-called pristine qualities of the remote and empty bush. Much of the present-day tourist industry in the Northern Territory is promoted on the basis of just these qualities on the northern frontier lands, popularly known as the 'last frontier' in Australia.[5]

If the creation of the Australian 'wilderness' was in part a fiction of European frontier mythology, the actual Aboriginal depopulation and disappearance in many landscapes was an historical reality. In this process of Aboriginal de-population of traditional lands there is an inexorable loss and disintegration of generational knowledge and life experience about the constituent symbolic meanings of the land and its topographical features. From an Aboriginal perspective the absence of a continuing residential presence within a landscape and the increasing remoteness of ancestral experience and knowledge creates new kinds of alienation. It may become a dynamic boundary of separation between a contemporary Aboriginal experience of everyday life, and an increasingly distant ancestral knowledge; a distinction between the familiar and local on one hand and the remote and external on the other. In this context it might be argued that Aboriginal Australians can experience an emergent form of the frontier, one constituted as a frontier of knowledge and experience.

In her article, Rose has drawn a sharp contrast between the cultural perspectives of settler and indigenous society in relation to landscapes in northern Australia. She argues that '[t]he white people who have conquered this country find themselves in a liminal and paradoxical time-space (time zero), unlike the

---

[5] For example, promotional material for media personality Troy Dann, refers to the outback as 'one of the last frontiers with a spirit and freedom all of its own' (Radio promotion NT May 2000). A travel magazine describes Darwin as 'a favourite today with backpackers, who like its frontier appeal' (Trips, 2000:74).

indigenous people for whom it is neither liminal nor paradoxical'.[6] The experience of the Fitzmaurice River indigenes however is that the consequences of colonial settlement of Australia are less categorical and more ambiguous than this analysis suggests. Just as the character of contemporary Aboriginal society reflects the historical experience of colonial settlement, so relationships to ancestral landscapes have taken divergent paths. Caught up in the colonial processes that have transformed their societies and reordered residential practices, the relationship between contemporary and ancestral knowledge of Aboriginal place can become increasingly tenuous.

The great tidal Fitzmaurice River in western Northern Territory, exemplifies many of these attributes of frontier mythology and practice. My purpose in the following paper is to explore the changing values and historical perceptions of this classic frontier in the Northern Territory. I am concerned to map out some of the historical interactions and contemporary realities of indigenous and settler community (exdigenous)[7] attempts alike to appropriate the landscape of the Fitzmaurice and convert it from the frontier to the familiar. I want to do so, however, from a particular perspective, one that arose out of a project to record and document Aboriginal toponyms and sacred sites on the Fitzmaurice River. This project developed over a number of years and coincided with a movement among affiliated Aboriginal communities to reinvigorate their historical and traditional ties with the Fitzmaurice, which had grown increasingly weaker in recent times.

The colonial frontier on the Fitzmaurice

The existence of the river, which became known as the Fitzmaurice, remained unknown to the colonial settlement of Australia until 1839. In that year Stokes and Wickham, aboard the *Beagle* ventured into the area with a view to completing a more detailed survey of the northern coast. The Victoria and the Fitzmaurice Rivers were both named by Stokes during this exploratory trip. The latter river being given the name of assistant surveyor L. R. Fitzmaurice on the *Beagle*, who led a small party 30 miles up river to confirm its existence and chart its lower reaches. No mention is made of any Aboriginal presence on the river at the time.[8][9]

The next European visits occurred some 17 years later when the redoubtable A. C. Gregory and party traversed the Macadam Ranges and crossed the

---

[6] D. Rose, 'The Year Zero and the North Australian Frontier', p. 31.
[7] The term is suggested as a neutral label for Australians with ancestral origins beyond the country.
[8] J. L. Stokes, *Discoveries in Australia, with an Account of the Coasts and Rivers Explored and Surveyed During the Voyage of the HMS Beagle in the Years 1837-38-39-40-41-42-43.*
[9] The curious date of 1814 found carved on a boab tree on the banks of the river has been attributed to the birth date of Fitzmaurice, possibly as they waited for the tide to turn and carry them back to the mouth of the river (Masters 1999).

Fitzmaurice on their journey south to the Victoria River. They make mention of the difficulties of finding a suitable route through the rugged topography, but report only two brief encounters with local Aborigines, both evidently in the Majalindi valley which extends from the northern banks of the river.

> Steering north-east and east for three miles along a salt creek, came to the termination of the salt water, where we saw four natives digging roots; on observing us they decamped.[10]

> Near the creek we saw a native man and two women, who were much alarmed at the sudden appearance of the party, and retreated across the plain.[11]

One of the consequences of Gregory's extensive explorations in the Fitzmaurice and Victoria River region, were his favourable reports for the prospects of rich grazing lands which lent weight to the increasing calls in southern capitals for the north to be opened up and developed. It wasn't until the early 1880s, however, that colonial interest was translated into practical effect through the burgeoning pastoral industry. Within a decade a series of pastoral runs was carved out on the land and large numbers of cattle introduced into the region. They included the huge Victoria River Downs (1883) and Auvergne Station (1886), and a string of other stations such as Leguna, Bullita, Delamere, Innesvale and Bradshaw's Run, Lissadell and Newry stations among others.

The consequences of pastoralism and the pressures placed on local Aboriginal populations in the region were little short of devastating and resulted in a major decline in population through a combination of introduced diseases and the 'clearing' of the land through shootings and reprisals. Between the 1880s and 1920s Aborigines across the region were rounded up and 'quietened' down on the developing stations[12] (see Shaw 1980, Riddet 1988, Rose 1991 and McGrath 1987 for examples). Ernestine Hill gives another insight in to the flavour of the times in her 1951 history of the Territory,

> To the new station you brought working blacks from some far country – no conspiracies, they were terrified of the 'bush niggers', and for protection of your 'muckity', musket, never ventured out of your sight. There was quiet nigger country and 'bad nigger' country....[13]

The great influx of cattle into the region provided local Aboriginal populations with an inadvertent new source of meat protein, which they took to securing with great alacrity. Indeed the spearing and later shooting of cattle was one of

---

[10] A. C. Gregory and F. T. Gregory, *Journals of Australian Exploration*, p. 103.
[11] ibid., p. 105.
[12] See B. Shaw, *My Country of the Pelican Dreaming*; L. Riddett, *Kine, Kin and Country*; D. Rose, *Hidden Histories*; and A. McGrath, *Born in the Cattle* for examples.
[13] E. Hill, *The Territory*, p. 175.

the major sources of friction between the settler pastoralists and the Aborigines. Massacres and murders of local Aboriginal groups suspected of cattle duffing or the intentional wounding of cattle went largely unreported although it is a theme frequently cited in local oral histories.[14] 'Dispersal' was the widely adopted euphemism of the times to describe the use of guns against any 'problem' Aborigines. As Hill has noted, '[A] big item on the books was ammunition, and it was not for shooting kangaroos'.[15]

On Bradshaw's Run, established in 1894, and which originally extended from the Victoria River to well north of the Fitzmaurice River into what is now the Daly River land trust, the story was little different. In a diary entry for April 1896, for example, it is noted that;

> ...the myalls made themselves obnoxious by spearing horses and cows so had to be dispersed near the stockyard at Angle point (Bradshaw Log Book 1894-1901)

The high number of rock paintings across Bradshaw station, which depict examples of carbines and other guns, is a striking if mute testimony to the importance and impact local Aborigines accorded this weapon (field observations 1996-98). However, it is also the case that most of the pastoral and mustering activity on Bradshaw's Run occurred in the southern part of the lease in the vicinity of the Victoria River that served as the supply route. The Fitzmaurice River region to the north remained for the most part a distant and largely unvisited region for European settlers.

In the turmoil of the frontier during this period into the early 20th century, the choices for surviving Aboriginal groups were limited. The distinction between the 'quietened down' blackfellas living in the comparatively safe haven of work camps on the station,[16] and so-called 'myall or bush blacks' who remained largely outside the pastoral system but foraged on its fringes, represented an uneasy compromise. Bush Aborigines maintained constant, if furtive, connections with the station camps that evolved within the pastoral leases.

From the early days of contact, tobacco figures as a major enticement for Aborigines to approach the European settlements, stock camps and mining areas. It is this theme which punctuates the following description of the life of old Pat Ngulunung whose ancestral lands lay in the middle Fitzmaurice River.

> Old Pat, he born Kartinyen.[on the Fitzmaurice] When he was a lad, till he come big kid, just around Fitzmaurice ... Kimul. Till he come big boy.

[14] B. Shaw, *My Country of the Pelican Dreaming*; B. Shaw, *Countrymen*; K. Mulvaney, 'What to Do on a Rainy Day'; and D. Rose, *Hidden Histories*.
[15] E. Hill, *The Territory*, p. 176.
[16] Life on the stations, however, was often marked by brutality and neglect (see Rose 1991 for example)

Took him from there to Bradshaw ... big station there. He stop one week, workin tobacco, they off again. Pat's father worry about bush, want to go back bush again. He trying to take Pat with him. Early day whiteman been there, they like those kids too. Stop them to make ringer. They caught Pat to hang on there. Pat's father take him away. All the time every night, take him to bush again. Take him level to Fitzmaurice again – Kartinyen. Big mob always bin there. Hang around there again. Follow that tobacco. When they come too short, they off again. All the family go, Pat's father take him down to Bradshaw get more tobacco. They never go daytime. Sneak in there in dark. Relations there. Come to them boy, get little bit tobacco, tea, then off bush to Fitzmaurice again. Round there they follow tobacco ... used to worry for tobacco. (Translated by Captain Waditj)[17]

The pattern described here for Pat Ngulunung was a common experience for all the groups and families living along the Fitzmaurice from the late 19th century. The river and its rugged dissected hinterland remained a comparative safe haven from which local families and individuals made forays across the frontier to engage the European settlers and hopefully profit from association. Unlike the violent encounters of early pastoralism and the notorious police 'dispersals' on pastoral leases along the Victoria River and beyond, the Aborigines of the Fitzmaurice do not appear to have been coerced from their riverine homes. Rather, as the anthropologist, Stanner, who worked in the region during the 1930s and 1950s (1936, 1950) has put it, 'there is no evidence ... that the exodus was other than entirely voluntary'.[18] Drawing on Aboriginal explanations he notes that:

They say that their appetites for tobacco and, to a lesser extent, for tea became so intense that neither man nor woman could bear to be without. Jealousy, ill will and violence arose over the division of small amounts which came by gift and trade. The stimulants ... were of course not the only, or the first, European goods to reach them...but it was the stimulants which precipitated the exodus. Individuals, families, friends ... simply went away to places where the avidly desired things could be obtained. The movement had phases and fluctuations, but it was always a one way movement.[19]

Although there is no clear record on the process of exodus from the Fitzmaurice, it is apparent that by the turn of the 20th century, an extensive migration of the riverine populations was already underway.[20] In the upper Fitzmaurice people

[17] A. McGrath, *Aborigines and Colonialism in the Upper Daly Basin region*, p. 9.
[18] W. E. H. Stanner, *White Man Got No Dreaming*, p. 46.
[19] ibid., p. 47.
[20] cf. ibid., p. 46

sought connections with Dorisvale and Claravale Stations in the east, Coolibah, Bradshaw and Auvernge Stations in the south and Leguna Station in the west across the Victoria River. Legune in particular attracted and retained a large population of Aboriginal groups from the Fitzmaurice and Macadam Ranges area. Known collectively as *Garamau*, and probably comprising Murrinhpatha and Murrinhkura speaking language communities, they utilised seasonal footwalk trails, which criss-crossed the western corner of Bradshaw's run, to move between Auvergne or Legune Stations and the Fitzmaurice River region. The practice of seasonal Aboriginal residence following the end of the annual cattle muster continued for decades as locals returned to live on country and attempted to maintain ritual links to ancestral estates. However, this pattern had little impact on the general trend of out-migration and the long-term demographic decline of the area as a focus for residential and ritual practice.

Just as local indigenous populations were moving away from their clan estates for extended periods, eventually all but abandoning them, the Fitzmaurice region also took on the reputation and status as a sanctuary or hideout for Aborigines evading capture or retribution. During the early 20th century, the so-called 'Blackfella wars' resulted in significant bloodletting between remnant populations of Aboriginal residents throughout extensive areas of the Victoria River District. This took the form of retaliatory killings and the mutual abduction of women from adversary groups. Social dislocation and the disruption brought about by pastoralism clearly exacerbated the situation. Some insight into this period is expressed in Shaw,[21] reporting the memory of a Jaminjung man from Bradshaw Station:

> All our people, the Yilngali, died out because all the blackfellas were killing, sneaking. That other mob who were in that country, the Garamau, they were the blackfellas who were running around the country murdering one another in the early days … The Garamau people were silly by killing my father, and then the Yilngali did the same. They were cruel. They smashed everything, his head. All my people, we were in the bush. If they lost a countryman, a brother or uncle like that, they'd come back and kill other people in cold blood. We wanted to kill that mob for our people, our mates.[22]

The emergence of the Fitzmaurice River region as an Aboriginal sanctuary for evading European legal and extra-legal process was based to a significant extent on the limited appeal of the region for settler society. The huge expanse of the riverine country of the Fitzmaurice, with its broken, rocky topography and tidal flats was never attractive grazing country and no serious attempts were made

---

[21] B. Shaw, *Countrymen*.
[22] ibid., p. 58.

to settle the area. European incursions remained sporadic and usually ill fated. Indeed, until well into the 20th century the threat of untimely death from murder and misadventure on the Fitzmaurice tended to confirm the continuing frontier reputation of the river. By way of illustration one well-reported incident that exemplified this reputation was the spearing murders of two European prospectors on the river in 1932.

Late in that year during the seasonal 'build up' of stifling humidity and big thunderstorms prior to the onset of the wet season proper, Alfred Koch, otherwise known as Alfred Cook, and his Russian colleague, Charles Arinski, (aka Stephans), set out on the motor vessel *Maroubra* from the Victoria River Depot to pursue prospecting interests on the Fitzmaurice River. They did so against the advice of the local policemen, Constables Fitzer and Langdon, who warned them against the dangers of their proposed venture. Aborigines of the Fitzmaurice River region were known to be 'particularly hostile to whites at the time'.[23] Undeterred, the prospectors arrived at the mouth of the Fitzmaurice where they lowered their supplies into a canoe and paddled away.

Some months later concerns were raised about their safety and, in the continuing the absence of any news, it was generally concluded that they had probably met their deaths.[24] Still, it was not until nearly a year later that the Timber Creek Police initiated a patrol to investigate their disappearances.

In October 1933 Constables Fitzer and Langdon left Timber Creek with four black trackers and a pack of horses and mules bound for the Fitzmaurice River. They covered some 100 miles of rugged sandstone country to the north and then spent eight weeks in the area tracking down likely suspects and interviewing witnesses. Deciding that the prospectors had indeed met an untimely death at the hands of local Aborigines, they set about rounding up eight offenders and six witnesses to the murders of Koch and Arinski. Following several gruelling months of travel, made difficult due to wet season flooding, they brought the accused Aborigines into town and 'to justice'.

The case was tried in the new courthouse in Darwin. The eight accused appeared 'with tousled hair and woolly whiskers wearing handcuffs attached to bright new chains'.[25] The eight included, Tiger (alias Tappin), brother of the even more notorious Nemarluk[26] , Barney (Waddawurry), Chugulla, Chalmar, Fryingpan (otherwise Chiniman),[27] Alligator (or Woombin, or Coonbook), Maru

---

[23] *Northern Standard*, 16 January 1934.

[24] I. L. Idriess, *Man Tracks*, pp. 297–8.

[25] *Northern Standard*, 20 January 1934.

[26] Nemarluk was renown for his involvement in the killing of a Japanese shark fishing crew near Port Keats in 1931, and his later exploits while evading capture by the authorities. He was also sought unsuccessfully by Police on the Fitzmaurice River, which only added to his fame. (see I. L. Idriess, *Man Tracks*).

[27] Mistaken spelling for Tjinimin – little bat – a key mythological figure on the river.

(otherwise Leon) and Harry (or Walung). All were charged with having feloniously, wilfully and with 'malice aforethought', killed and murdered the two prospectors.

Evidence during the case certainly identified Tiger as a primary participant in the murders, the motive for which was said to be desire for tobacco, flour and rations. One witness stated that 'Tiger and Barney bin chukem spear. Three spears hit short fellow (Koch) and three the longfellow (Stephans)'. The bodies of both men were carried to the bank [where they were] hacked to pieces by Tiger with an axe taken from the canoe. He cut off their heads, arms and legs, the severed portions being placed in the canoe'.[28] The canoe was then sunk in the river.

It is apparent from the newspaper reporting of the trial that the prosecution evidence was contradictory and at times 'most unsatisfactory' with the Barristers 'experiencing considerable difficulty in getting coherent replies'.[29] Nevertheless, and despite strong argument by the defendants' counsel, the Judge duly found that 'a cold-blooded and diabolical murder had been committed and there were no extenuating circumstances whatever'.[30] A sentence of death on all accused was pronounced, later commuted to life in prison and, indeed further commuted as all were subsequently released after serving up to 10 years in prison.

As an Australian version of the theme of the conquering victim,[31] the case of these murders on the Fitzmaurice in the 1930s is an exemplary text of its time. It provides a snapshot of social conditions in the region, the uneasy relationship between Aborigines and settler Australians and the contested nature of the colonial frontier. At the same time the qualities of the riverine environment as an Aboriginal sanctuary and hideout in the context of an inexorable depopulation are also exemplified. Living as they did on the northern margins of the pastoral grasslands of the Victoria River District, the Fitzmaurice River people escaped some of the worst excesses of colonial violence and invasive pastoralism, but ultimately they could not resist its subversive attractions.

Images of the contemporary frontier

Unlike the bounteous grasslands of the central Victoria River District which, in the space of a few short years, became subject to the proliferation of pastoral establishments, the Fitzmaurice River basin held little attraction for pastoralism. Difficulties of terrain, poor grazing potential and access problems meant that the river always lay on the margins of pastoral settlement and never attracted significant settler interest. This remains the situation into the present day where

[28] *Northern Standard*, 2 February 1934.
[29] *Northern Standard*, 29 May 1934.
[30] *Northern Standard*, 1 June 1934.
[31] R. White, 'Frederick Jackson Turner and Buffalo Bill', p. 29.

the Fitzmaurice River region lies largely beyond settled society and continues to exhibit a range of enduring qualities of liminality or transition. While the overt violence of the river frontier receded, many of the qualities that characterised frontier perceptions of the river persist in a variety of ways. This can be understood from the perspective of both settler and indigenous society alike.

Ecologically speaking, the river defines the changeover between the wetter, more heavily forested, swamp country of the Moil and Daly Rivers to the north, and the drier open savannah lands of the Victoria River District in the south. This ecological distinction contributed to the development of social differences between Aboriginal communities. The 'cowboy' culture, with its social origins in the mustering camps of the cattle stations contrasts with the mission culture that developed north of the river around Port Keats and the Daly River.[32] The latter experienced an entirely different history of religious-based discipline and orientation. The distinction persists to this day despite increasing interaction between the respective communities.

These distinctions between Aboriginal communities separated by the river, however, have much earlier origins. In traditional and historical terms for example the river marked the limits of the subsection naming system, the skin system, that extends throughout the Victoria River District. It also formed the northern extent of ritual subincision practices with their attendant ceremonial and ritual support structures.[33] Contemporary myths support this conclusion. All told it seems that in times past the river may well have formed a long-standing social barrier or filter that constrained the extent of direct communication. Stanner, for instance commented on the apparent recent adoption of the subsection and *ngurlu*[34] naming system among the Murrinhpatha people. 'Both [he noted] have undoubtedly spread from the Djamindjung to the Murinbatha, perhaps in the last twenty years'.[35] Given the likely strong pre-colonial history of the subsection naming system in the region, the recent adoption by the Murrinhpatha suggests a shift in the nature of ritual communication between the neighbouring communities, possibly as an inadvertent effect of colonial intervention.

From a somewhat different contemporary perspective, the 1996 acquisition by the Australian army of the Bradshaw Pastoral Lease which extends to the southern edges of the Fitzmaurice River, represents a modern and rather ironic expression of the river frontier within Aboriginal Australia. On the northern banks of the

---

[32] J. Pye, *The Port Keats Story*.

[33] cf. N. B. Tindale, *Aboriginal Tribes of Australia*.

[34] What Stanner (1936) refers to as a non-cult, non-local and directly matrilineal form of social totemism. Ngurlu systems are still extant in the region but only weakly articulated.

[35] W. E. H. Stanner, 'Murinbata Kinship and Totemism', p. 197.

Fitzmaurice River is the expansive Aboriginal freehold territory of the Daly River Land Trust. Thus the tidal flow of the river, demarcates a new and enduring legal and cultural boundary between Aboriginal land on one side and army or federal state land on the other.

In this context of multiple boundaries and transit points, which coalesce on the river, we can recognize something of the continuing expression of the colonial frontier in the contemporary world. But it is one in which the frontier experience has different consequences for Aboriginal and settler society alike.

From a settler perspective it is the 'pristine wilderness' quality of the river that conveys the frontier character and persists into the present. This conception is well demonstrated in one of the distinctive features of the construction of frontier landscapes, namely its representation in cartography.

The business of map-making might be described as one of those classic handmaidens of colonialism.[36] The construction of maps and more particularly the appropriation of new topography and named landscapes through the creation of toponyms form a primary vehicle for asserting hegemonic ownership over land. It represents the cartographic equivalent of the erasure of indigenous identity in land and its replacement by more 'familiar' European referent points and orientations. Indeed, it might be said that the very process of map-making itself in the development and expansion of colonial settlement served to effect a transformation of the 'wild' and unknown frontier into a domesticated space, remade into a familiar landscape.

In this process Aboriginal toponyms and cognitive or iconic maps of places within landscapes[37] are simultaneously erased, subsumed, or converted into the language of the dominant nomenclature. Hence the contemporary maps of northern Australia are replete with evidence of the naming process of colonial settlement. Regional toponyms such as the Victoria River itself, the Pinketon Ranges, Blackfella Creek, Massacre Creek as well as all the Sandy Creeks, Lilly Waterholes, Top Yards and so on, all represent the historical legacy of this cultural appropriation of landscape.

At the same time, and by contrast, one of the striking features of the Fitzmaurice river basin is the comparative absence or paucity of named topographical features on current map sheets of the region. This vast riverine landscape boasts just a handful of European names mapped onto the country. Most of these derive from the 1839 maritime visit of Stokes and Wickham on the *Beagle* and are focused to a significant degree on the major riverine features of the area. They include names such as Keyling Inlet, Quoin and Clump island, and the Fitzmaurice River

---

[36] J. Jacobs, 'Resisting Reconcilation'.
[37] P. Sutton, 'Icons of Country'.

itself. The few other official place names generally derive from Aboriginal terms and for the most part are erroneously located on the maps.

Now, the absence of named places is not an uncommon feature in Northern Territory mapping and there are numerous map sheets for example, which are largely devoid of any named topographical features (see Australian Topographic Map Survey series). For the most part, however, these official maps reflect landscapes that exhibit relatively minor topographical variation. The regularity of the sand deserts, the stone plateau country and the contiguous single-species eucalypt scrub are examples.

The Fitzmaurice River, on the other hand, is a region of rich topographical diversity and landscape variation. It has multiple islands, inlets, waterholes, rock bars, cliffs, waterfalls, rivers, creeks, mountain ranges and so on, virtually none of which carries a European toponym. In other words, from an exdigenous (settler) perspective the river and its environs might be said to constitute an unnamed land, a *terra innomena,* that speaks to the ineffective or stalled appropriation and resolution of the river frontier. In other words, settler society resolved the opposition of the indigenous river population by absorbing it into pastoral and mission society but it failed to fully incorporate or domesticate the 'wild' river environment into the 'settled' world. In these terms the river remains an empty frontier, rarely visited, unmodified and cast imaginatively as a wilderness. Even for the rangelands which lie within the Fitzmaurice River basin and which operate on informal pastoral maps with their top paddocks, bores and yards, there is no extension of this nomenclature into the river environment proper.

Figure 11.1. Topographic map section of the Fitzmaurice River

Source: Extract from the National Topographic Series SD52-11 Port Keats, scale 1:250,000. Commonwealth of Australia 1984)

This great sense of the 'emptiness' of the Fitzmaurice River, I would argue, is not simply a construction expressed in and by the symbolism of settler society. In many ways it is also a social reality for many members of contemporary Aboriginal communities and families who represent the present traditional owners of country within the Fitzmaurice River basin. Their distance and separation from the river began with the early and inexorable long-term demographic decline of local Aboriginal resident populations on the river.

Accompanying the physical absence of the indigenous presence was a corresponding decline in traditional patterns and knowledge of nomadic life and a weakening of meaningful ties to Fitzmaurice River estates. For young members of these communities the Fitzmaurice has become, over time, a newly mythologised and remote ancestral space. Barber describes this generation shift of population and settlement especially after the Second World War and into recent times in the following terms:

> The Fitzmaurice River basin became a social desert. No one visited, or lived there and only the oldest of the community had been there. Those born since the establishment of the Mission (Port Keats 1935) are as a

result, almost without exception, ignorant of the totemic geography of the area.[38]

In other words, for many Aborigines with traditional affiliations to the area, the sense of ancestral belonging to the river is tempered, even detached from everyday social reality through its remoteness from present-day settlements. In the decline of personal lived knowledge of the land and its traditional places, and the disappearance of the 'old people' who walked its paths and spoke its language, I would argue that the Fitzmaurice might also be seen as an emergent Aboriginal frontier. No wilderness to be sure, but as a known environment of Aboriginal significance, the river echoes absences as much as it does the presence of Aboriginal history and residence. It is the 'absent' presence of a once thriving riverine culture that abandoned the relative security and familiarity of the river and voluntarily entered the world of the missions and mining camps to the north and the mustering stock camps to the south. In this context, concepts of liminality and absence in relation to Aboriginal home countries become an imagined reality for a growing community of younger affiliated members to the Fitzmaurice.

The notion that there could be an Aboriginal frontier, is perhaps stretching the definition and sense of the term from its more classical meaning. But frontiers are rarely clearly demarcated, and similarly the subjective experience of frontier realities varies markedly between individuals. In this sense my point is made more heuristically, and serves to highlight the complex impact of colonialism on Aboriginal lives. Mission and town life and its focus on settlement and sedentary living have greatly contributed to a growing sense of separation and detachment from traditional lands. Apart from the physical separation of Aboriginal people from ancestral lands for extended periods, social activity became increasingly focused on the sedentary world of housing complexes and fixed communities. Welfare dependency, the disabling effects of unemployment and drug abuse of various kinds, combined with a marked enthusiasm, especially among younger Aborigines, for European consumer goods and commodities, all contributed to a turning away from ancestral pathways.

It is fortunate then that at the very moment, historically speaking, when the links between ancestral country and contemporary life were at their weakest, there emerged processes of reclamation by those among the Aboriginal community whose ties to country remained grounded in personal experience. In this case, it was the select groups of older Aborigines whose youth was spent camping, foraging and hunting within the riverine environment.

The possibility of renewing ties to the Fitzmaurice was to some extent a reflection of broader trends in Aboriginal aspirations in northern Australia for a return to country. The emergence of the out-station movement and the possibilities offered

[38] K. Barber, *History of the Mystification of Culture*, p. 14.

by land rights and native title legislation generated a renewed interest in reasserting land-based identities.

More particularly, however, one significant development in the nascent revitalisation of Aboriginal ties to the Fitzmaurice River, was the opening up of an access track in the early 1990s to the 'Bele' (Majalindi valley)[39] for mustering stock owned by the Aboriginal community at Palumpa. This encouraged affiliated families from the neighbouring communities of Wadeye and Palumpa and Peppimenarti to begin regular dry season camping visits to the valley. For the older community this provided a belated opportunity to re-acquaint themselves with the ancestral sites and food resources, which the Majalindi holds in abundance.

When the Australian army subsequently acquired the southern pastoral lease of Bradshaw Station for training purposes in 1996 and sought a general site clearance for the lease, there was an opportunity to explore Aboriginal connections and knowledge of the river on a wider scale. Between 1996 and 1998 detailed site and place name surveys were undertaken in cooperation with a number of older Aboriginal affiliates to the river country whose personal origins and early experiences were intimately tied to the area. Using a variety of field transport including helicopters, trucks, and boat trips, substantial areas of the river could be visited.

What emerged from these mutual explorations of country was a patchwork of detailed place-based knowledge and named sites, although gaps emerged in the toponymic map of the country, reflecting the localised consequences of demographic decline among the populations of the river estates. Collectively the cultural mapping revealed a detailed abundance of landscape-based cultural knowledge, in striking contrast to the comparative paucity of official European place names.

To date, over 100 place names and sites of significance have been recorded, located and documented in varying degree.[40] Figure 2 illustrates the results of this cultural mapping in general terms. The map reflects the knowledge of a comparatively small group of traditional owners who, individually, may only have a detailed knowledge about segments or particular regions of the river, but who can collectively identify a unique world of place-based cultural meanings.

Place names recorded for the river estate known as Yambarnyi are a case in point. This region lies in north-west Bradshaw Station on the western reaches of the Fitzmaurice and there are no longer any living traditional owners with detailed

---

[39] The valley is an extensive, more or less flat black soil plain with a number of freshwater tidal tributaries of the Fitzmaurice and contained by an amphitheatre of rocky hills and gorges.
[40] A. R. McWilliam, *Big River Dreaming*.

knowledge of the locations of significant places on the estate. Access to a comparatively rich store of this knowledge, however, was made possible by the enthusiastic participation of an elderly Aboriginal woman, Polly Wandanga, now resident in Kununurra (WA). Polly was married to a former senior man of the Jaminjung language patri-country of Yambarnyi, and spent her youth footwalking between the Fitzmaurice and Legune Station where she worked for many years as a cook. In a series of extended helicopter surveys it proved possible to follow in Wandanga's earlier footsteps, so to speak, and identify with her the places and prominent cultural features of the landscape. In this way she located two prominent footwalk trails and their sequence of place names. One path followed the hills and shallow waterholes that fringe the estuarine mud flats for use in the wet season. A second dry-season track followed a large tributary of the Fitzmaurice inland past the cliffs of Wiritmangiung to the Victoria River near Purulun or Entrance Island.

Through these exercises, Wandanga was able to reveal unique sequences of place names across a broad landscape that remains otherwise unknown and un-visited by other Aboriginal affiliates to the country, and largely devoid of any cartographically named natural features.

Figure 11.2. Map showing general location of place names on the Fitzmaurice

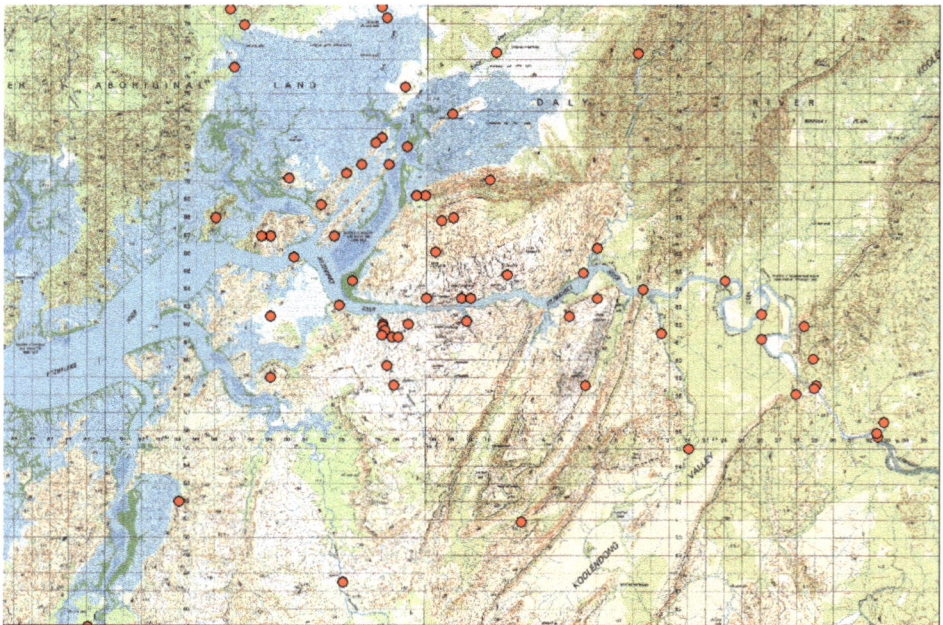

Source: Aboriginal Areas Protection Authority cartography

Conclusions

The Fitzmaurice River[41] in the western Northern Territory remains an enigmatic region of the north, arguably for both Aboriginal and non-Aboriginal people alike. From a broader Australian viewpoint, since the first exploratory European journeys into the north west until the present day, the Fitzmaurice River has been regarded as a remote or wild region beyond the scrutiny, security and comforts of settled Australia. In the popular imagination, the river is a place of physical dangers and hostile nature; latently so in its remote unpeopled expanse of some 10 000 km², and manifestly so in its treacherous currents and sand bars, as well as the many large saltwater crocodiles that populate the river channels and banks. In the past one measure of the frontier character of the river, for non-Aboriginals, lay in its threat of attack from hostile Aborigines. Today its wilderness status is couched in terms of remoteness, 'scenic beauty and superficially unspoiled pristine state'.[42]

I have also argued that the historical process of colonialism on the Fitzmaurice River and its dislocating effect on resident Aboriginal populations has contributed to the emergence of frontier-like perceptions of the river among the descendants of the Fitzmaurice River ancestors. Physical separation from the river and an emergent alienation from the historical experiences and cultural knowledge of the past contribute to this sense of a frontier quality.

In recent years, this disjuncture or emergent frontier in contemporary Aboriginal perceptions of the river is undergoing a process of re-affirmation and reclamation. Drawing on the threads of knowledge and personal memories from a small group of senior affiliates, there has been a concerted effort to recall and reinvigorate traditional relationships to the Fitzmaurice landscape. In this sense one might speak of a double notion of the contemporary frontier on the river, one which remains in a kind of dynamic tension. First, there is the conventional settler frontier, a frontier which remains in the process of appropriating the 'new', although seemingly stalled through an absence of settlement and domestication. Second, one can speak of an incipient Aboriginal frontier which is undergoing another kind of appropriation, that of the old and once familiar, as contemporary Aboriginal communities reassert long-standing associations with the river. Perhaps in the recent collaborative and consultative exercise of mapping place names and mythologies along the river, a collaboration of indigenous and exdigenous, are the tentative steps towards a post-frontier reconciliation on the Fitzmaurice.

---

[41] I use this name as a device to describe or encompass the whole length of the river. There is no satisfactory Aboriginal equivalent term to describe the whole river. Yitpiling ngala is a Murrinhpatha phrase referring to the 'big river'.

[42] H. Messell et al., *The Victoria and the Fitzmaurice River Systems*, p. 45.

Acknowledgments

A version of this was presented as a paper at the Northern Landscapes Symposium 23-4 September 1999. Field material referred to in the text has been assembled under the auspices of the Aboriginal Areas Protection Authority. Additional funding for work undertaken on the Fitzmaurice River was provided under an AIATSIS small grant. Grateful acknowledgment is extended to Kuiyen Jebinyi, Patricia Karui, Veronica Dumu, Polly Wandanga, Marcia Keringbo, the late Gypsy Mudthayi, Captain, Rusty, Robin and Mabel Waditj and Mark Crocombe who have all participated in place name mapping and supported the site-recording exercises on the river. The title of this paper was suggested to me following a discussion with Debbie Rose about the marked contrast between the evident abundance of Aboriginal place names and the comparative paucity of European ones.

References

Barber, K. 1987, *History and the Mystification of Culture: A Site Survey of the Western Fitzmaurice River Basin*, AAPA Consultancy Report. Darwin.

Gregory A. C. & Gregory F. T. 1981 [1884], *Journals of Australian Exploration*, James C. Beal Government Printer, Brisbane, Facsimile edition: Hesperian Press.

Hill, Ernestine 1951, *The Territory*, Angus and Robertson, Sydney.

Idriess Ion L. 1943, *Man Tracks: With the Mounted Police in Australian Wilds*, Angus and Robertson, Sydney.

Jacobs, Jane 1997, 'Resisting Reconciliation: The Secret Geographies of (Post)Colonial Australia, in Steve Pile and Michael Keith (eds) *Geographies of Resistance*, pp. 203–18, Routledge, London.

Log Book of Bradshaw's Run and associated material 1894–1901. Australian Archives Accession CRS04. Darwin, Australia.

Masters, B. 1999, '1814 Boab Tree-Bradshaw Station (NT) A Medieval Whodunnit', in *The Bulletin of the Australian Institute for Maritime Archaeology*, vol. 23, Perth.

Messell, H. et al. 1979, *The Victoria and the Fitzmaurice River Systems. Survey of Tidal River Systems in the NT of Australia and Their Crocodile Populations*, Pergamon Press, Sydney.

McGrath, A. 1983, *Aborigines and Colonialism in the Upper Daly Basin region: Historical Submission. Upper Daly Land Claim*, Northern Land Council.

— 1987, *Born in the Cattle*, Allen & Unwin, Sydney.

McWilliam, A. R. 1999, *Big River Dreaming: Aboriginal Toponyms and Cultural Heritage on the Fitzmaurice River. Report to the Aboriginal Areas Protection Authority*, Northern Territory, Darwin.

Mulvaney, K. 1996, 'What to Do on a Rainy Day: Reminiscences of Mirriuwung and Gadjerong Artists', *Rock Art Research*, vol. 13, no. 1, pp. 3–20.

Pye J. 1974, *The Port Keats Story*, J. R. Coleman (printer).

Riddett, L. 1988, *Kine, Kin and Country: The Victoria River District of the Northern Territory 1911-1966*, PhD Thesis, James Cook University.

Rose, Deborah Bird 1991, *Hidden Histories: Black Stories from Victoria River Downs, Humbert River and Wave Hill Stations*, Aboriginal Studies Press, Canberra.

— 1997, 'The Year Zero and the North Australian Frontier', in Deborah Bird Rose and Anne Clarke (eds) *Tracking Knowledge in North Australian Landscapes*, pp. 19–36, ANU North Australia Research Unit, NT.

Shaw, B. 1980, *My Country of the Pelican Dreaming* as told to Bruce Shaw, Australian Institute of Aboriginal Studies, Canberra.

— 1986, *Countrymen: The Life Histories of Four Aboriginal Men*, Australian Institute of Aboriginal Studies, Canberra.

Slotkin, Richard 1985, *The Fatal Environment: The Myth of the Frontier in the Age of Industrialization, 1800-1890*, HarperPerennial, New York.

Stanner, W. E. H. 1950-60, *Daly River Field Note*, AIATSIS Archives, Canberra.

— 1936, 'Murinbata Kinship and Totemism', *Oceania*, vol. 7, no. 2, pp. 186–216.

— 1979, *White Man Got No Dreaming: Essays 1938-1973*, ANU Press, Canberra.

Stokes, J. L. 1969 [1846], *Discoveries in Australia, with an Account of the Coasts and Rivers Explored and Surveyed During the Voyage of the HMS Beagle in the Years 1837-38-39-40-41-42-43*, T. and W. Boone, 2 vols, London.

Sutton, P. 1998, 'Icons of Country: Topographic Representations in Aboriginal Traditions', in David Woodward and G. Malcolm Lewis (eds), *Cartography in the Traditional African, American, Arctic, Australian and Pacific Societies*, vol. 2, book 3, pp. 353–86, The University of Chicago Press, Chicago & London.

Tindale, N. B. 1974, *Aboriginal Tribes of Australia: Their Terrain, Environmental Controls, Distribution, Limits and Proper Names*, University of California Press, Berkeley.

Turner, F. 1994, 'The Significance of the Frontier in American History 1893' in J. Faragher (ed.), *Rereading Frederick Jackson Turner: 'The Significance of the Frontier in American History' and other essays*, pp. 186–216, Henry Holt & Co, New York.

The Northern Standard 1933-34, selected issues, State Reference Library of the Northern Territory, Darwin.

White, Richard 1994, 'Frederick Jackson Turner and Buffalo Bill', in James R. Grossman (ed.), *The Frontier in American Culture, Essays by Richard White & Patricia Nelson Limerick*, pp. 7–65, University of California Press, Berkeley.

Index

Aboriginal Benefits Trust Fund
  and Central Mount Wedge station, 51
Aboriginal collectors of scientific
  specimens, 108, 113, 114–16
Aboriginal frontier
  Fitzmaurice River region as, 190, 193
Aboriginal knowledge
  appropriation of, 15, 17, 56–8
  decline in, 189–90
  of desert, 93–4
  and philosophy, 18, 165
  relationship between contemporary
    and ancestral knowledge of
    Aboriginal place, 179, 189–91
  unlearning of, 95
Aboriginal-owned pastoral stations, 146–
  7, 152, 153
Aboriginal people
  as aggressors, 36
  changing place of in Kimberley
    pastoral industry, 146–7
  cowboy culture and mission culture,
    186
  depopulation of in Fitzmaurice River
    region, 180, 181, 185
  depopulation of traditional land, 178
  and mission and town life, 190
  as 'other', 13–14
  out-migration of, 16, 18, 19, 183
  in pastoral histories, 72
  and process of settlement, 8
  and reassertion of land-based
    identities, 191
  relationship of pastoralists to the land
    and, 78
  relationships of to ancestral lands,
    179, 183, 188–91, 193
  rodeo and perceptions of land of, 151,
    154
  and savagery, 165–6
  and scientific tourism, 117
  and settler identity, 149
  White Australia policy and presence
    of, 128–9

see also desert people; Fitzmaurice
  River Aboriginal people; indigenous
  people; indigenous people–settler-
  colonist encounter on the frontier;
  Kimberley Aborigines
Aboriginal power, 9, 165, 168–9, 174
  Boxer and, 166, 175
  persistence of in face of white power,
    171–2
Aboriginal rodeo, 17–18
  and frontier theory, 147, 159
  and regional society, 159
  staging of, 145–6
  see also Kimberley rodeo
absence
  and alienation from ancestral
    experience and knowledge, 178, 189
      see also alienation; exile
  of civilised man, 49
      see also wilderness and wildness
  see also emptiness; presence; terra
    nullius; wilderness and wildness
agriculture
  and science, 125, 132
Alexander, Fred, 11
Alice Springs pastoral district
  production and consumption of
    memory and history in, 67
alienation
  Aboriginal depopulation of traditional
    lands and, 178, 193
      see also absence; exile
ancestral lands and experience
  absence and alienation from, 178, 189
  and decline in traditional patterns and
    knowledge of nomadic life, 189
  and depopulation of traditional land,
    178
  mission and town life and separation
    of Aboriginal people from, 186
  reclamation of ties to, 190–1, 193
  relationships of Aboriginal people to,
    179, 183, 189–91

echidna
    classification of, 103
    collection of, 114
    eggs, 101, 103, 112
Elsey Station, 8
the empire
    and science, 99, 100, 101
        English–French rivalry, 103
emptiness
    and Aboriginal depopulation, 178
    and Aboriginal separation from
        Fitzmaurice River region, 189
    and development, 126–7, 128
    of Fitzmaurice River region, 19, 189
    see also wilderness and wildness
encounter see indigenous people–settler-
    colonist encounter on the frontier
energy industry, 17
ethical dialogue
    violence and, 49
European stock
    and transformation of the land, 74
exile
    sense of, 16, 179
        of desert people, 91, 94, 95
    see also absence; alienation

farm dams, 86, 88
Fitzmaurice River Aboriginal people
    attractions of station camps for bush
        Aborigines and consequent out-
        migration, 181–3, 185
    decline in population, 189
    decline in traditional patterns and
        knowledge of nomadic life, 189, 193
    'dispersal' of, 180, 181, 185, 193
    and reassertion of land-based
        identities, 191
    reclamation of ties to ancestral lands,
        190–1, 193
    relationships of to ancestral lands,
        179, 183, 189–91
Fitzmaurice River region
    as Aboriginal frontier, 190, 193
    cultural mapping of, 191–2, 193
    as dangerous for Europeans, 184–5
    European exploration of, 179–80, 193

impact of pastoralism on, 180–1, 185,
    193
river as frontier, 18, 186–7, 188, 193
as sanctuary for Aborigines, 183, 185
topographical diversity of and lack of
    place names, 188
Fitzroy Crossing, 91, 95, 145
Forster, Michael, 110
Forster, William, 107
the frontier
    in Canadian and Australian anti-native
        title discourse, 31–40, 42–3
    closure of, 79–80, 99
    concepts of, 7, 8–9, 12–13, 14, 30–1,
        129, 147–8, 177–8
        'classical' frontier, 8–9, 177, 179
        cultural determination of, 93
        environmental wilderness, 177
        ethnocentricity, 30–1, 148
        'genuine' frontier, 8
        linear/sequential, 49
        in spacial sense, 67
        Turner's, 24–5
    and crises, 148, 150
    dislocating, 13, 14
    Fitzmaurice River as, 18, 186–7, 188,
        193
    Fitzmaurice River region as Aboriginal
        frontier, 190, 193
    and the future, 17
    and gender, 10
    of knowledge and experience for
        Aboriginal people, 178
    and national identity, 7, 42–3, 147,
        149–50
    and science, 16–17, 99, 100–1, 125–6
    and scientific frontier, 113–16
    suburban living on, 133
    in USA see under United States of
        America (USA)
    violence on see violence on the
        frontier
    see also land; settlement
the frontier
    and clash of old and new, 130
frontier metaphors, 100–1
the frontier myth see under Slotkin,
    Richard

frontier mythology
  and pastoralism, 67, 68–9, 76
  and presence and absence, 49–50,
    177–8
frontier science, 99
frontier studies, 12, 14–15, 23–31, 148
frontier symbolism, 30, 31
  in Canadian and Australian political
    discourse, 14–15, 42–3
frontier theory
  Aborigines and rodeo and, 147, 159
  and otherness, 147–8
frontier thesis see under Turner, Frederick
  Jackson
the future
  and the frontier, 17
  frontiers of, 138
  making of, 137–8
  and progress, 121–2

Gallipoli, 11, 36
Garamau people, 183
garden landscape, 69, 79
  effect of stock and, 74
Geary's Gap, 85, 87, 88
gender
  and Aboriginal station workforce, 153
  and the frontier, 10
  and rodeo events, 152, 153, 154
globalisation
  as progress, 136–7
Great Sandy Desert, 91, 94, 95
Gregory, A. C., 18, 179–80
Groom, Jessie, 124
Groom, Littleton, 122–3, 137, 138
  and development of Northern
    Territory, 127–8, 129
  and new liberalism (progressive
    liberalism), 123, 124
  and project of establishing of a Federal
    Bureau of Agriculture, 123–4, 125,
    126, 128
  vision of progress of, 129
  and White Australia policy, 128
Gunn, Jeannie (We of the Never-Never),
  8, 16
Günther, Albert, 106

Gympie gold rushes of 1867, 107

Haacke, William, 112
Hanson, Pauline, 32–5, 41
  as battler, 36
  see also One Nation (Pauline Hanson's
    One Nation)
Haynes, Roslynn, 92
Hill, Edward Smith, 105
Hill, Ernestine, 177, 180, 181
Hiroshima, 130, 132, 135
historical writing see pastoral memory and
  historical writing
history wars, 7
Hoare, Michael, 99–100
Home, Everard, 102, 113
Huxley, T. H., 110

Idriess, Ion (Lasseter's Last Ride), 55
Ien Ang, 34
indigenous people
  relationships of to land, 15–16
  see also Aboriginal people
indigenous people–settler-colonist
  encounter on the frontier, 7, 8–9, 13, 17,
    149, 150–1, 177–8
  cross-cultural, 13, 14, 15
    and Aboriginal rodeos, 18
    and Boxer's Djanba, 18
    and scientific classification of
      platypuses, 17
  see also settlement; violence on the
    frontier
initiation
  Aboriginal people's relationships to
    land through, 155
insider and outsider, 167, 168, 169, 172,
  174
  see also order and disorder
Isaacs, Isaac, 124, 125

Jungian universal archetypes
  and paintings of Ainslie Roberts, 55,
    56, 57

Kalkatungu battle (1884), 171
Kalkatungu people, 18, 165

McCord, W. F., 111
McGregor, Bill, 172
Macintyre, Stuart, 137
McLean, Ian, 10–11
Macleay, W. S., 113
McMahon, Billy, 132
Mahood, Marie and Joe, 77
Maitland, Francis, 110
Majalindi valley, 191
Mangarrayi people
    and title to Elsey Station, 8
Maralinga, 130, 131
Marxism, 165, 174
memory *see* pastoral memory and
    historical writing
Menzies, R. G., 133–4, 135
Mirdinan, 173
mission and town life
    and separation of Aboriginal people
        from traditional lands, 186
mission culture
    and cowboy culture, 186
monologue
    and frontier violence, 58, 59
Mount Isa, 42
Mountford, Charles, 15, 53
    and Central Mount Wedge station,
        53–4
    on landscape and nationalism, 56, 57
    and power of place, 62–3
multiculturalism
    Pauline Hanson's One Nation and, 34
multinational companies
    and progress, 133
Mulunga, 171
Munro, Morndi, 160
murder of Koch and Arinski in
    Fitzmaurice River region, 184–5
Murrinhpatha people, 186

naming
    and colonisation, 102
    and hegemonic ownership, 187
    see also place names
national identity
    battling and battlers and, 36
    and the frontier, 7, 42–3, 147, 149–50

and legal entitlement, 14
violence and, 11, 12
see also settler identity
see also under Canada; United States of
    America (USA)
national science, 99, 100
national security
    and forward defence, 135
    and projects for development of
        Northern Territory, 127–8
    and White Australia policy, 128
native title, 13–14, 32, 41–2, 78
    evidence in claim for, 61
        painting, 92
        song, 52, 61
    and reassertion of land-based
        identities, 191
    see also anti-native title discourse;
        Central Mount Wedge station
nature
    ideals of of non-indigenous people, 93
new liberalism (progressive liberalism)
    protectionism and, 123
New Western History, 27–8
Ngulunung, Pat, 181–2
ngurlu naming system, 186
Nicker family, 71–2, 74, 75
Nicols, Arthur, 107–8
North West Mounted Police (Canada), 38
Northern Territory
    Commonwealth takeover of, 122–3
    projects for development of, 121, 122–
        3, 127–8, 129
        and atomic energy, 132–3
        and national security, 127–8

One Nation (Pauline Hanson's One Nation),
    32–3
    anti-native title discourse of, 33, 37,
        41
    opposition to Asian immigration, 34,
        35
    reasons for public support of, 33–4,
        37–8
One Pound Jimmy, 54, 59
Ord River scheme, 168

order and disorder
  Boxer's *Djanba* and, 168
  and Kimberley Aborigines, 167
  settler-patoralists and, 167, 168, 172
  see also insider and outsider;
    wilderness
otherness, 13, 14
  Aboriginal people, 13–14
  comprehension of, 16
  frontier theory and, 147–8
  frontiers and, 129
  platypus, 103
outback mythology *see* frontier mythology
outside *see* insider and outsider
Owen, Richard, 103, 105, 106, 115

painting
  as evidence in native title claim, 92
Palka-karrinya, 15, 51–2, 54
  painting by Ainslie Roberts, 59–60
Palumpa, 191
pastoral landscape
  discovery of, 72
pastoral memory and historical writing, 67
  arrival as homecoming, 71–3
  and central Australia, 69–71
  and closure of the frontier, 79–80
  knowledge of the land, 75–8
  and legitimation of rural settlement,
    68–9, 78–80
  transformation of the land, 73–5
pastoralism
  and frontier mythology, 67, 68–9, 76
  impact of on Fitzmaurice River region,
    180–1, 185, 193
  and taming process, 177
  see also European stock
pastoralists
  and knowledge of the land, 75–6
  relationship of to the land, 78
    and Aboriginal people, 78
  self identity of, 68–9, 76
  see also settler-patoralists
paternalistic benevolence *see* benevolence
philosophy
  and Aboriginal knowledge, 18, 165
  true, 166
Pike, Jimmy, 16, 94, 95

piosphere, 88
place names, 18, 19
  and colonialism, 187
  and cultural mapping of Fitzmaurice
    River region, 191–2, 193
  erasure of Aboriginal presence
    through, 187–8
  paucity of in Fitzmaurice River region,
    188
  see also naming
platypus, 110, 113, 117
  and Australian otherness, 103
  classification of, 103
  collecting specimens, 107–8
  debate over, 16–17, 101–4
  eggs, 101, 103, 112, 113
  naming of, 102
  in 19th-century Australian scientific
    history, 100
  trade in skins of, 110
platypus frontier, 117
Portus, G. V., 134
Powell, P., 70, 73
power *see* Aboriginal power; white power
presence
  Aboriginal
    erasure of, 178
      through place names, 187–8
  and absence
    and frontier mythology, 49–50, 57,
      177–8
    see also love/desire and death
  of pastoralists in the land, 78
Price family, 71, 75
progress, 129, 137
  and atomic bomb, 131, 132
  and the future, 121–2
  and globalisation, 136–7
  and moral perceptions, 136
  and profits of multinational
    companies, 133
  science and, 17, 122, 132
  threats to, 134
  see also development
progressive society, 124
protectionism
  and new liberalism (progressive
    liberalism), 123

www.ingramcontent.com/pod-product-compliance
Lightning Source LLC
Chambersburg PA
CBHW061245270326
41928CB00041B/3429